Also by Robert Kuttner

Going Big

The Stakes

Can Democracy Survive Global Capitalism?

Debtors' Prison: The Politics of Austerity Versus Possibility

A Presidency in Peril

Obama's Challenge

The Squandering of America

Everything for Sale: The Virtues and Limits of Markets

The End of Laissez-Faire

The Life of the Party

The Economic Illusion

Revolt of the Haves

Family Re-Union (with Sharland Trotter)

Notes For Next Time

Surviving Tyranny, Redeeming America

Robert Kuttner

JPZ

J. P. Zenger Books

One Must Imagine Sisyphus Happy

— Albert Camus, The Myth of Sisyphus

Contents

Chapter 1

Sisyphus Happy

It seems a bizarre moment to write a memoir about a lifetime working to enlarge democracy and advance social justice. But if we are ever to emerge from Donald Trump's nihilism, we need to understand how we got here. As this book will suggest, we are at a fateful crossroads. As Trump's popularity continues to decline, his recklessness continues to increase. Though the MAGA base still loves him, most Americans are weary of Trump and ready for new leadership. Republicans have begun to defy him, and some courts have overruled him. Democracy may yet endure.

If democracy does hold long enough for there to be relatively fair elections in 2026 and 2028, we could begin the process of repairing the damage, strengthening democratic institutions, and restoring a more just America. But even if everything breaks right, this process will be far from easy. Conversely, if Trump's desperation makes him a more effective despot, the American democratic experiment could be over. The "Next Time" of my title could be decades, if not centuries, away.

In this political memoir, I hope to use the arc of my own story to shed some light on the political and economic odyssey of America in my lifetime. My project, as a journalist, political intellectual, and activist, has been to pursue arguments and practical strategies for a decent society. That quest has taken me into a variety of pursuits, including writing fourteen books, working as a Senate investigator, a college professor, a magazine writer, an editor, and a syndicated columnist. I've been both a witness and a player.

In the 1980s, when progressivism was on the defensive and neoliberalism was ascendant, I co-founded two institutions to fight back intellectually and politically. One was the Economic Policy Institute, launched in 1986. I still serve on its board. EPI has become the premier economics think tank defending and advancing the model of a dynamic, egalitarian economy, not with rhetoric but with well-documented research.

The other was *The American Prospect*, founded in 1989, where I continue to serve as co-editor. The Prospect, with deep reporting and analysis, details how the neoliberal ascendancy undermines the life prospects of ordinary people and creates political debacles. The Prospect poses alternatives. It connects policy to politics to narrative, and to the disparity of power. The two enterprises incubate many of America's most important progressive thinkers and arguments. Both punch above their weight.

I've always located myself at the left edge of the possible, in Michael Harington's phrase, as more of a left-liberal than a revolutionary. Unlike many of my sixties chums, I never had much use for Marxism, which seemed archaic. When I was young, the proletariat that was supposed to be undergoing immiseration was part of a prosperous blue-collar middle class, represented by vigorous trade unions. Prosperity was broadly shared.

Lately, I've become more of an economic radical. Capitalist

America has become a kleptocracy. Corporations have become more extractive than entrepreneurial. Trade unions have been plundered. Even professions are becoming immiserated. It is no longer risible to use the word, capital, as a collective noun. I don't think I've become more Marxian. I think the world has become more Marxian. The liberation of rapacious finance from its constructive New Deal moorings is central to the disparity of power as well as wealth in America.

Our democracy was weakened by economic concentration long before Trump savaged it politically. By the late 20th century, America was well on the way to becoming an oligarchy, with both political parties allied with financial elites and ignoring the ever-greater insecurity of working families. Money became the currency of politics. A small number of progressives in mainstream electoral politics, such as Elizabeth Warren and Bernie Sanders, kept warning us about this trend and proposing far-reaching remedies. When they remained prophetic outsiders and Democratic presidents from Carter to Obama became all too cozy with finance, it was Trump who reaped the political benefit of class resentments with a cultish brew of ethno-nationalism that also managed to intensify the power of the financial elite.

One of the chapters in this book is titled Winning the Arguments, Losing the Politics. In the 1990s and 2000s, reality demolished the fundamental tenets of neoliberalism. Deregulation of several industries did not promote greater efficiency or consumer choice. Mainly, deregulation produced greater concentration and monopoly pricing power, insider enrichment, and financial speculation that ended with a collapse and a prolonged recession.

Globalization, as defined in corporate terms, helped China, but it mostly harmed the United States, which lost industry after industry and ended up with an ever-increasing chronic trade deficit. Globalization was good for American corporations and investment bankers, but destroyed the prosperous blue-collar middle class, killing a key constituency of the Democrats. Race was a complicating factor. The full redemption of the promise of civil rights would have been a heavy political lift in the best of circumstances. But it was far more divisive with Democrats largely abandoning the white working class.

Why did we win the arguments and lose the politics? Why did three Democratic presidents before Biden join Republicans in pursuing neoliberalism? The corruption of politics by big money and the debasement of well-governed capitalism fed on one another. There was a great deal of money to be had if you dismantled the New Deal, the better to enrich the rich, and not much to be had for defending and modernizing it. Much of my work, and that of The Prospect and the Economic Policy Institute, has been about investigating, explaining, and publicizing how this downward spiral occurred, and posing alternatives. I tell this story in the chapters to come.

———

I was born during World War II, near the end of Franklin Roosevelt's presidency, a time that produced stunning advances both for broad prosperity and the expansion of democracy. I came of age in the early sixties, another hopeful period that was cut short first by the Kennedy assassination and then by the collateral damage of the Vietnam War. But along the way, the struggle for a decent America made great gains.

In the 1940s, the US began a three-decade era in which the pursuit of happiness was possible for a larger share of its citizens than at any time before or since. Many of the people of my generation almost floated upwards — graduated from college without any debt, purchased a first house when that dream was still attainable without the aid of wealthy parents, and got on track for fulfilling careers that included real jobs and not gigs. Working-class people, as well as college grads, enjoyed reliable jobs and increasing prosperity.

That unusual era was not the result of dumb luck. It was the fruit of a social compact bequeathed to us by the New Deal that transformed American capitalism from a predatory system into a well-managed and egalitarian one. The postwar boom was a rare period when the economy not only grew at record rates but actually became more equal. It was, in the title of a book by the historian Jefferson Cowie, *The Great Exception* to most of American history, when the norm was laissez-faire, small government, and creditor rule.

After the experience of the Crash of 1929, followed by the Great Depression, the New Deal tightly regulated the more destructive aspects of financial capitalism so that bankers could play their textbook role of supplying capital to the real economy, not just enriching themselves. The New Deal dramatically expanded public investment and social insurance. It legalized trade unions as a worker counterweight to corporations. These policies created a society of broader security, prosperity, and possibility.

My generation pursued politics at a time when constructive change was possible. And we had a rollicking good time. The system was indulgent. It permitted us to drop out and turn on, and then when it was time to put away our childish things, to resume mainstream career tracks. Some of us even had careers in which we were paid good money to do what we loved, antics and all. To be sure, not everyone in our generation was so fortunate, but it was a rare era when good fortune was broadly spread, for working-class people as well as professionals.

Many of our parents had a tough time of it, first in the Great

Depression and then in World War II — sixteen arduous years. My own father was one. Great hopes were invested in their children—us—and the economy delivered the preconditions. Our children and grandchildren will have it even tougher.

My dad was born at the wrong time. I got to live out his dreams. That was true of my generation generally. We did not need a head start from family resources.

When I was born in 1943, we lived in a newly completed moderate-income housing project called Parkchester, in the East Bronx. It was subsidized by land purchases and tax abatements. My parents, who had spent the Depression in cramped apartments in Queens, felt like they had won the lottery. Their talk must have sunk into my young consciousness — something called the government helped provide decent places for working people to live.

My dad was soon drafted. His unit landed at Normandy, helped liberate Paris, stumbled into the Battle of the Bulge in December 1944, and he barely survived four months in a POW camp. In 1948, my parents and grandfather moved to a very modest house just inside the Scarsdale line so that I could go to a good school. When I was nine, my father became ill with what would be a fatal cancer. My mother and I began to have adult conversations. I learned that he was getting excellent care at a new VA hospital; that if he died, we wouldn't lose our house, thanks to his veteran's pension and something called Social Security.

Parkchester. The VA. Social Security. Long before I ever studied Roosevelt, I was a New Dealer in my bones.

The year after my dad died, our very reform synagogue had a charity drive. My Sunday (sic) School class was asked to make small donations and to pick from an approved list of mostly Jewish charities. I told the teacher that I wanted my entire contribution to go to the VA. The teacher, knowing from my mother why I felt this way, gently explained that the VA did not need my money. It was supported by the US government. I insisted. To this day, I don't know whether some bewildered clerk at the VA got a small check from the Westchester Reform Temple.

Growing up as a poor kid in a rich town also taught me something about class. One day, in seventh grade, I made a play date with a new friend from one of Scarsdale's wealthiest neighborhoods, called Murray Hill. As his mother dropped us off, he looked at my 900-square-foot house and said, in a not unfriendly, almost anthropological tone, "This little bungalow?"

Given my personal encounters with social class, the sense of infinite possibility of the late fifties, followed by the civil rights struggles and my personal experience of what FDR's legacy had done for my own family, it would have been odd if I didn't grow up to be some kind of liberal. This was reinforced by my years at Oberlin, in the sweet, hopeful first half of the sixties, before politics turned ugly.

A lot of my work has been about challenging the conventional wisdom of the economics profession, which has functioned as the ideological department of American conservatism. If markets are basically efficient, as standard economics teaches, then government intervention can only make things worse. If labor markets pay appropriate wages based on supply and demand, then minimum wage laws, trade unions to represent workers' interests, unemployment compensation, and health and safety laws are drags on prosperity. My lifelong critique of the undertow of standard economics is the subject of one of my chapters.

————

This political memoir is part personal history and part political history. I've departed somewhat from the usual sequence of proceeding chronologically. After this introduction, I continue with a chapter titled "Falling Upward," about my own early adult life and the experience of my generation. I follow with some emblematic accounts of different facets of politics and my involvement in them.

At the time I began writing, in the heyday of Lyndon Johnson's Great Society, it looked as if America might be moving toward broader social justice. But over the more than half-century of my life as a journalist and activist, our country has moved further away from that vision of a just and dynamic economy.

With the election of Ronald Reagan in 1980, the right wing seemed to have won both the intellectual and the political debates. America would now reject the vision of the New Deal and the Great Society in favor of a free market dystopia. Democrats became more like Republicans. Yet those policies, culminating in the financial collapse of 2008, produced mainly catastrophes—an economy of weaker performance, wider risk, and worsened inequality and insecurity.

Under Obama, the Democrats blew what should have been a Roosevelt moment to put finance back in its box and restore an economy of broadly shared prosperity. Obama helped Wall Street to recover quickly, while working families continued to suffer. Those outcomes, in turn, discredited elites in both parties and paved the way for disgruntled citizens to elect Donald Trump.

I've had the grim satisfaction of winning the intellectual arguments based on the practical failure of neoliberal policies, while the right kept gaining and the center became corrupted. With Joe Biden, Democrats temporarily regained something of their souls. But it is not enough to win intellectually or provisionally. You have to win politically and keep winning.

Beyond the widening inequality and insecurity generally, America, since Reagan, has been increasingly hard on younger people. Each succeeding generation, after mine, has faced a tougher time gaining traction because the rules of the game have turned brutally against the young. My generation had unearned tailwinds. The generation that came before, and the ones that came after, faced unearned headwinds.

Today, in the absence of family wealth, the non-rich must look to government programs to provide a boost — or not. And those programs have become threadbare. Young adults begin with college debt, unaffordable housing, unreliable health coverage, and jobs that are more likely to be temporary gigs rather than real payroll career positions. My grandchildren's horizons are still less auspicious, even without the added complication of pandemics and global climate change. Their lives began at a time when opportunities are stunted, even though America is more than twice as rich on average as when I was a child.

For the most part, younger Americans do not have the sense of generational or political solidarity that comes with a mass depression, yet the terms of engagement have turned brutally against them. Many internalize these reverses as purely private struggles and failures. Issues that ought to be deeply political are taken as merely personal. The right-wing success in disabling helpful government becomes a self-fulfilling prophecy, and some younger Americans embrace the conservative story that we are all on our own.

There is also a misleading narrative that appeals to some Millennials and Gen Z-ers to the effect that "the boomers took it all," as if there were a finite pot of economic resources. The reality is that the postwar generation benefited from a functioning social contract that was the result of a different constellation of influence, wealth, and deliberate policies. The challenge is to restore something like it. That is better understood in terms of class and power than generational conflict. I will also have more to say about this in succeeding chapters.

One has to hope that we may yet reverse these trends and that American democracy, anchored in a society of far more decency, may yet endure. This would have been easier had Trump not been elected to a second term. But the optimist in me perceives that the Trump coalition and its policies are a bundle of contradictions. There are massive schisms between the corporate globalist wing of his base and the racist/nationalist MAGA wing. Many of Trump's policies are based on fantasies. His voters may soon notice that migrants have been deported and trans athletes banned, while their own economic lives are still a shambles.

————

The epigraph of this book is Sisyphus Happy. It comes from the last line of Albert Camus' celebrated essay, "The Myth of Sisyphus". It has become a kind of credo for me. Camus writes, "One must imagine Sisyphus happy."

Sisyphus Happy? Every time Sisyphus rolls the rock up the hill, it comes tumbling back down. Every task he undertakes is futile. When I first encountered that last sentence, at 19, in a philosophy class at Oberlin, I thought the claim of happiness, well, absurd.

I then imagined the Myth of Sisyphus as an argument between existentialists and believers—Camus versus the Book of Job. For the observant, the parable of Job is about trusting in the Lord, even when the sadism of the natural world makes no sense. You reconcile yourself to the apparent absurdity by believing that there must be a divine plan. But what kind of benevolent Providence would afflict a child with leukemia? Job seems to me utterly unconvincing—a powerful if unintended argument for the *non-*

existence of God, or for the non-existence of a loving god. A New Yorker cartoon expressed it perfectly. God is confiding to an angel, "First I was trying to teach Job a lesson, now I'm just messing with him."

Reading the essay again, I accepted the metaphor of Sisyphus to mean that even if we often fail, we make meaning from endeavor. "The struggle itself towards the heights is enough to fill a man's heart," Camus wrote. Yes, okay, fair enough. And then I finally got it. The rock, ultimately, isn't just the plans that often come to naught. The rock is death. In the end, it crushes us all. But along the way, this life is all we have. One must imagine Sisyphus happy.

Some of the time, anyway, and only for some people. Another of the cruelties of a morally incomprehensible natural order, compounded by the injustices of the political order, is that most people don't experience much happiness. As a bumper sticker puts it, "Life is a bitch and then you die". Thoreau aptly wrote, *The mass of men lead lives of quiet desperation.* That is reality, for far too many souls.

So our calling, as progressives, is to offset the injustices of the natural order and to keep pushing the rock up the hill, appreciating that sometimes it does stay put for a long time. In the half-century between the Wagner Act, when the New Deal made it possible for workers to organize and join unions, and the Reagan presidency, when the destruction of unions became a government priority, two generations of blue-collar workers were able to enjoy a secure middle-class life. The post-Civil War Reconstruction lasted long enough for many former slaves to get educated, so that the children of slaves could include intellectuals of astonishing reach who created the Harlem Renaissance. The Second Reconstruction, of the three great civil rights acts of the 1960s, was cut short by Nixon's "Southern Strategy" of making the Republicans the party of racism. Court decisions weakened the Voting Rights Act. Eventually, even affirmative action was ruled unconstitutional, and DEI became a term of scorn. But along the way, millions of black Americans did gain the right to vote, joined professions, and became part of the middle class. And then racism gained back some ground, fomented by a President and a Supreme Court.

Thus, Sisyphus. Each generation needs to keep pushing the rock back up the hill.

As a high school student, reading Thomas Hardy, I recall my English teacher explaining that Hardy tended to view the structure of the natural order and human fortune as random, bordering on cruel. His characters strive, and many succumb to chance mishaps that don't even rise to the level of tragedy. That touched me, as all too accurate.

The randomness of good luck and bad luck is staggering: Who happens to get cancer; who comes of age in a great depression or a pandemic just when the economy is collapsing; who is born Black in a racist society; whose seemingly loving marriage is randomly upended by a husband's midlife crisis.

Yet some of the cruelty isn't random. Children born to privilege find that the cosmic deck is not stacked against them the way it is for poor kids. For the affluent, there is a family welfare state. Government policies can partly even the odds – or worsen them. In the recent pandemic, nobody was safe, yet it was lower-income people who bore disproportionate risks, delivering packages, staffing supermarkets and warehouses, while the fortunate could conduct professional business from home with computers, or repair to summer homes in less infected locations.

So, in both my writing and political work, I pursue ways for us to make both the natural order and the political order a little less randomly cruel. Temper Thomas Hardy with Franklin Roosevelt.

This is not just a matter of politics but also compassionate personal behavior. Yet all the charity and random acts of kindness in the world will never make up for a universe whose natural propensities and usual political rules are both stacked against ordinary people.

In John Kennedy's inaugural address, he declared, somewhat impertinently, "Here on earth, God's work must surely be our own." The trouble with the sentiment is that people have antithetical conceptions of God's work. That's why we have religious wars, and why Jefferson insisted on a secular state. For progressives, our calling is to behave as we would like the Divine to behave, if the natural order were less cruel, and to enlist government in that enterprise.

As the Sisyphus parable suggests, political victories are provisional and reversible; they need to be fought and won, over and over again. Nobody gets through a lifetime without personal reverses that can be devastating, but that need not be disabling.

When Trump was first elected in 2016, I imagined that America would feel like a fundamentally different place. But one of the oddities of the Trump era is that daily life goes on, coexisting all too readily with the destruction of democracy, which has only a remote personal impact on most people.

One might expect that the incipient Trump dictatorship would cast a shadow over everything. But that's not how despotism works. Life feels all too normal, especially for those with discretionary income not personally affected by Trump's closures of federal agencies or drastic cuts in research funding. For the very rich, life is sweeter than ever. This is one of the many sinister aspects of the Trump era.

If you were not a Jew or a homosexual or a social democrat, Nazi Germany could be a pleasant place to live before Hitler destroyed it with a second world war. In occupied Paris, the cafes and music halls were full. In America today, Broadway has plenty of shows, and Netflix has never been more prolific. You can listen to an item on local public radio about Trump's latest outrage, juxtaposed to an ad for a trendy sushi bar.

This somehow feels wrong, if not surreal. Yet it also feels essential, however paradoxical, to resolve that Trump's attempt to destroy everything good about America is not going to ruin our personal lives, too. While I do everything I can to resist Trump in my role as journalist and agitator, I also cherish time with friends and family, cooking, playing tennis, writing poems, and going to the theater.

Would the struggle against Trump be more authentic if I became a revolutionary ascetic? I think of Ira Gershwin's lyric from the 1930s: *No, no they can't take that away from me.*

I've had more than my share of loss. I mentioned that my father died when I was nine. My wife, Sharland Trotter, died of cancer when we were both 54. And our wonderful, antic, actor/director/theater teacher son, Gabriel, who always lived on the edge, died of an accidental drug overdose at 45.

And yet, at age 82, with the full knowledge that I only have a few years left in my own lifetime, I am somehow a joyous person. One must imagine Sisyphus happy.

I've thought a lot about how this can possibly be. Either I'm shallower than I admit, in denial about grief, or there is something in my experience or temperament that allows me to resolve that losses are not going to destroy my own life. I don't attribute that to superior character. A lot of it, like so much in life, is luck, as coming chapters will recount. I give a lot of credit to my mother, Polly, who also endured several personal losses but remained a cheerful person and a role model of resilience. I must have internalized the idea that people who suffered reverses picked themselves up and went on.

We are right on the verge of another collective loss, the loss of our democracy. Our country will need all the resilience it can muster. We may yet get another chance to reclaim a functioning democracy and a politics of broadly shared prosperity, maybe even in my lifetime. We'd better maximize it. I hope these Notes for Next Time will help.

Chapter 2

Falling Upward

In October 1969, I was offered the job of program director at Pacifica Radio's flagship station, WBAI, in New York. I had been working for Pacifica as half of a two-person Washington bureau. I'm picking up the story at this period of my life partly to give a sense of who I was in those years. But mainly, I want to explain how I managed to impersonate a rich man by the time I was 40 on the salary of a journalist—due to larger economic trends that gave my generation an undeserved lift at the expense of my children and grandchildren.

The offer was a chance to take a very cool job in New York and move in with my fiancée. I was 26. Sharland and I had been dating long-distance for about six months, and we were thinking seriously about spending our lives together. I had never lived with a woman before.

Nothing illustrates how my generation was able to fall upward economically better than our household budget in those years, what we paid for housing then and afterward, and how we accumulated wealth. It certainly wasn't by putting aside savings.

Sharland was living in a second-floor walk-up with four small rooms on the fringe of Greenwich Village, at 344 West 11th Street, a block from the Hudson River. The bathtub was in the kitchen. The rent was $64.55 a month. Rent control had been introduced nationally during World War II. Some cities, such as New York, with a chronic housing shortage and large numbers of politically active tenants, never gave it up. So I was acquiring not just a live-in girlfriend, but a funky apartment that was a lot hipper and not much more costly than what my parents were paying when I was born in 1943.

This was the period before the Village became ultra-trendy and very expensive. It was still bohemia. In those years, the far West Village was a mix of rundown apartments and warehouses. For the first few weeks I lived there, the trucks would wake me up as they rumbled in around 4 a.m. You'll get used to it, Sharland said. And I did.

I was making $12,000 at WBAI. Sharland was making $10,000 as a junior editor at the publisher Crowell, Collier & Macmillan. Her job was not very stressful. It amounted to selecting books for the Behavioral Science Book Club and two others operated by Macmillan. She had long lunches with authors and editors, read lots of books, and in her spare time got very into cooking.

On the way home from the subway stop, at 7th Avenue and 12th Street, she would stop at the butcher, J. Ottomanelli and Sons on Bleecker Street, the greengrocer (a word I learned from her), maybe the bakery, and then prepare a meal. We bought serious Bordeaux wines at $20 a case. Ours was the sort of lifestyle that is available today to professionals with high six-figure incomes. But we could easily afford it on my salary working for a hippie radio station and Sharland's with a very junior job in publishing. I even had an MG.

Long before NPR, Pacifica had invented listener-sponsored non-commercial radio in the 1940s. WBAI, a circus of brilliant news and public affairs programming, antiwar activism, and radical cultural experimentation, was then at the peak of its influence. We were the first to have a correspondent in Hanoi. We covered the major antiwar protests with live remote broadcasts, and some of our reporters went to jail along with the protestors. We did live radio theater, and one of our regulars was John Lithgow. For a week, we read all of *War and Peace*, 24 hours a day, with Broadway actors and local politicians as well as the station staff stopping by to read passages. (Mine was the Battle of Borodino.) Allen Ginsberg regularly dropped in to read poetry. Pete Seeger sang at our on-air fundraising marathons.

Our morning man, Larry Josephson, was a New York institution, as was the late-night host, Bob Fass. We had the first feminist talk show, featuring Nanette Rainone and guests, under the arch title, "Electra Re-wired." The station regularly got into trouble. Just before I arrived, during a bitter teacher strike that pitted the heavily Jewish teachers union against Black activists demanding local control, host Julius Lester invited a teenager to come in and read a poem that began, "Hey, Jew Boy." This and similar provocations eventually cost WBAI its property tax exemption as a nonprofit.

Not long after I stepped down as a manager, our noon hour host, Paul Gorman, decided to play George Carlin's classic bit, "The Seven Words You Can't Say on TV" (shit, piss, fuck, cunt, cocksucker, motherfucker, and tits). A man named John Douglas, a member of Morality in Media, heard the broadcast while driving in his car with his fifteen-year-old son and complained to the FCC.

In the case that ensued, the issue turned less on whether the material was per se obscene than on whether management had control. We were advised to dissemble. Station management told the FCC that this had not been Gorman's spontaneous provocation, but a carefully considered decision based on Carlin's socially valuable commentary. After five years of contention, the US Supreme Court in *FCC vs. Pacifica Foundation,* by a 5-4 vote, decided that WBAI would be fined for using material that was "indecent" but not obscene, and would not lose its license.

On one occasion, I sent a reporter upstate to cover the prison uprising at Attica. When he landed at Buffalo airport, the Hertz rental agency refused to rent him a car because he didn't have a credit card. I phoned the agency and offered mine to guarantee the rental. They still refused to rent him the car. So we went on the air, gave out the agency's phone number, and asked the listeners for help. After dozens of calls jamming his line, the harassed manager went to a phone booth, called and asked me to relent, and rented our man the car.

As program director, I was often in the role of the slightly queasy left-liberal adult in the room with provocative radicals whose goals were to push boundaries. We had the first gay talk show. It was terrific. We pre-taped it, and one of my jobs was to negotiate with the host, Richard Lamparski, about what sexually explicit material might get us thrown off the air.

I made several lifelong friends at WBAI, the most influential of whom was Carolyn Goodman, the board chair, a woman of real grace and kindness. Carolyn and her husband Bobby, who died the year I started working for Pacifica, had been fellow travelers in the 1930s. The family construction company, which specialized in deep tunneling, had built the Moscow subway for Stalin, who presciently ordered it extra deep for use as bomb shelters in case of war. Their son, Andy, was one of the three civil rights workers murdered in Mississippi in 1964. He was exactly my age.

The first time I visited Carolyn at home, in her gracious apartment on West 86th Street, with original paintings by Ben Shahn and Picasso, I was stunned to realize that there were lefties who lived well, even elegantly. When her three sons were young, Carolyn went back to school and earned a doctorate in psychology. She founded a pioneering day-treatment program at Bronx State Hospital for severely disturbed women who had young children. The entire therapeutic program was built around having the mothers bring their kids and learn parenting skills. Knowing that they did right by their children gave them focus and relieved one major source of stress. Carolyn became a role model for Sharland, who also went back and earned a doctorate in psychology when our kids were young.

I had a hell of a good time at WBAI, knowing that when it came time to pursue a more grown-up career, I'd have opportunities. I was also writing columns for the Village Voice. As things turned out, when I left Pacifica for good in 1974, it was to go to the Washington Post.

———

I may be an extreme case of falling upward economically, but not an exceptional one. A lot of people in my generation can tell variants of the same story. It is said that people who will tell you all about their sex lives are very circumspect with disclosures about their money. In this book, I will keep my sex life private. But I want to provide some details about my net worth and how it accumulated, to show the utter injustice of the generational tailwinds and headwinds during my lifetime.

After we were married in 1971, Sharland and I moved back to Washington, where I stayed with Pacifica as bureau chief, and she got a job as the house editor for Ralph Nader. I was still writing columns for the Voice and beginning to freelance for other magazines. We were making about $25,000 between us. We bought our first house in 1973, for $65,000, in the Adams-Morgan neighborhood. It had been a boarding house in a slightly dicey area. We converted it to a single-family home with a rental unit.

What happened next is almost indecent, especially given the struggles that my children's generation has faced. We owned that house for not quite six years. In 1979, I was offered a fellowship to spend a year at Harvard, where I worked on my first book.

As inflation took off in the mid and late 1970s, our Washington house soared in value. Housing prices rose not just because prices were rising generally. A house was seen as a good hedge against inflation because it was something real. While the stock market fell, demand for housing rose, pushing up housing prices further. We were also lucky, if that's the right word, in that our "changing" neighborhood was actually becoming more yuppified, increasing the value of our house even more.

So the house that we had bought for $65,000 less than six years earlier sold for $250,000 in 1979. Some of this reflected the improvements we had made, but most of it was lucky timing. Our actual cash investment—the down payment—had increased about tenfold. After paying off the mortgage, which had financed some improvements, we walked away with over $170,000 in cash, none of it earned.

The story gets even more lopsided, again due to sheer luck of time and place. When we decided to stay and purchase a home in the Boston area in 1979, interest rates were sky-high. That depressed housing prices since it made mortgages very expensive. Boston in those years was also in an economic slump, whereas Washington, in every presidency until Trump, was recession-proof. Housing prices in Boston were a bargain compared to those in DC. As economists would put it, we had "arbitraged" the two housing markets to our advantage, selling in an expensive one and buying in a cheap one.

None of this was a deliberate economic maneuver; we had not compared the two housing markets in order to maximize our housing wealth. We simply moved to Boston so that I could take a fellowship at Harvard and my wife could apply to graduate school and, she hoped, resettle the family in greater Boston. The windfall was dumb luck.

As it turned out, we were able to buy a lovely home in a good Brookline school district, just in time for our son to start kindergarten. Because we could buy it for cash at a time when mortgages were expensive and hard to get, an anxious and grateful seller dropped his asking price by $30,000. So now we had a spacious house and no mortgage. This was fortunate, since I was now working as editor of a small left magazine, Working Papers for a New Society, and earning less than I had been making in Washington.

When I sold the Brookline house 23 years later, its value had increased eightfold. So I was able to achieve the same trick twice, over four decades, entirely by accident. Most of my net worth is the value of my current house, which has also doubled since we bought it in 2002. On the income of a journalist, I am impersonating a rich man, thanks to unearned housing wealth.

I may be an extreme case, and my personal experience may reflect more random luck than most. But this is the economic experience of my generation, as well as those a little older and younger: Housing is cheap when you buy, it increases in value at windfall rates, then builds net worth and ultimately provides a comfortable cushion for your retirement. Meanwhile, the inflated housing prices create almost insurmountable entry costs for succeeding generations, at a time when most incomes are lagging behind the average rate of economic growth.

I recently looked up our apartment at 344 West 11th Street. It is now a condo. It was combined with the identical one across the hall and spruced up. Zillow lists its value as $3.1 million. To live the kind of sumptuous hippie life in the West Village that Sharland and I did in our mid-twenties, today you would need to be a multi-millionaire. Young people who have the sort of jobs that we had in the 1960s are paying fortunes for cramped rental apartments and can't imagine becoming homeowners unless they have affluent parents to help.

———

The grotesque injustice of how the rules of the game have been turned against successive younger generations was only compounded by the COVID pandemic. Young adults who were having difficulty getting traction in their economic lives before COVID struck found themselves even further disadvantaged.

If we consider the elements of the good life for the aspiring middle class, they include the ability to afford a home without consuming an excessive portion of one's income; the wherewithal to attend college or send one's children to college without disabling debt; the prospect of good jobs and a rewarding career; decent and affordable health coverage; secure retirement; and the capacity to accumulate modest wealth over one's lifetime.

Every one of these has become less reliable and more expensive over the three generations who were born since about 1960—and with each succeeding one, it gets worse. Avoidable catastrophes such as the 2008 financial collapse, the deepening onset of global climate change, and partially avoidable crises such as the 2020 pandemic and its economic costs, only intensify these trends. And as if to mock the darkening horizons for ordinary middle-class people and their kids, extreme wealth has only become more concentrated during this entire period.

The statistics of the great generational tailwind and its reversal are stunning. Of men born between 1940 and 1945—my generation—more than 90 percent would go on as adults to earn more than their fathers had. (These numbers are adjusted for inflation.) By the time the generation born in 1961 came along—late "baby boomers"—the figure had dropped to 60 percent. And by 1984, men born in that year had less than a 50 percent chance of earning more than their fathers, according to the Harvard economist Raj Chetty. The trend has only worsened for people born later.

As Chetty and his colleagues have documented, as the cost of making it into the middle class has increased, the affluence of one's parents matters far more than it once did. The percentage of people likely to end up as adults in the same income quartile as their parents has steadily risen.*

The ability of well-off parents to pass on their status has increased, as socially-provided ladders have been weakened. It begins literally before birth, as affluent families tend to have better prenatal care. It continues as well-off children have better pre-kindergarten, attend either good suburban public schools or private ones, enjoy a multitude of costly enrichment activities, and have a big head start at getting into a good college.

They are likely to graduate college free of debt, get parental help with their first down payment, and when (grand-)children come along, their own parents often help with expenses. In other countries, some of these expenses, such as high-quality universal pre-K and daycare, are provided socially. Not in the US. According to economist Chetty, a young person whose parents are

---

* Chetty, "The Fading American Dream," https://opportunityinsights.org/national_trends/

in the wealthiest one percent is 71 times more likely to get into an Ivy League college than one in the bottom 20 percent.

Here is the core point to keep in mind: If we take a closer look at the elements of the good life that got away from younger Americans, each reflects a different blend of random shifts and deliberate political choices, mostly the latter that might have been different.

Take the case of debt-free college. Free higher public education in America goes back to the Morrill Act of 1862. Free higher education was also provided to vets by the 1945 GI Bill of Rights, which even included living stipends. Beginning in the 1960s, Pell Grants covered a substantial share of tuition for those of modest income. In 1975-76, a Pell Grant covered three-fourths of the cost of attending a public university. Today, it covers less than 30 percent, and debt must make up the rest.*

Of course, it was relatively easier to finance free higher education at a time when a relatively small fraction of Americans went to college. As late as 1960, only about 8 percent of Americans had a college degree. Today, the number exceeds 40 percent.

However, demographics tell only part of the story. Beginning in the 1980s, state legislatures went on a tax-cutting binge, setting off a four-decade process of shifting public colleges from tax support to reliance on tuition and fees, and hence debt. Today, less than one-quarter of public university costs come from appropriated public funds. The federal student loan system was also structured as a mostly for-profit operation guaranteed by the government. A side effect was that even as interest rates began falling, interest charges on most student loans stayed high.

So there was an awful rendezvous of several perverse policies that led to a situation nobody would have voted for. In 1980, no

---

* Pell Grants, National College Attainment Network. https://www.ncan.org/page/pell

politician would have flatly declared, Let's create a system that cuts spending for free public institutions and instead encumbers young adults with debt before their economic lives even begin. But that is exactly what occurred.

And while it is obviously more costly to finance free or cheap higher education for a population where half of young people go to college, some European countries with comparable college graduation rates still manage it. Free public university for all Americans who qualify would cost about $100 billion a year—not chicken feed, but a lot less than the cost of recent tax cuts. The student debt crisis and the burden on younger people are mainly the result of bad policy. Different choices could have been made — and still could be.

Private colleges and universities were also less costly fifty years ago, in part because they were simpler affairs. Colleges did not play the rankings game. They did not construct costly amenities to attract well-off students whose families could pay expensive sticker prices. Administrations were far less bloated.

I went to Oberlin on a mix of summer and part-time jobs, a small scholarship, and some savings my mother had put aside from my father's veterans' benefits. In those years, Oberlin cost about $10,000 for four years all-inclusive—tuition, fees, room, board, and books. The ratio of college tuition to median income, public as well as private, has steadily worsened. Had I not been able to afford Oberlin, I could have gone to one of the State University of New York campuses for free.

The debt-for-diploma part of America's escalating war against the life chances of its young could be fixed, if we had the political will. Today, total college-loan debt exceeds $1.8 trillion, and the average graduate carries over $40,000 of debt. There is a direct connection between increased college debt and declining home-ownership rates for the young. The average age of first-time homeownership is now 40, an all-time record. An individual or couple carrying debts that require monthly payments of several hundred dollars will have more difficulty obtaining a mortgage. And once again, the averages are misleading. Rich people generally pay tuition for their kids and so their offspring graduate debt-free. Black families have suffered the most extreme drop in homeownership rates.

But housing, the other prime badge of membership in the middle class, is tougher to restore to what it was when Sharland and I accumulated windfall housing wealth, because of unique circumstances that no longer exist. In the 1930s, the New Deal put the federal government squarely on the side of mass homeownership. Three separate federal agencies created long-term, low-interest-rate mortgages, insured them, and created a secondary market to purchase them, in order to replenish the funds of local savings and loans and community banks. After the war, cheap mortgages were available through either the FHA or the VA.

But that is only part of the story. Housing was cheap in the years after World War II, partly because so much cheap farmland was being converted to suburbia. Today, land costs are a big part of housing costs. The federal government helped promote the move to suburbia by building highways. The rise in housing prices was one part the accident of inflation that began in the 1970s, one part the removal of policies aimed at helping people become first-time homeowners, and one part the end of cheap land.

Those policies might have been different. But the policies pursued, such as the tax-deductibility of mortgage interest and the almost total absence of subsidies to help prospective first-time home buyers get their foot in the door, only exacerbated the underlying trends. It will take a reversal of subsidy policies to help young people become homeowners. Even with that, the windfall appreciation in housing values was almost surely a one-time event.

We will need other strategies to promote wealth-building for the non-rich. I will have more to say about those in later chapters.

The reversal of the great economic tailwind included not just higher education and housing. There were also drastic transformations in the organization of employment. When I was a young adult, most jobs were payroll jobs. You worked for an employer as a regular employee, and you received a W-2 tax form. That meant the employer paid half the cost of your Social Security payroll deductions. Whether in the blue-collar economy or among professionals, if you did a good job, you could expect something like lifetime employment. More than half of all jobs came with health and pension benefits.

Fifty years ago, the typical worker in a decent job had a true pension. The pension was based on years of service times wages paid in the final few years. Workers could retire with 80 or 85 percent of their final wages. These so-called defined pensions operated not just in unionized companies but in Fortune 1000 employers generally.

In the 1970s, when industry had a bad decade, major companies began shifting to 401(k) plans, in which workers paid more of the cost and bore all of the risk. Today, only 11 percent of workers have traditional pensions, and only a small fraction of workers in their fifties and sixties have enough money in 401(k) plans to finance more than a few years of retirement. Workers risk outliving savings, getting caught in a down stock market, and making bad choices in terms of which financial companies hold and manage their accounts.

All told, 401(k) accounts hold about $7 trillion of assets. If Wall Street middlemen take 2 percent, that's $140 billion a year. Comparatively speaking, the public Social Security system is simplicity itself. You pay FICA taxes during your working life, and when you retire, the government cuts you a check that reliably comes every month. It's adjusted for inflation. It comes as long as you live. Administrative costs are trivial, and no fees are taken out by middlemen. There is no risk of making bad investments.

We are unlikely to return to a traditional pension system. We don't have the stable corporate structure of that era, and it was easier to build such a system during the postwar boom when the ratio of workers to retirees was more favorable. The sensible and radical remedy is to create a second tier of Social Security, as a universal, portable pension.

This system of broad economic justice has gotten away from us because of a transformation of political power, in favor of capital and against labor. As I've suggested, these generational shifts were the result of both fortuitous circumstances and deliberate policies. If we want to change them to give younger people without affluent parents a shot at the good life, that will take both better popular understanding and deliberate politics.

In 1975, I took a sabbatical from journalism to work as chief investigator of the Senate Banking Committee. At the time, it felt like a safe haven after a humiliating career misstep, a painful temporary time-out. But it turned out to be one of the best jobs I ever had—a major education about the economy, politics, finance, and the strategy of how to achieve structural change. My experience investigating the banking system became foundational for my subsequent career as an economics journalist, at a pivotal time when the well-regulated financial system of the New Deal era began escaping its moorings, to the detriment of the broader economy.

Chapter 3

The Rewards of Failure

In the brutal turning of the terms of economic mobility against each succeeding generation, the increasingly predatory financial economy played a key role. Wall Street's excesses were enabled by presidents of both political parties. Due to improbable luck, good and bad, I had a front row seat to the process of the liberation of finance from its New Deal regulatory constraints and the political consequences that followed. But first, I had a major career humiliation.

In late 1973, a position on the national staff of the Washington Post came open. In that era, the entire Post national staff was just 25 people. An editor at the paper whom I knew socially, Larry Stern, encouraged me to apply for the job. It seemed like a preposterous long shot.

At the time, the national editor, Dick Harwood, was feeling upstaged by two young police reporters on the Metro Desk named Woodward and Bernstein, who had broken the first Watergate story and kept running with it, while the national staff reporters were adding just about nothing. Harwood wanted his own answer to Woodward and Bernstein.

For reasons I'll never grasp, he hired me. To say this was a set-up for failure is the mother of all understatements.

I had never worked on a daily. Most of my print work was for the Village Voice. I had done several feature pieces for a wonderful insurgent journalism review called (More), where my mentors were Dick Pollak, who later became literary editor of The Nation, and the great historical journalist and author J. Anthony Lukas. I had only just published my first major magazine piece, an investigative article for the New York Times Magazine on Nixon's failed efforts to weaponize the IRS. I had an assignment from Harpers to write a piece about the impact of campaign finance.

In my job interview with executive editor Ben Bradlee and national editor Dick Harwood, I pitched a new investigative beat on money and politics. They must have liked it. That idea intersected with Nixon's corruption and major aspects of the Watergate scandal. But of course, Carl and Bob had a nearly two-year head start on Watergate. They owned the story.

That winter, there was a strike at the Post, which delayed my start date. When I reported for work in April 1974, our first child had just been born. The newsroom was organized into carrels with four desks. My carrel mates were two legends more than a decade my senior, Bill Greider, later the Post's national editor; Mort Mintz, scourge of the drug industry and the Pentagon; plus the Post's virtuoso Supreme Court reporter, Jack MacKenzie.

On my very first day on the job, Mort Mintz asked if I could do him a favor. Mort was covering the effort to keep a government entity called the Renegotiation Board alive. Mort, characteristically, was both reporter and protagonist. He was doing everything he could to keep Nixon and industry allies of the Pentagon from killing the board.

During World War II, when there was crash production of supplies for the military, defense contractors profited handsomely from cost-plus contracts. The Renegotiation Board was created to conduct audits after the fact. If profits turned out to be excessive, the contractor had to repay the government. The board saved taxpayers tens of billions of dollars. Miraculously, it had survived from the early 1940s into the 1970s.

But now Nixon appointees at the Board were on the verge of shutting it down. Mort had developed some sources on the board, who kept him apprised of the infighting, and he had a major piece about to run in tomorrow's Post. He had gotten hold of a staff list of the Board with phone numbers, and he had devised a plan to protect his sources.

Bob, he said, you and I are going to divide up this list. You call each number, and you say, "Hello, this is Bob Kuttner from the Washington Post. I'm doing a story on the Renegotiation Board. Can I talk with you?" They will, of course, say no. Try to keep them on the phone for a little while, then call the next one. That way, Mort continued, when my story runs tomorrow, and they interrogate the staff to find the treacherous leaker who talked to the Post, there is a record that they all did.

I don't recall if my jaw literally dropped, but I was gob-smacked by Mort's ingenuity. I must have made sixty phone calls. I still smile when I imagine the meeting where the whole staff is asked, Who's the SOB who talked to the Post? To this day, one of the things I coach young reporters on is the importance of protecting sources.

After that, my first several weeks went decently. I had a few stories on page one, but there was no way I was going to scoop Woodward and Bernstein. Then disaster struck. The Post purchased the Trenton Times. They needed a Post veteran to run it. So they dispatched Dick Harwood.

My new boss as national editor was Harry Rosenfeld, the Metro editor who had championed Woodward and Bernstein and fought to keep them in charge of the Watergate story. He was incensed when the Post went outside to hire me to fill the national desk position rather than promoting Woodward or Bernstein or both. Worse, I was still on my probationary six months.

Harry reassigned me to cover the Justice Department, a fool's errand. Woodward and Bernstein had been getting their scoops everywhere but at the Justice Department, which was filled with Nixon loyalists. Meanwhile, my wife had been struggling as a new mother. I had promised her three Saturdays in a row that we would have some family time, and each Saturday, I was called into work.

On a Friday night, before the third Saturday, the phone rang. The desk was calling to say that Harry wanted me to come in to cover a press conference. It's a nothing event, I said, we've already had that story in the paper. Please tell Harry there's no point in covering it. When I came in on Monday, Harry was livid. I explained that we had already run the story, that my wife and I had a new baby, and that I had promised her some family time that had already been cancelled twice. Harry looked at me icily: "My wife would have understood."

My probationary period was extended. I knew it was only a matter of time before I would be fired, or maybe demoted to cover the school board in Montgomery County. I began looking for a job. As luck would have it, the great progressive Wisconsin Senator, William Proxmire, was about to take over as chair of the Senate Banking Committee. The current chair, John Sparkman of Alabama, a friend of the financial industry, was moving over to chair the Foreign Relations Committee.

As chair of the Banking Committee's subcommittee on Consumer Affairs, Proxmire had held several investigative hearings on banking abuses and had succeeded in getting Congress to pass one piece of reform legislation after another. The bankers hated him and did what they could to block his ascent, but they failed. Now the highly effective staff director of the consumer subcommittee, Ken McLean, would become staff director of the full committee, and he and Proxmire would get three more staff slots. One was the position of chief investigator. The Post was not a bad credential, even if I was falling on my face. For the moment, I was still employed there. Ken and I hit it off. The final job interview was with the senator.

Proxmire was a unique specimen. He took no campaign contributions. He abhorred waste in government and gave out a facetious annual "Golden Fleece" award to mock foolish uses of federal spending. He jogged to work every day, long before jogging became fashionable, running the four miles from Upper Connecticut Avenue to the Senate. He had been defeated three times in runs for governor before finally winning a special Senate election in 1957 to fill the seat formerly held by Joe McCarthy. Unlike some legislators who are tyrants to their staff, Prox was a sweetheart, and utterly principled.

Most Senate offices are festooned with photos of the senator with presidents, celebrities, constituents, and other public officials, almost like a delicatessen. Prox had just one item on his wall. It was a framed quote, in the manner of an old-fashioned sampler. It read, "Success is the Ability to Survive Failure." I stared at the quote. It sure as hell spoke to me. I later researched the source of the quote. It was original to Proxmire. I was in the right place.

I had about a month to kill before the new Senate convened in January 1975. So I took a temporary job as part of a stealth campaign to depose right-wing House Committee chairs. As long as anyone could remember, committee chairs had been filled by seniority. Even though the Watergate class, elected in November 1974 in the wake of Nixon's ouster, was overwhelmingly Democratic, many of the key Committee chairs were still held by conservative Dixiecrats, a throwback to the days going back to FDR when Dixiecrats had a lock on the Democratic congressional party, which they used to block progressive legislation.

The Watergate class was obsessed with process reform. If ever there was a time to end the automatic seniority tradition, it was now. In the 1960s and 1970s, progressive Democrats were very well organized in a large caucus called the Democratic Study Group (DSG), which included nearly all northern Democrats. Its chair and architect was Rep. Phil Burton of San Francisco. Its staff director, Dick Conlon, was a strategic genius. The DSG put out its own analysis of bills, took positions, and whipped its membership on votes.

Burton and Conlon strongly favored killing seniority but did not want to go public with that demand, lest they split the Democratic caucus, whose members included some progressive but controversial committee chairs who owed their posts to seniority, such as the great eccentric populist Wright Patman of Texas, chair of the House Banking Committee. So Conlon cooked up a scheme. He met with Ralph Nader of Public Citizen, then at the peak of his prestige, and David Cohen, who headed the reform group, Common Cause. The idea was that Public Citizen and Common Cause would jointly research, write, and release a report showing the voting record of all House committee chairs and spotlight those who regularly voted against a majority of House Democrats.

Conlon had a pretty good idea of which conservative committee chairs would likely flunk the test, and he targeted several. The report was timed to be released on the eve of the key

Democratic Caucus meeting, where chairs would be picked. In the past, it was just done automatically, by seniority. The reformers' demand was that it should now be done by a vote of the whole Democratic Caucus. The Public Citizen/Common Cause report would provide ammunition for deposing several offending chairmen.

I was hired to write the report. But I was spared the onerous chore of tabulating hundreds of votes, roll call by roll call. That information was leaked to me by Conlon, though the DSG's fingerprints were never on the plan.

After our report was released, the House Democratic Caucus succeeded in ousting two of the most loathsome and racist Dixiecrat chairs, F. Edward Hébert of Louisiana, the right-wing chair of the Armed Services Committee, and W.L. Poage of Texas, the agribusiness-friendly chair of the Agriculture Committee. In voting them out, the Caucus overruled the recommendations of the Democrats' own Steering and Policy Committee. However, there was collateral damage. The populist Texan Wright Patman, now 81, who had made his share of enemies over the years, also lost his chairmanship.

I learned something about strategy and power. Progressives could also play hardball, in this case with a hidden-ball trick.

But nothing lasts forever. The DSG mastermind, Phil Burton, 56, died of a heart attack in 1983. Dick Conlon, at 57, died in 1988 in a freak boating accident. When Republicans took back the House in January 1995, substantially the result of Bill Clinton's missteps, one of the first actions of the new Speaker, Newt Gingrich, a wily hard-baller himself, was to kill the DSG. He did it by prohibiting House members from allocating a portion of their staff allotments to finance independent caucuses. My takeaway, of which more just below, is that these windows of opportunity open only periodically, and it's essential to maximize them.

On my first day on the job at the Senate Banking Committee, Ken handed me a thick folder marked Redlining. The consumer subcommittee had been working with community groups around the country to combat the standard practice in the banking industry of literally drawing red-lined maps of minority or integrated neighborhoods where standard mortgage credit would not be available. This was the legacy of government-sponsored redlining. As late as the 1950s, the FHA underwriting manual required lenders to avoid racially mixed or changing neighborhoods.

Now the full committee would take over the investigation, and it would be my project. Community groups in dozens of cities, I learned, had been conducting painstaking research projects. To find out which banks were redlining, they had to go to recorder-of-deeds offices and look up property transfers, one at a time. They tabulated which banks and S&Ls were taking money out of the community but not putting it back in. Then they organized pressure campaigns against the offending banks and used bad publicity to encourage local citizens to withdraw savings. Only a few banks had relented.

This was mighty impressive. A couple of weeks in, I met with about twenty community activists from different cities and their national leaders. In Chicago, a stay-at-home mother of six named Gale Cincotta lived in the Austin neighborhood on Chicago's West Side, a prime target of racial blockbusters. In the late 1960s, Cincotta, the daughter of Latvian and Greek immigrants, organized the Organization for a Better Austin (OBA) to resist blockbusters and press for normal bank credit; then, in 1972, she created National People's Action on Housing, later renamed National People's Action. With her immense blond bouffant hairdo and street-smart bravado, Cincotta was great newspaper copy for her David-and-Goliath battles.

Cincotta connected with an organizer named Shel Trapp, who had been trained by the great theorist and practitioner of neighborhood organizing, Saul Alinsky. Their strategy was classic Alinsky: Organize your neighbors, do your homework, embarrass the bad guys, work the press, and win some modest victories, which then energizes neighbors to fight for bigger victories.

A second inspired national leader was Monsignor Geno Baroni, a Pittsburgh-based radical priest. Local parishes in Pittsburgh and elsewhere were contending with racial blockbusting and dwindling congregations. Most of these neighborhoods were Catholic and ethnic—Irish, Italian, and Eastern European. Like Cincotta, Baroni taught that the enemy was not Black families seeking housing, but the cynical bankers and brokers exploiting fear and dividing neighbors by race.

Msgr. Baroni founded the National Center for Urban Ethnic Affairs to help local groups exchange information and strategies, working closely with Cincotta. A lot of these local groups were spearheaded by progressive parish priests. A not-so-secret source of their funding was Catholic Charities, the most progressive local face of the Church.

It was a man-bites-dog story: white ethnics battling banks on behalf of racially integrated neighborhoods. Remember, this was only a few years after the civil rights movement split, and militant groups like the Student Non-Violent Coordinating Committee insisted that there was no place for white people in the movement. Civil rights in many quarters became a separatist quest for Black Power, rejecting the role of white allies.

The activists in the anti-redlining movement included Blacks and Latinos whose communities could not get credit, but it also included white people in neighborhoods that were redlined because they were beginning to become integrated. They wanted to resist racial blockbusting and steering by corrupt real estate investors and brokers. The brokers' tactic was to warn whites about the risk of declining property values and to pressure them into panic-selling. They could then flip the property to Blacks, creating a self-fulfilling prophecy. If these neighborhoods could get normal mortgage flows, integration could proceed in a manner that might be sustainable.

The political sophistication of the groups was formidable. Likewise, their knowledge of how banking and real estate worked, as well as their genuine grassroots base and their sense of multiracial coalition and the uses of power. I learned a lot just from meeting with them. But what did they want from Proxmire?

First, they wanted the Banking Committee to hold hearings to publicize the abuses of redlining and the need for reinvestment by local banks. Second, they wanted to spend less time mining files in recorder-of-deeds offices and more time organizing. Their idea was a modest piece of legislation that would require lenders to disclose, by zip code or census tract, the number and value of loans made. Then the organizers could easily tabulate the results, tell the good guys from the bad guys, and marshal community pressure.

I was impressed and totally sold. I briefed Ken and Prox, and they were sold, too. The remedy was pure Proxmire, who was a tight-money progressive. It cost the government nothing and changed corporate behavior by energizing citizens as counterweights. I got the green light to draft what became Senate Bill 1281, the Home Mortgage Disclosure Act of 1975, sponsored by Proxmire, and to organize several days of hearings. What followed was more fun than I'd had since WBAI.

I had worked in both radio and television. Producing a Senate hearing is not that different from producing a large-scale radio or TV show. I went all out. Our four days of hearings, beginning in

May, had 27 live witnesses. The hearing record included more than 1,633 pages of research reports and other exhibits.

Opening the hearing and welcoming community witnesses, Proxmire declared: "Banks welcome their business at the deposit window, but when it comes time for the dream of homeownership," urban savers "find that they live on the wrong side of the tracks." Leaders of community groups such as the East Oakland Housing Committee, the Cincinnati Coalition of Neighborhoods, the Jamaica Plain Community Council in Boston, and several more presented documented findings of pervasive redlining. Joining them in support of the legislation was an impressive array of civil rights leaders, including Clarence Mitchell of the NAACP and Ron Brown, then of the Urban League, as well as Gov. Dan Walker of Illinois and Ken Gibson, the mayor of Newark, on behalf of the US. Conference of Mayors.

Banking representatives of the major banking trade all testified against the bill. Proxmire had a great time interrogating them. We found two community bankers to testify enthusiastically in favor. One was Ron Grzywinski of the South Shore Bank of Chicago, the first community development bank, which had been created to provide credit to Chicago's South Side neighborhoods. The other was Todd Cooke, president of the Philadelphia Savings Fund Society, at the time one of Philadelphia's largest nonprofit savings banks, and a big booster of inner-city reinvestment. The Ford Administration did not send live witnesses but sent statements opposing the idea and warning darkly against government "credit allocation."

We managed to catch the bankers off guard. They didn't think we had the votes to pass it, and they didn't go all out to kill the measure. They overlooked the power of very broad coalitions across several states to work their senators via grassroots lobbying.

The bill was reported out of committee and scheduled for floor action. We knew that the vote would be very close. My job was to call other Senate offices, see what commitments I could get, and report the tally to Proxmire, who would then personally work the phones with uncommitted senators. Prox explained to me that he had two extra votes in his pocket, if he needed them when the bill came to the floor. Senators Bob Byrd and Jennings Randolph of West Virginia didn't really want to vote for the bill, but promised him that they would support it if he needed them. In the end, it passed by two votes, and Byrd and Randolph voted nay. Prox got his bill attached to a must-pass omnibus housing bill in the House, and President Ford signed it.

———

For me, all this was a potent education in the uses of power—grass-roots power, legislative power, and the synergy between the two, as well as an education about economics and banking. In Chicago, where redlining was a major public issue, the Chicago Tribune ran the story of the passage of the disclosure bill as a front-page banner headline and credited local activist Gale Cincotta.

And we weren't finished. We still had our working majority on the Banking Committee, and the community groups were jubilant and newly energized. What else might we do?

In 1976 and early 1977, I continued to meet with community activists. I floated the idea of going beyond mere disclosure and requiring banks to affirmatively seek out ways to increase their lending in formerly redlined communities. And the banks would be scored by regulators on their records. Those with bad records would be denied requests requiring regulatory approval, such as new branches and mergers. The best part of this approach is that the front-line "regulators" keeping bankers honest were community people, not distant bank examiners.

Later, as an editor, I commissioned a piece titled "Regulation as an Organizing Tool."

The community groups got on board, and so did Proxmire. I named the new bill the Community Reinvestment Act (CRA). And again, we held extensive hearings in March 1977. This time, we had the support of the AFL-CIO and several state banking commissioners. And the new Carter Administration didn't oppose it. The bill once again passed narrowly in both the House and the Senate and was signed into law.

After nearly five decades, the Community Reinvestment Act is one of the best pieces of banking legislation. It has reinforced the power of community groups to monitor and pressure banks and has significantly increased the flow of mortgage and small-business credit to lower-income communities and communities of color. The National Community Reinvestment Coalition, relying on both community and regulatory pressure, regularly negotiates agreements with banks with low CRA scores to increase verifiable targets for increased community lending.

But the story has a dark side. Over the decades, CRA was regularly renewed and strengthened by Congress. For Wall Street, fighting hard to resist tougher regulation in more fundamental areas, CRA was a form of what the theologian Reinhold Niebuhr liked to call cheap grace. It showed that bankers could be good guys. But meanwhile, Wall Street was winning much bigger fights.

FDR's regulatory schema of the 1930s, with its tight regulation of commercial banks, investment banks, and stock markets, has been gradually gutted. New tactics, such as leveraged buyouts, and new players, like private equity firms, did end runs around the old regulatory constraints. New opaque products, such as credit derivatives and subprime loans backed by bonds, enabled massive leverage, in which there was no real money backing speculative instruments. It was Bill Clinton, more than either of the presidents

Bush, who was a prime sponsor of the toxic deregulation. His top advisers, Robert Rubin and Larry Summers, were a prime source of bad advice; Rubin for self-interested reasons, since he would soon return to Wall Street even before Clinton's presidency ended.

After the financial collapse of 2008 crashed the larger economy and helped elect Barack Obama, Rubin became a prime architect of Obama's feeble reform program and successfully promoted his protegé, Larry Summers, to serve as Obama's top economic adviser. The resulting reforms did almost nothing to rein in Wall Street's business model. The biggest banks were bigger than ever. And thanks to Clinton's repeal in 1999 of the Roosevelt-era Glass-Steagall Act, which had separated commercial banking from investment banking, the biggest banks had the entire financial system as their playground.

When the house of cards came crashing down in 2008, it was Black and moderate-income white homeowners who paid the price. Some had been talked into taking out subprime loans, whose interest rates would soar after two or three years. Others had standard mortgages, but the value of their homes was caught in the general downdraft. All told, some six million Americans, disproportionately Black, lost their homes to foreclosure.

Three decades of work to increase homeownership, spearheaded by the Home Mortgage Disclosure Act and the Community Reinvestment Act, were wiped out. In the years after the Fair Housing Act of 1968, HMDA in 1975, and CRA in 1977, the rate of Black homeownership peaked at 49.1 percent just before the 2008 collapse. By 2019, it had fallen to 40.1 percent, the lowest in six decades.

And one of the pioneers of community banking, who appeared at our hearings back in 1975, Ron Grzywinski of South Shore Bank, was wiped out in 2011. The bank, renamed Shore Bank, had never made a subprime loan, but the general collapse of property values meant that too many of the bank's mortgage loans were worth less than their collateral, pushing the bank's balance sheet into the red. Obama's people at the Treasury and the Fed found trillions of dollars to bail out the biggest Wall Street bankers who had caused the collapse, but they refused to spend less than $200 million to save Shore Bank.

Citibank, Goldman, Morgan, and the other behemoths were too big to fail, but Shore Bank was too small to matter. Disgracefully, one of the contributing causes of the government's refusal to help an exemplary small bank was that it was located in Barack Obama's old neighborhood, the South Side of Chicago. Obama's political advisers warned that bailing out Shore Bank wouldn't look good, never mind how bad bailing out Citibank looked.

I came to appreciate that community activism needs to connect to the larger project of containing financial capitalism generally. But I got my basic education on banking from my years with Senator Proxmire and the anti-redlining activists.

And it pains me to add one other detail. The road to the repeal of Glass-Steagall in 1999 and the financial collapse that followed began with my hero, Senator Proxmire. In the mid-1970s, inflation was eroding commercial banks' profits. A business loan with a fixed term of five years and a fixed interest rate of six percent would quickly become a money-loser when inflation rose to eight percent.

Later, the system would partly solve this problem by relying more on so-called commercial paper, where the terms are reset more frequently. Banks also reduced their risks by securitizing and selling off their loans. But at the time, the commercial bankers, who were losing money, looked enviously at their investment banker cousins, who were still making fortunes as a kind of cozy cartel. Their pitch to Proxmire and his staff director, Ken McLean, was to let commercial bankers do some investment banking. That way, there would be more competition, which would lower costs; consumers and investors would have more choices; and profits from investment banking could offset losses from commercial banking. Everyone would gain.

Proxmire and McLean both accepted the idea. I was the only member of the Banking Committee senior staff to express skepticism. What happened, of course, was that rather than commercial banks and investment banks competing in each other's markets, a few trillion-dollar giants took over all financial markets.

There is one other important takeaway, which informs the larger story of this book. The period that ended in 1980 was something of a golden age of Congressional investigations, especially investigations of predatory capitalism. There was a virtuous triangle of vigorous public interest groups like Nader's, and the network pulled together by Gale Cincotta, crusading investigative journalists like Mort Mintz, and House or Senate Committees that would take the findings, run with them, add to them, and produce reform legislation. Then public consciousness would be reinforced, activism galvanized, and the groups, the journalists, and the legislators would do it again.

Before the Reagan revolution of 1980 ended the long era of Democratic control of the Senate, there were dozens of progressive senators, operating in the spirit of the New Deal, chairing powerful committees and subcommittees, and producing major reforms. It was one of the ways that the New Deal lived on, long after FDR's death. Unless you lived through that era, or are a history buff, names like Philip Hart, the great Michigan senator and antitrust champion, or Gaylord Nelson of Wisconsin, who exposed abuses in multiple industries, or Frank Moss of Utah, (Utah, no less), scourge of nursing home abuse and profiteering under Medicaid, are just vague names from the past.

Democrats did manage to take back control of Congress at a few points since then. There were some epic investigations, not least of which was the impeachment of Donald Trump, and some world-class investigators like Rep. Jamie Raskin of Maryland and Senator Elizabeth Warren of Massachusetts. But the ongoing legacy of the Senate investigation, as an art form that operated as a counterweight to predatory capitalism, was seriously weakened, just as capitalism was becoming ever more extractive. Meanwhile, the Democratic leadership in Congress often fell to people like Chuck Schumer of New York, long known as the Senator from Wall Street. It is part of the story of how the New Deal social contract got away from us.

———

After CRA was enacted in 1977, it was time to return to journalism. Looking at other senior Senate and House staffers, I saw a pattern. Some made jobs in Congress their life's work, but that wasn't for me. I'd been in the right place at the right time, learned a lot, and made a difference. I did not want to become a lifer. Others used their Capitol Hill experience as a stepping stone to a lobbying career, adding many multiples to their salaries. Even less was that for me.

I spent part of the next year as executive director of the National Commission on Neighborhoods, a panel created by another piece of legislation sponsored by Proxmire to dig deeper into the relationship between healthy urban neighborhoods and bank credit. But I was ready to call it a day; my wife was even more eager to end our time in Washington.

I won a visiting fellowship at Harvard to research what became my first book, *Revolt of the Haves*, on the great California tax revolt, as expressed in Proposition 13. Taxes were almost as interesting and instructive as banks. We decided to stay in Boston, where my career would take off.

After the fellowship ended in 1979, I was hired to serve as editor of the journal, Working Papers for a New Society. When I left Working Papers after three years, BusinessWeek was looking for a token leftish monthly columnist, and I got the job. The Boston Globe took me on as a weekly columnist as well, and I was also hired as economics editor of The New Republic. My specialty was the intersection of economics and politics.

Success is the ability to survive failure.

Chapter 4

Spies Like Us

The political and economic struggles of my adult lifetime were pursued against the backdrop of the Cold War. It's easy to tell a story of the Cold War wrecking American liberalism. Money that might have gone for social outlay went for arms. Anti-Communism pushed American politics to the right generally, as Democrats had to prove their patriotic bona fides in the McCarthy era and radicals were blacklisted, weakening the labor movement. The East-West conflict became a cover for old-fashioned imperialism, as the US sponsored pro-business coups in Guatemala, Chile, and Iran.

But the reality is more complex and more interesting. Until the catastrophe of Vietnam, the welfare state coexisted surprisingly well with the warfare state. The immense buildup of World War II finally ended the mass unemployment of the Great Depression, and the government never shrank back to its pre-Roosevelt size. A much expanded government was useful for properly regulating capitalism and justifying steeply progressive taxation.

In theory, the military sucked up money at the expense of domestic spending, but in the prosperous postwar period, we managed to have both guns and butter. The Pentagon, with its need for new technologies, also served as a closet industrial policy that bolstered American competitiveness.

Under Eisenhower, huge public works projects received broad bipartisan support as long as they included the magic words National Defense tacked onto the legislation. The federal highway program was enacted under the 1956 National Defense Highway Act. (The highways were needed for military transport, but civilian motorists were free to use them, too.) Federal aid to education expanded under the 1958 National Defense Education Act (NDEA). Through the NDEA, I was offered a National Defense Foreign Language graduate fellowship to learn an obscure language needed in the Cold War struggle—Spanish.

Some of my lefty friends would argue that the Vietnam debacle was the inevitable outcome of an American imperium obsessed with containing communism. But as the great German postwar chancellor Konrad Adenauer once observed, history is the sum total of things that might have been different.

Consider: When John Kennedy ran for president in 1960, he ran to Nixon's right on national defense, campaigning on a "missile gap" that turned out to be fictitious. As a defense hawk, he appointed as secretary of state one of the most rigidly anti-communist figures in the foreign policy establishment, Dean Rusk. However, by mid-1963, Kennedy's own views had evolved, and he had opened the door to East-West detente.

In November 1963, just before he was murdered, Kennedy was well on his way to ending active US military involvement in Vietnam. Had Kennedy lived, history would likely have been different. But Lyndon Johnson, a master of domestic legislation, was far more insecure on foreign policy than Kennedy. LBJ listened to Kennedy's hawkish advisers and their domino theory that if Vietnam fell, all of Southeast Asia would fall with it. So Johnson went all-in on Vietnam.

Vietnam was the great needless tragedy of our era. The war ultimately wrecked the most expansive domestic program since the New Deal, LBJ's Great Society. Vietnam splintered the New Deal coalition. The young protestors who opposed the war and the patriotic blue collar union workers who supported it—both onetime Democratic voters—saw each other as the enemy. The civil rights movement, once LBJ's allies, became part of the antiwar movement. Martin Luther King broke with Johnson over the war. College students managed to avoid the draft in large numbers, while working-class kids served. Those who survived, often maimed, were not given parades.

I stayed out of Vietnam thanks to a misdiagnosis of a stomach bug as an ulcer by an incompetent student health service doctor. Had that not worked, I was prepared to join the Peace Corps or go to Canada. A good friend tells the story of being at a draft physical and hearing an announcement that everyone with a doctor's note should go to one side of the room. That entire group was white and educated, while the other side of the room was working class and substantially Black. We all carried around some shame, imagining who served in our place.

These several splits allowed Richard Nixon to narrowly win the 1968 election. It ushered in a mostly Republican era that undermined civil rights and began Nixon's "Southern Strategy" of using racism to convert the Dixiecrat Solid South into a Republican Solid South. In the era spanned by Nixon and Reagan, the problem wasn't just Republicans. Many elected Democrats, competing on Republican turf, strayed from their New Deal roots, distancing themselves from the trade union movement and supporting serial forms of deregulation and privatization that undermined economic security. (See Chapter 7.) The defection of the white working class from the Democrats, and the reciprocal defection of Democrats from policies that served the working class, began a long and winding road that led to Donald Trump.

———

The era defined by civil rights and Vietnam also sheds light on the uneasy alliance between radicals and liberals. The early civil rights protests of the 1950s used radical means—civil disobedience—for liberal ends: a society of equal justice under law, as proclaimed by a unanimous Supreme Court in *Brown v. Board in* 1954. But from the carefully planned arrest of Rosa Parks in 1955 for refusing to sit in the back of the bus, to Dr. Martin Luther King's repeated use of civil disobedience, to the lunch counter sit-ins and freedom rides of the late 1950s, it was radicals who opened up space for liberals. That alliance culminated with the Selma to Montgomery march of 1965, where federal marshals had to countermand state authority to allow Dr. King and his peaceful marchers to reach the Alabama state capital on the third try.

The brutalization of marchers by police on the Edmund Pettis Bridge gave Lyndon Johnson the momentum and backdrop for his greatest speech, calling for Congress to finally pass a federal voting rights act. Johnson ended by declaring, "We shall overcome," embracing the anthem of the movement and associating himself and the power of the presidency with courageous radicals who were breaking the law to vindicate the Constitution. And it worked.

The antiwar protests displayed the same uneasy alliance between radicals and liberals. In 1964, when the left was still appreciative of Johnson's Great Society and civil rights efforts but increasingly opposed to the deepening Vietnam War, a Students for a Democratic Society button circulated at the Atlantic City Democratic National Convention captured the ambivalence perfectly. The SDS button punned on the campaign slogan, All the Way with LBJ. It read: "Part of the Way with LBJ." Johnson's Great Society would get America only part of the way to where we needed to get domestically. And we were only partly with LBJ, on civil rights, but not on the war.

Our support for Johnson was skeptical and conditional, and with good reason. Just two weeks before the convention, Johnson had used a grossly exaggerated attack by North Vietnamese patrol boats on two US destroyers in the Tonkin Gulf to get a blank check resolution from Congress to escalate the war.

I still have that button. I had gone to the Atlantic City convention with the Young Democrats in order to smuggle floor passes to members of the Mississippi Freedom Democratic Party (MFDP). The official Mississippi Democratic Party, which resisted any Black participation in our democracy, had sent an all-white delegation to the convention. Civil rights activists led by Fannie Lou Hamer and Aaron Henry had organized an integrated Freedom Democratic Party and asked the convention to seat their delegation. Johnson dispatched Hubert Humphrey, the party's most credible civil rights leader, who Johnson would soon name as his vice president, along with Walter Reuther and Walter Mondale, to negotiate a deal.

But the insulting final offer proposed seating the regulars as the official Mississippi delegation and giving the MFDP two token at-large seats. Instead, the MFDP walked out. "We didn't come all this way for no two seats," said Ms. Hamer. "All of us is tired." The defection did not hurt Johnson in 1964, but it foreshadowed terrible divisions in 1968 when it was the war that tore the party apart.

As the antiwar movement broadened, once again, radicals

created space for liberals. In 1965 and 1966, it was the radicals who led anti-war protests. In 1967, Jules Feiffer, the cartoonist for the Village Voice, captured the moment perfectly with a drawing of an anxious liberal carrying a sign that read, "A Little Less Bombing." A little less bombing didn't work, as a slogan or as policy, and Johnson kept escalating the war.

Now it fell to liberals to make antiwar sentiment mainstream. Allard Lowenstein, a longtime organizer and later New York Congressman, began to organize what became the Dump Johnson movement, an idea that was dismissed as preposterous—nobody had ever dumped a sitting president who wanted to run for re-election. But Lowenstein and several others managed to enlist Sen. Eugene McCarthy as the antiwar candidate. McCarthy went on to narrowly lose the New Hampshire primary but did well enough that Johnson soon decided to abdicate. And it was thousands of "Be Clean for Gene" kids, working in primaries as patriotic liberals, who contributed to that result.

In the same way, the giant Moratorium marches on Washington, in October and November of 1969, were organized by liberals to demonstrate the widest possible opposition to the war. Extensive negotiations enabled both radicals and liberals to participate. Historians later confirmed that the scale of those protests persuaded Nixon to abandon plans to carpet bomb Hanoi and destroy North Vietnam's system of dikes.

But by 1969, the political damage had been done. Too many activists of my generation could not bring themselves to vote for Hubert Humphrey, who had waited too long to break with Johnson, and his break was only modest. We were partly responsible for the election of Richard Nixon.

The bracketing of civil rights and Vietnam for my generation was captured by an episode at my commencement at Oberlin in 1965. Our commencement speaker was Martin Luther King. The college, ever pursuing balance, had also decided to give an honorary degree to Dean Rusk, a prime architect and defender of the war.

Large numbers of students wanted to boycott commencement, but that would have been an affront to Dr. King. So the student council proposed a compromise. Rusk would agree to a lengthy meeting with student leaders, including me, to discuss the war. At the meeting, we pitched a plan. Why not have the great powers guarantee Vietnam's neutrality? In return, the US would recognize North Vietnam, which was winning on the ground, as the legitimate government of all Vietnam, and call off the war.

Rusk ridiculed us as preposterously naive. In reality, history delivered something very much like our naive plan -- but ten years, tens of thousands of American lives, and millions of Vietnamese lives, later. A bunch of 22-year-olds at Oberlin knew better than Lyndon Johnson's best and brightest.

There was one other serious piece of collateral damage from the Vietnam disaster, known as blowback. The excesses of the Cold War abroad undermined democracy at home. It began in the 1950s with McCarthyism. It continued with J. Edgar Hoover's efforts to ruin Dr. King on the grounds that he was a communist sympathizer or agent, and only worsened after the attacks of 9-11, with the incursions of the USA Patriot Act and the secret FISA Court, which allows spying on Americans.

Quite inadvertently, I became intimately involved with one of the epic chapters of Cold War blowback, the use of the National Student Association as a front for the CIA.

———

As an undergraduate at Oberlin, I had been active in the local chapter of the National Student Association. The NSA, which was a big deal at the time, had an international program that ran exchanges with other national unions of students. The NSA hired desk officers for each region of the world, who got to travel a lot. For some reason, if you worked for the NSA, your all-important draft deferment would be continued, presumably because you still had some kind of student status. The real reason, I would soon learn, was much darker.

I applied to spend a year directing NSA's Latin America program. In 1965-66, I was a graduate student at Berkeley, studying international political economy. My master's thesis was on the influence of colonialism on South American political parties, and my Spanish was decent. Before I was offered the job at NSA, I had an extensive interview with NSA officers and alums who probed my knowledge not just of Latin America but of US politics and my own ideological leanings. Since I would be attending the NSA national convention that August as an incoming staffer, the student council at Berkeley offered to credential me as a Berkeley delegate.

I also applied for a summer internship at the State Department and was delighted and somewhat surprised to be accepted. At Berkeley, I had been volunteering to do press work for an antiwar candidate for Congress, the radical journalist Bob Scheer, who came close to defeating the incumbent mainstream Democratic incumbent, Jeffrey Cohelan. I had also been volunteering at KPFA, a sister station to Pacifica's WBAI in New York.

The people responsible for granting security clearances somehow missed all that. When I reported for work at the State Department that June, having prudently shaved my full beard and gotten a haircut, I was ushered into an orientation session and handed a badge that read, ARA/CCA.

That turned out to stand for American Republics Area/Coordinator of Cuban Affairs. I had been assigned to the Cuba desk, with a top-secret security clearance.

There, I learned something about how the Cold War was actually conducted. This was 1966, only seven years after Fidel Castro had come to power and just five years after America's humiliating defeat in the abortive Bay of Pigs invasion. After Kennedy and Khrushchev had brought the world to the brink of war in the Cuban Missile Crisis of October 1962, they had made a deal where Khrushchev would pull offensive missiles out of Cuba, and the US would withdraw some missiles from Turkey, and cease trying to overthrow Castro, at least overtly.

But the US doubled down on a strategy of trying to strangle the Cuban economy by denying Cuba necessary imports from other nations, not just from the US but from any friendly country with which Washington had some leverage. This was the Cuba boycott, known in State Department-speak as the Quarantine. At age 23, fresh from Berkeley with antiwar views, my summer job was helping to enforce the boycott.

I was assigned to assist the economics desk officer, an affable and eager foreign service officer in his thirties named Charlie Carlisle, who would later turn against the Cuba policy. At the time, he was a ferocious supporter.

Charlie explained to me how it worked. We at the Cuba desk would get classified cables from sources who Charlie called our friends across the river—the CIA. Our friends would advise us that they had learned of a pending shipment of anything from auto parts to oil from a country that traded with Cuba. Our job at the State Department was to contact our embassy in that country and request the embassy to do whatever it took to kill the deal.

Judging by the state of Cuba's economy, the strategy was all too successful. But there was always more to be done. One day,

Charlie had an intoxicating idea, and he was eager for me to hear about it firsthand.

We headed down the hall to the Panama desk, where Charlie pitched the following plan. Several US companies whose assets in Cuba had been expropriated by Castro had won judgments against Cuba in US courts, but had no way of collecting. Suppose, Charlie suggested, the companies went into a Panamanian court, got a judgment against Cuba, and then, when a Cuban ship was steaming along the Panamanian coast, en route to the Panama Canal, the Panamanian coast guard could seize the ship.

The Panama desk officer, an old hand at least two decades Charlie's senior, peered over his glasses. "This time, Charlie," he said, "You've really lost your mind. For one thing, our closest allies, the British, have this thing about freedom of the seas? Second, we've been fighting with the Latinos for decades over whether we recognize a 3-mile limit or a 12-mile limit, and this would be a de facto 3-mile limit. And Charlie, (long pause) Panama doesn't have a coast guard."

Charlie, never one to accept defeat, said. "Maybe we could lend them a ship?"

I spent the rest of the summer helping Charlie and his friends across the river deny the Cuban economy necessary goods, appalled by the whole idea. Six decades later, astonishingly, the boycott is still in effect. Those cute antique 1940s and 1950s Chevys and Fords in Havana are not there as tourist attractions. Cuba is still prohibited from importing US cars or parts, and the US pressures allies, with mixed success, not to sell the Cubans any of their cars. Cuba may be poor partly because of economic mismanagement, but the boycott is a big part of the story.

———

In late August, I headed off to the annual NSA convention, called the National Student Congress, at the University of Illinois at Champaign-Urbana. There, delegates from some 350 member colleges and universities spent the better part of a week debating issues, listening to speakers, passing resolutions, partying, and electing officers for the following year.

Student opinion against the Vietnam War had hardened since the previous summer's National Student Congress in 1965, and this widened tensions between NSA's domestic program and its international one. Domestically, NSA had been on the left edge of student politics, active in the civil rights movement, defending civil liberties, and working for various brands of educational reform. But its international program had been consistently liberal anti-communist. The international program was mysteriously well funded, while much of the domestic program had to scrounge. The NSA Washington headquarters was a double townhouse on S Street in the stylish neighborhood just west of Connecticut Avenue, somehow financed by the international program.

I found myself among the leaders of a group of student delegates who wanted the student congress to take a much more critical position on Vietnam. The US needed to stop the bombing, de-escalate, and negotiate peace. Before I quite appreciated what was happening, I was nominated to run as the antiwar candidate for International Affairs Vice President. The establishment candidate was Rick Stearns, student body president at Stanford, who later became something of an antiwar activist himself, working in the 1972 McGovern campaign. But at the time, he was the moderate. It looked like I had the votes to win.

At that point, something creepy happened. My old friend Ed Schwartz, an Oberlin delegate, was a candidate for National Affairs Vice President. The night before the vote, Ed took me aside and said in a very ominous tone, "Bob, if you win this election, it will ruin your life. I can't tell you why yet, but you will find out very soon. You need to drop out."

My initial reaction was that maybe Ed felt that it would appear unseemly when people found out that, despite my Berkeley credentials, we were both actually from Oberlin. Or perhaps he was thinking that my candidacy for the one job would upstage his for the other. But there was something about the way he talked that made me take him seriously.

So I sought out Rick Stearns, who had far more NSA experience than I, and suggested that the student congress needed unity on Vietnam rather than a split. I offered to drop out and support him if he would agree to stronger antiwar language. The next day, I announced to the assembled delegates that I was ending my candidacy and supporting Rick, in exchange for a tougher resolution opposing the war. I urged a vote for Rick. There were scattered boos, but Stearns was elected almost unanimously.

I then drove back to Washington to take up my new post as the NSA's director of Latin American affairs. I organized a trip to Peru and Bolivia in October to set up exchange visits by delegations from their national student unions. The trips and return visits went swimmingly. In January, the reason for Ed's warning became clear.

The US National Student Association was organized in 1947, one of several so-called national unions of students. They were affiliated with a worldwide body called the International Union of Students (IUS). This was at the dawn of the Cold War, and the IUS was based in Prague, soon the site of the communist coup of 1948. The Soviets and student organizations in satellite countries managed to take over the IUS. The CIA responded by creating its own anti-communist front, the International Student Congress, and began covertly pouring money into non-communist student organizations through dummy foundations.

One of these was the National Student Association. By 1950, the NSA's international program was effectively a CIA front.

Why did the CIA do this? For several reasons. One quiet facet of the Cold War was the US effort to combat communist influence in trade unions, student and youth organizations, and other cultural institutions. The CIA also found it useful to have a covertly affiliated student organization report on foreign student organizations through the NSA's international activities.

A more subtle twist was that the National Student Association could have relationships with radical foreign student organizations that were off-limits to official US government institutions, and thereby cultivate contacts that could prove useful in the future. Student leaders often became national leaders. This was during the period before Britain and France liberated their African colonies, and the official US policy aligned with its close allies. But the NSA could and did have relationships with anti-colonial movements.

At the time, the US officially supported the apartheid regime in South Africa. The illegal anti-apartheid movement included a blend of nationalists and communists. The movement did not trust the US government. But its student wing, the multiracial National Union of South African Students, had good relations with the NSA.

By 1950, all of the NSA's international officers and staffers were effectively CIA agents. They were required to sign a national security oath, which risked a long prison term if they divulged classified information that they learned. To a person, these young student agents were enthusiastic about their work, in part because the CIA was a great place for a liberal anti-communist during the McCarthy era. They not only spied on foreign student movements; they ran operations. By offering travel grants, they could position favored students to win top leadership positions and go on to leading positions in politics.

The NSA staffers could even consort with communists occasionally, as in the case of the anti-colonial movement. Freelance activists doing the same thing risked being red-baited. But because the NSA was de facto a CIA operation, McCarthy and his crew left them alone. A number of radical liberals, such as Yale's influential chaplain William Sloane Coffin, worked for the CIA in those years, as did the feminist Gloria Steinem.

Remarkably, the secret held for sixteen years, from 1950 to 1966. But as students turned increasingly against the Vietnam War, tensions increased to the breaking point. In the anti-communist fifties, the young students had signed the national security oath and begun working as agents willingly, even enthusiastically. But by the early 1960s, as student opinion turned against Cold War excesses like the Bay of Pigs invasion (a CIA operation) and then against Vietnam, many NSA staffers were tricked into signing and cooperating.

The routine worked like this. After being vetted by the CIA and given the job, a new NSA international staffer would be called into an orientation session with an NSA alum who was actually a CIA agent. The new staffer would be told that the NSA's international program had found it useful to be able to have candid conversations with the State Department about conditions in this or that country, subject to signing a national security oath. The staffer would duly sign the oath—and then be told that he was now working for the CIA. Sometimes, spouses were required to sign as well.

Karen Paget, author of the book *Patriotic Betrayal,* tells the story of how she was trapped into signing the oath. Her husband, Mike Enwall, had been hired to work for the NSA's international staff. He had also been tricked into signing. As Paget tells the story, an older man whom she had seen at NSA meetings told her that "my husband was doing work of great importance for the United States government" and handed her a document to sign. "My host then revealed that he worked for the CIA, that the CIA funded the NSA international program, and that he was my husband's case officer." Paget was twenty. The marriage did not withstand the strain.

Until the mid-1960s, CIA agents in the role of NSA staff and alums had been able to manipulate the election of officers to make sure that each incoming class of NSA leaders would continue the CIA relationship. Promising future officers were invited to spend the summer at an institute called the International Student Relations Seminar. The seminar speakers were identified as NSA alums now in foreign policy careers. They were actually CIA agents. Those attendees with the right politics and leadership skills were vetted and groomed to run for election as officers. For fifteen years, the CIA was literally able to pick who would be elected to top NSA posts, in the same way the CIA sought to rig elections overseas.

But as antiwar sentiment grew, the leaders elected to run NSA at the 1964 and 1965 conventions were increasingly skeptical of NSA's international program. Steve Robbins, a UCLA student leader, was not the CIA's choice for president, but he was elected at the 1964 congress and spent the year sparring with the NSA's CIA handlers. Phil Sherburne, from the University of Oregon, elected at the 1965 congress, resolved to end the tie with the CIA. Over the course of a year, Sherburne negotiated an arrangement with the CIA whereby the NSA's international program would gradually seek other funding. The CIA would quietly help with the transition. In return, the NSA officers would never disclose the history.

But this tentative bargain came off the rails. Sherburne, like other officers, had signed a national security oath, and he came under excruciating pressure to accept the CIA's terms. In 1966, he hired a Pomona College dropout and community organizer named Mike Wood to work for the NSA as a fundraiser. Wood had not signed a national security oath but had been told that several foundations were off-limits. He suspected that something was fishy and began asking more questions. Sherburne finally told Wood the truth. The tainted foundations were CIA cutouts.

It was Wood who had spilled the story to my Oberlin friend Ed Schwartz, which was the basis for Ed's ominous warning to me at the NSA 1966 convention. And Wood not only told Ed. In January 1967, he took the story to the leading radical investigative magazine of the day, *Ramparts*, meeting with Ramparts editor-in-chief Warren Hinckle at the Algonquin Hotel in New York. It was only a matter of weeks before the story blew.

This was not Ramparts' first exposé of CIA domestic activities. In June 1966, the magazine published an investigative piece about the CIA's use of Michigan State University to train advisers to the South Vietnamese President Ngo Dinh Diem, who was later assassinated in a coup orchestrated by the CIA. Several of the Americans at Michigan State were, in fact, CIA agents under cover. The piece was written by economist Stanley Sheinbaum, who had been hired by Michigan State to work in the program. He soon learned about the CIA connection, which violated US law prohibiting domestic activity by the CIA, and he took the story to Ramparts. Sheinbaum's co-author was Robert Scheer, the same Scheer in whose antiwar campaign for Congress I had worked at Berkeley.

Tipped off by Mike Wood about the far more consequential NSA operation, Ramparts immediately began researching the dummy foundations that the CIA had created to finance the NSA's international program. This was easily done because foundations are required to file so-called 990 reports with the IRS listing their donors and grantees. It turned out that the CIA officials in charge of the NSA operation had made an elementary tradecraft error. They had failed to compartmentalize their covert funding of several other groups.

By looking up the front foundations that funded NSA, the Ramparts investigators quickly learned that the CIA was also financing the international operations of the AFL-CIO, Encounter magazine, the Congress of Cultural Freedom, MIT's Center for International Studies, and several other supposedly non-governmental institutions. By February, the New York Times had also gotten wind of the story, and there was a race between Ramparts and the Times to publish first.

In late January, NSA President Gene Groves called an emergency meeting of the NSA staff and board to explain the history and its imminent public disclosure. Thanks to Sherburne's resistance to the CIA's demands, international staffers in my year had been spared having to sign a national security oath. We were not told of the CIA connection. Only Groves and Stearns had signed.

Both the outraged staff and the equally appalled board insisted that the NSA go beyond what even Groves and Stearns had been prepared to do in severing all links to the CIA. We needed to cooperate with the press, open our files, and make the whole sordid history public. One of the key leaders of those demands was the chair of NSA's board, Sam Brown of Redlands University, later a key architect of the successful Dump Johnson movement of 1967-68.

Officers and staff then scrambled to protect innocent people. I had made several friends among local student leaders on my two trips to Latin America. Several had come to the United States on exchanges that I had arranged. Now I had to write them and warn, in oblique language, that the US press would soon be publishing articles claiming that the NSA was entangled with the

CIA and that they might be at risk of being branded CIA collaborators.

The NSA had given international credentials to an American graduate student in Poland. The student, Roger Pulvers, had no idea about the CIA tie. When the story broke, the Communist government in Warsaw would take it for granted that Pulvers was a CIA spy. He could be sentenced to a long prison term, or worse. Rick Stearns sent a telegram to Pulvers, told him that his mother was desperately ill, and directed Pulvers to take the next plane home.

It fell to me to warn some other close allies of the NSA of the impending story and the political embarrassment. The NSA had worked closely with the labor movement, especially the United Auto Workers (UAW), still under the inspired leadership of the Reuther brothers. Walter Reuther was the UAW president. Victor Reuther ran the UAW's international program. The Reuthers were quintessential liberal anti-communists. In the 1940s, they had purged communists from their union.

I called Victor to arrange a meeting. There, expecting shock and outrage, I sheepishly informed him of the NSA's long history as a CIA front and the imminent news story. "Oh, no," said Victor, slapping his forehead, "You too?" And he told me, with some chagrin, that the international programs of the UAW and the AFL-CIO had long been financed by the CIA.

Ramparts, a monthly, was planning to publish the article in its March 1967 issue. This was decades before the internet, and there was no way of publishing it online. When it became clear to the Ramparts editors that the Times had much of the story, Ramparts decided to scoop itself and publish its own story as a full-page ad in the Times in February.

As the story was about to break, top CIA officials began getting calls from the Times. They did not want NSA officers to confirm the reports. I was sharing a house with Stearns and two other NSA staffers. One morning, Rick came down for breakfast white as a sheet. He had gotten a call at 4 a.m. from one of the CIA's senior officials, warning that if Stearns corroborated the story, they would make sure that he was sent to the front lines in Vietnam.

All those months, we scared each other and ourselves silly. We had no idea how deep this went or what sort of retribution we faced. We now knew that the CIA had penetrated a wide range of ostensibly private institutions. For all we knew, there was a secret state, run by the CIA, and they would find a way to get us.

I had applied for a Fulbright to spend a year in Chile. But there was obviously no way I could go to Chile and have any credibility with people I'd hope to meet. I would be pegged as a CIA agent. This was far from an idle concern. When Chile's leftist president, Salvador Allende, was ousted and murdered in a vicious coup in 1973, the CIA was behind it. That was the end of my budding career as a Latin Americanist.

————

I took a job as assistant to the legendary independent left journalist I.F. Stone, who ran a weekly newsletter. Stone, known universally as Izzy, was the weekly's editor, and his wife Esther was the publisher. At any given time, they had one young assistant. Others had included Carl Bernstein and Peter Osnos, later national editor of the Post. Izzy had been a hero of mine since I started subscribing to his weekly at Oberlin. Working for the greatest radical journalist of the age seemed both a thrill and good penance for my time at NSA.

I was surprised and pleased to get the job. Oddly, the position came open with great frequency. While working for I.F. Stone sounded like a dream job, the daily reality was all too routine and lonely.

Izzy's assistant had a desk in the basement, surrounded by piles of the Congressional Record, hearing transcripts, and arcane government reports. Izzy was severely hard of hearing, and his signature technique was to find material on the public record that others had missed and to connect the dots. It was his assistant who combed through the material and find the proverbial pony in the manure pile, while Izzy cultivated live sources.

Other than reporting hidden treasures to Izzy, I got to emerge once a day for lunch, served by Esther at the kitchen table. I lasted a couple of months.

Izzy was friends with another hero of mine, Rep. William Fitts Ryan, who represented the Upper West Side of Manhattan in Congress. Ryan was the most left-wing member of the House, the first New York Reform Democrat to oust a Tammany incumbent in a primary, and the first Member of the House to call for an end to the Vietnam War.

Ryan was looking for a legislative assistant. Izzy recommended me for the job. This was another wonderful opportunity, but also frustrating in its own way. I got to draft speeches, do press work, and conduct legislative research. But as a far-left back-bencher who did not chair even a subcommittee, Ryan had zero influence except for his bully pulpit.

Once, I composed a major speech on the war, using quotes from Yeats' celebrated poem, "The Second Coming," which seems to fit far too many ominous historical moments. I knew the poem almost by heart, but asked the Library of Congress for a text just to be sure. Several days went by. Finally, I got a call from a puzzled researcher who reported that there was no record of Rep. Sidney Yates of Illinois ever having written any such poem.

On the side, I began writing articles for Commonweal, of all things, a left-Catholic magazine, which was in need of a Washington correspondent. To avoid compromising Ryan, I had to write under a pseudonym. I came up with Ernest Garvey, a pun on Ernesto Guevara.

After about a year and a half with Ryan, I moved over to Pacifica Radio, which had just opened a Washington Bureau. My experiences during those years, from working on the State Department's Cuba desk through the NSA affair and then working for I.F. Stone and Bill Ryan as the war kept escalating, radicalized me somewhat when it came to US military excesses, but I was still something of a left liberal. I opposed our government's policies but had no sympathy for communism.

Yet the pro-communist protestors who chanted, "Ho-Ho-Ho Chi Minh, NLF is going to win," turned out to be right. Ho and the National Liberation Front of Vietnam did win. The domino theory, in whose name the war was fought, turned out to be totally wrong. Today, communists rule Vietnam, but they view close trading relations with the US as a bulwark against their ancient enemy, China. Communism had one meaning when it was carried out by Stalin. It had a different meaning when Marxism was embraced by national liberation struggles. Yet in power, communists of all stripes were invariably dictators.

On economic issues, however, I became more radical. Divisions over the war had destroyed the New Deal-Great Society coalition. That in turn let in Nixon and then Reagan. In the absence of New Deal counterweights, the resurgence of raw capitalism eviscerated what was left of the Roosevelt social contract, in which working people got a fair shake. Things have only gotten worse since then. That is the defining story of our age. As a writer, editor, and organizer on political economy, my personal project for the past half-century has been all about how we once again regain the insights and the political coalition to housebreak increasingly predatory capitalism.

Chapter 5

The Marketplace of Ideas

In June of 1978, there was a political earthquake in California that created a fault line between the legacy of the New Deal and the turn to conservatism that followed. Voters in the Golden State, by a margin of almost two to one, approved a ballot initiative known as Proposition 13, rolling back property taxes by more than six billion dollars annually, despite the devastating effect on public services. Commentators treated the vote as a spasm of almost nihilist repudiation of government.

Proposition 13 looked to be an anti-government revolt, but it turned out to be something more complicated and interesting. It was really a revolt against the grossly unfair allocation of taxes. Nonetheless, Proposition 13 played into the hands of the newly resurgent right and signaled the end of the long era of activist government. Two years later, Reagan won the presidency in a landslide.

A friend suggested that this was an excellent topic for a book. Intrigued, I found an agent and got a contract from Simon & Schuster for what became my first book, *Revolt of the Haves*. I won a fellowship to spend a year at Harvard's Institute of Politics researching and writing it. The book advance would pay for some travel to California.

This came as welcome news to Sharland. My wife experienced Washington as a company town, and she didn't enjoy the company. If you weren't involved in government and politics, you were nobody. Her passion was psychology. She had been working as editor of the American Psychological Association's monthly magazine, but she was interested in getting a degree that would enable her to practice as a therapist.

With my fellowship at Harvard, we could move to Boston for at least a year and hope to stay there. It seemed a better place to raise kids than DC. Sharland was accepted to a doctoral program at Harvard. Although I had grown up in New York, my mother's family, a large matriarchy, was all from Boston, the site of holiday reunions with cousins. I viewed the move to Boston as a homecoming.

Proposition 13 turned out to be a perfect topic for my brand of political economy. Despite the commentators' cliches about a revolt against government, Proposition 13 was mainly a revolt against a tax system that had become grossly unfair. Mainstream liberals had several chances to fix what was broken, but they bungled the job. The initiative thus passed to the far right to be the tribune of popular discontent. If that formulation seems familiar, the liberal failure to address the grievances that led to Proposition 13 was a distant harbinger of Trumpism.

Here's the basic story. The gory details are recounted in *Revolt of the Haves*. Property taxes are based partly on assessments and partly on tax rates. If your house is assessed at a market value of $400,000 and the tax rate is 2 percent, your annual property tax is $8,000. Simple arithmetic. But not so simple in practice. For starters, one agency sets the tax assessment while other agencies set the tax rate. In California, county assessors, who are popularly elected, reassess property values every three years.

As the horrific Los Angeles fires of 2025 showed, Los Angeles suffered from too many intersecting and overlapping local government jurisdictions. Exactly the same problem afflicted property tax policy. Each jurisdiction sets its own tax rate, which adds up to the total homeowner tax. Once inflation spiked property taxes, assigning political responsibility was all but impossible. This was a recipe for a general, know-nothing tax revolt.

In the 1970s, housing prices in California soared. In previous decades, elected assessors would assess houses at less than their market value, winning the gratitude of homeowners. But after a series of scandals in which several assessors went to prison for taking bribes, the legislature passed a reform requiring assessors to closely track actual market values and make assessments according to a strict formula.

In this climate, as assessments skyrocketed, many taxing districts took a free ride on rapidly rising property values and enjoyed windfall increases in their budgets. That in turn saved the state budget a lot of money, since state aid to localities is based on shortfalls in local budgets.

The governor at the time was Jerry Brown, who was hoping to challenge Jimmy Carter for the Democratic nomination in 1980. The same inflation that caused California property taxes to soar had made a wreckage of Carter's presidency. Brown's calling card for national office was that he presented himself as a fiscally responsible progressive. The proof was that California's state budget ran a huge surplus, about $4 billion in 1978. But Brown's dirty little secret was that the state surplus was built on exorbitant property tax increases on homeowners. The more money localities took in, the less money the state aid formulas required Sacramento to part with.

In the year before Proposition 13 passed, Brown and the state legislature dithered and never managed to provide property tax relief. In that climate, a fringe figure named Howard Jarvis was treated as the homeowner's savior. Jarvis, age 76, had been involved in far-right California politics for decades and was not taken seriously even by most Republicans. But as property taxes began to literally price people out of their homes, Jarvis managed to qualify a ballot initiative that limited property taxes to one percent of the value of the property, and limited annual increases to two percent, regardless of the rate of inflation. Actual property taxes would be rolled back to the levels of 1975-76. The government would be out six billion dollars.

Respectable opinion in California viewed the remedy as draconian. But as Gov. Brown and the legislature deadlocked over tax relief, and people found their property taxes doubling and even tripling, Jarvis's initiative became all too mainstream. As luck would have it, one of the counties due for reassessment in the spring of 1978 was Los Angeles, with the state's largest and hottest housing market. The county assessor, a liberal with the poetic name Alexander Pope, knowing the firestorm that would result, tried to delay making public the new assessments until after the election. But Pope could not withstand the pressure, so he came up with a compromise that was the worst of all worlds. His office would not mail the new assessments, but citizens were free to come to his office and look them up.

Predictably, long lines formed, staked out by TV camera crews. People staggered out of the assessor's office, often weeping. With their new tax bills, they would lose their homes. In the space of two weeks, Proposition 13 surged 20 points in the polls. When teachers warned that schools would close, Jarvis replied, "Hell, the schools aren't teaching the kids to read anyway." He became the loveable curmudgeon and avenging angel of the political establishment's failure to listen to the citizenry. The Proposition 13 script prefigured Trump.

My book came out in 1980 to respectable reviews. By now, I was absolutely hooked on writing about topics that blended the economic with the political. Proposition 13 was a good story. Upon investigation, it wasn't quite what you thought it was. It cried out for reportage and explanation.

Despite my efforts to explain what had actually happened, Proposition 13 became part of a simplified narrative of the era, marking a turning away from Big Government. The right took full advantage. The battle of ideas over the meaning of Proposition 13 was as important as the tax revolt itself. The real lesson, tragically overlooked, was that when liberals ignore valid grievances, conservatives and eventually tyrants fill the vacuum.

———

As my fellowship at Harvard was ending, I began writing more magazine pieces. But I really needed a job. As it happened, the editorship at a small magazine of the practical left, called Working Papers for a New Society, came open. I was offered the post.

Working Papers, based in Cambridge, was founded in 1973 by a group of scholars and activists who hoped to salvage something useful out of the political era just ended, in which the long ascendancy of New Deal-Great Society progressivism was definitely over, and so was the more radical Movement of the 1960s. The New Left had fragmented into a violent fringe of Weathermen and a more reformist group without practical influence.

Working Papers was a voice in the wilderness that aspired to learn from recent blunders, plumb progressive history for a usable past, and report on hopeful initiatives, both to inform organizing and to influence the mainstream with evidence and argument.

The editorial board and regular writers included people I admired, then mostly in their thirties and forties, many scholars of the first rank, such as Christopher Jencks, Robert Heilbroner, Jane Mansbridge, Richard Barnet, Emma Rothschild, Frances Fox Piven, and Paul Starr, who would later become my collaborator and close friend in founding The American Prospect.

In its first six years, before I became its editor, Working Papers covered what brands of progressive politics and economics gained some traction, which efforts failed, and what could be learned. It was admirably curious and modest, never sloganeering or strident. Its essays were empirical as well as good-humored. Unlike so much of the left, which tended to fragment into narrow ideological factions that argued about such things as who was the true heir to Trotsky, Working Papers was blissfully free of sectarianism. Like small magazines at their best, it reflected and created an intellectual community. It was a model of the kind of journalism I hoped to carry forward.

In looking back over Working Papers articles, I'm reminded again of how the same struggles and the same temporary gains, often followed by defeats, keep recurring. It's why my hero is Sisyphus. Although the rock eventually comes tumbling back down the hill, sometimes it stays put for a long while. The industrial labor movement that took root in the 1930s and 1940s has been decimated by a combination of union-busting, outsourcing, and deindustrialization. But for two generations, it allowed blue-collar workers a decent, middle-class life. There likewise have been two partly aborted efforts at Reconstruction, first in the 1870s and again in the 1960s. Along the way, there have been undeniable gains. We must now attempt a third Reconstruction.

In short, the same conflicts repeat and sometimes produce results. Some people stay the course for a lifetime. I don't know whether this makes me an optimist or a pessimist, maybe a realist who has retained some idealism. But if we are serious about understanding history, yesterday's struggles can inform tomorrow's.

This small magazine was all about practical radicalism at all levels of government, hence the name, *Working Papers for a New Society*. When we founded The American Prospect two decades later, Working Papers was something of a model.

The first cover piece that I assigned at *Working Papers* was by the left economists Bennett Harrison and Barry Bluestone. It was the germ of pioneering work that they did over the next two decades on the de-industrialization of the American economy. The piece showed that most of the factories that closed were, in fact, profitable. But outsourcing production was even more profitable.

At the time, industrial policy was a dirty word. It smacked of central economic planning and even socialism. If market forces dictated that production should move to low-wage countries, with the role of markets played by large multinational corporations, that had to be sufficient. The displaced workers just needed to find something else to do.

In 1953, Charles E. Wilson, the former president of General Motors, who had been nominated to serve as Eisenhower's Defense Secretary, was asked at his confirmation hearing whether he saw any conflicts of interest in his two roles. He famously replied that what was good for General Motors was good for the country. The comment was widely ridiculed. But in the 1950s, when there were virtually no auto imports and the UAW was at the peak of its strength, assuring that autoworkers got their fair share of GM's profits, Wilson was substantially right.

A quarter of a century later, as giant multinational corporations became globally footloose and far less committed to domestic workers and communities, the corporate interest and the national interest diverged. Industrial policy was an effort to right that imbalance. It had been central to the New Deal and would only become semi-respectable in mainstream Democratic circles again under Joe Biden, after so much domestic industry had been lost.

The work of Harrison and Bluestone chimed with my lifelong critique of standard economics and my interest in how economics influenced, and was influenced by, politics. Like Proposition 13, the disdain expressed toward factory workers was another early taproot of Trumpism. Industrial policy remained anathema in mainstream economics, which in turn had far too much influence on the Democratic Party. Barry and Ben both became friends. Ben died in 1999, but Barry, alive and well at this writing, lived long enough to see industrial policy be embraced by the Biden administration.

Working Papers, like other small magazines, was a financially fragile enterprise. By 1983, the publishers were becoming weary of subsidizing a small circulation magazine and came up with the idea of making it a slicker, mass-market publication. They also decided to change its name to Modern Times, but they lacked the money to do it properly. It seemed a good moment to part company. As it turned out, Modern Times lasted one more year and then folded.

———

My friend Rick Hertzberg, then the editor of The New Republic, offered to put me on half-time salary. My title was economics correspondent, then economics editor. In fact, I did no editing but soon became the magazine's main writer on economic topics.

In those years, the once liberal New Republic was schizophrenic and increasingly conservative. Its latest owner, Marty Peretz, was involved with the New Left in the 1960s, but got disgusted with some of its excesses, and had become a neo-conservative. Peretz was also an ardent Zionist. As Israel became more right-wing, so did Peretz. But the quirky Peretz was also loyal to his friends, one of whom was Rick Hertzberg, one of the most talented and personally kind journalists of his generation. Nobody didn't like Rick Hertzberg. So Marty had his stable of neo-con writers and Rich had his stable of liberals.

The liberals included Hertzberg himself, Sid Blumenthal covering politics, Jack Beatty as literary editor, and me. The neo-cons were Morton Kondracke, Charles Krauthammer, and Fred Barnes, as well as Peretz. There were also first-class arts writers and editors, including Stanley Kauffman, Robert Brustein, and Robert Pinsky. Depending on your tastes, it was either an eclectic symposium of different views or an incoherent mash-up.

For almost a decade, the editorship alternated between Hertzberg, who was my sort of left-liberal, and Michael Kinsley, an iconoclast. Kinsley was also going through various personal crises, and at one point fired Hertzberg and me on the same day, and then fired himself. Rick was soon back as editor and reinstated me.

I was profiled in Newsweek as an interesting young left-of-center writer on economics. Not long afterward, the editor of BusinessWeek, Steve Sheppard, got in touch to explain that the magazine was starting a feature called Economic Watch. Four economics columnists would write in weekly rotation: a conventional conservative, an unconventional conservative, a conventional liberal, and an unconventional left-liberal. The mainstream liberal was Princeton economist Alan Blinder, later vice chair of the Federal Reserve. The conservatives were Gary Becker, a leader of the free-market Chicago school and later a Nobel laureate; and Paul Craig Roberts of the Center for Strategic and International Studies, a leading proponent of supply-side economics who had been a Reagan Treasury official. I was the only one without an economics degree. It was nice company.

I also began doing op-eds for my new hometown paper, the Boston Globe. The column was soon syndicated by the Washington Post, which had forgiven me for my earlier lapses.

The 1980s were an awful time for the country, especially if you were any sort of progressive. The decade was good to me personally. I was launched as a national writer on economics. I was something of a minor celebrity in my neighborhood, thanks to the Globe column. One day, after watching me interviewed on TV, my 7-year-old daughter Jess asked, "Daddy, are you famous? I said, "I'm a little bit famous." For better or worse, that has been my lot.

In those years, I worked at home. Having lost my own father at age 9, I loved being the father of young children. I loved that I could be there to greet them after school and be on call for emergencies. Sharland had entered graduate school in 1981. Her schedule allowed her to be home a lot, too, first while she was doing her coursework, then while she was working on her dissertation, and later when she began a private practice in a home office.

I had a great deal on my plate—writing weekly columns for the Globe, the monthly column for BusinessWeek, an average of one feature piece a month for The New Republic, and always working on the next book. I remember it as a time that was both hectic and joyous. I still have a framed 1985 note from my internist: "Bob, your blood tests are fine. Slow down!!"

I began writing more feature pieces for The Atlantic. When the editor, Bill Whitworth, offered me a staff job, I was torn between the opportunity and my loyalty to Rick Hertzberg and The New Republic, and I ended up staying at TNR.

———

In the meantime, the right became increasingly systematic about putting a thumb on the scale of the supposedly free marketplace of ideas. Despite the latent economic power of business and despite the Nixon presidency, liberals had been dominating policy discourse. In August 1971, just before accepting Nixon's nomination to the Supreme Court, Lewis Powell, then a prominent corporate lawyer, was commissioned by the US Chamber of Commerce to write a confidential memorandum for the Chamber entitled "Attack on the American Free Enterprise System," a blueprint for conservative business interests to exercise their dormant political muscle.

Powell was particularly indignant about Ralph Nader, whose 1965 exposé of GM, *Unsafe at Any Speed*, helped Nader build an activist consumer movement that worked closely with progressives in Congress. Powell argued that if Nader could have such anti-corporate influence on a relative shoestring, business, with its far greater resources, needed to systematically pursue Naderism in reverse. As a director of Philip Morris, Powell also believed that the tobacco companies were being treated unfairly by the consumer movement and in the press. (Nader, of course, was right about both the auto industry and tobacco.)

"There always have been some who opposed the American system, and preferred socialism or some form of statism (communism or fascism)," Powell wrote. "But what now concerns us is quite new in the history of America. We are not dealing with sporadic or isolated attacks from a relatively few extremists or even from the minority socialist cadre. Rather, the assault on the enterprise system is broadly based and consistently pursued. It is gaining momentum and converts."

Powell's purpose was to mobilize the business elite to fight back in a systematic fashion. "The painfully sad truth," he wrote, "is that business, including the boards of directors and the top executives of corporations great and small and business organizations at all levels, often have responded — if at all — by appeasement, ineptitude and ignoring the problem."

The influence of Powell's Memorandum can be overstated, but Powell has broad contacts. His efforts helped catalyze the creation of a network of right-wing think tanks, well-funded by conservative foundations. These included the Heritage Foundation, the Cato Institute, the Manhattan Institute, the American Legislative Exchange Council, the Business Roundtable, and the Federalist Society. The sleepy American Enterprise Institute was transformed from a modest research organization into a massive and aggressive think tank. The well-mannered US Chamber became a more forceful lobby.

Meanwhile, conservative funders such as the Coors, Scaife, Olin, and Bradley foundations connected ideology to institutions to strategic politics to policy. They invested in public intellectuals and in media. They saw their common project as movement-building, and they provided long-term funding. New right-wing funders, such as the Koch brothers, joined the movement. By the 1980s, the organized right wing was spending billions of dollars on the creation of a cadre of intellectuals to propagate business-friendly capitalism.

All this was a delayed reaction to the suppressed political influence of capitalists in a capitalist economy, another legacy of Roosevelt. For a time, large corporations believed that labor unions were here to stay and tried to get along with them. The New Deal had divided financial capital into separate, well-regulated industries, and each stayed in its lane. The disgrace of the stock market crash and the success of the New Deal system had pretty well annihilated the intellectual free-market right.

The combination of the bad decade of the 1970s and the indignation of conservatives like Powell created a stunning resurgence. Reagan's election gave it political muscle. And once activated, there was no shortage of money.

This new generation of right-wing donors and think tanks was part of an ecosystem. You could serve in a Republican administration, publish articles in conservative journals, work at one of several of the new think tanks, influence the mass media, and then provide ideas for the next GOP president. This new conservative infrastructure had what the left once had—a movement culture. There was nothing remotely comparable on our side.

I vividly observed this firsthand. In 2003, I was invited to the annual conference of the Philanthropy Roundtable, an association of conservative funders, to debate Bill Kristol, then the editor of *The Weekly Standard*. We were to be the after-lunch entertainment.

I agreed to do it on the condition that they let me stay for the afternoon program. The afternoon panel was made up of the presidents of four of the most influential right-wing think tanks: the American Enterprise Institute (AEI), Heritage, Cato, and the Manhattan Institute. The audience was their funders, the heads of the leading right-wing foundations.

Each think-tank president thanked the foundation presidents in the audience for their long-term financing, with commitments of ten and even twenty years. Ed Crane, president of Cato, pointed out that change takes time. Cato had been investing in the Federalist Society for many years before it became powerful enough to pick federal judges. Chris DeMuth, president of AEI, cited the right's long-term investment in the case for school vouchers, which took decades to become mainstream. As the panelists pointed out, conservative funders gave long-term support to right-wing intellectuals such as Charles Murray and Robert Bork for many years before their work became influential on public debate and policy.

By contrast, the big center-left funders did not view themselves as part of a movement. The idea that they were engaged in a long-term ideological struggle made them uncomfortable. Program officers who were liberals were constrained by business-dominated boards of trustees. Outfits like Ford, Rockefeller, Carnegie, and MacArthur supported a wide range of community causes. Charity and the arts were far less risky than politics. Their philanthropy, which did support social change, was typically project-based and faddish. Priorities and grantees changed with new presidents. Grants were notoriously short-term—a three-year grant was considered a long investment—and nervous program officers tended to meddle.

Even worse, as Karen Paget wrote in 1990 in an early issue of The American Prospect titled "Many Movements, No Majority," the habits of foundation funders reinforced the disabling fragmentation of the American left. As Paget observed, "A major consequence of the necessity to compete for an always scarce dollar is that a 'market niche' mentality has come to dominate many organizations and funders alike. To succeed in raising money, the leaders of each organization are forced to argue that their constituency, geographical domain, issue, or approach to the issue warrants support because it differs from all other competing groups."

The other source of funding for the battle of ideas was individual large donors. Very rich people supporting left institutions was anomalous, especially when it came to constraints on capitalism. There was a natural affinity between wealthy donors and the conservative intellectuals whom they supported to hone rationales for shielding wealth from taxation or regulation. But there was no such affinity on the left. Liberal billionaires tended to lean conservative on economic issues but liberal on "woke" cultural issues, which complicated the left's relationship with its working-class base.

In 2010, the details of what became the Dodd-Frank Act to reform Wall Street were being debated, setting up a classic David-and-Goliath battle. There was a small, underfunded progressive coalition called Americans for Financial Reform (AFR) pushing for strong reforms versus the concentrated lobbying power of Wall Street. AFR was having a terrible time raising foundation money. I was enlisted as half of a two-person delegation to seek support from George Soros, whom I knew slightly. By then, Soros had been a generous benefactor of a range of liberal causes and a large donor to Democratic candidates.

My partner in this effort was a longtime senior employee and confidant of Soros. For 45 minutes, we pitched our hearts out. Soros listened. Finally, he responded. "As you know," he said, "I am conflicted," referring to the fact that his multibillion-dollar fortune came from his speculations as a hedge fund operator. "But I will tell you one thing," he continued. "If anyone is going to criticize Wall Street with my money, it's going to be me."

Needless to say, AFR did not get any money from Soros, nor did Soros support any other efforts to tighten regulation of Wall Street. As I wrote in one of my magazine pieces criticizing the conservatism and unreality of free-market economics, the free marketplace of ideas is one more market that doesn't work like the model.

The big mainstream foundations and individual large donors poured billions into every moderately liberal cause, except the most important one—how to contain predatory capitalism. AFR operated on a modest budget of about $4.5 million. The other main group pressing for reform of financial abuses, Better Markets, depended on the generosity of a handful of dissenting people in the financial industry who resented the rigging of markets.

In 2006, a group of large donors, seeking to bring strategic coherence to liberal funding in order to offset the immense conservative idea-infrastructure, created the Democracy Alliance. The prime donors were billionaires. They included Soros, Hedge fund billionaire and climate activist Tom Steyer, and Peter Lewis, an auto insurance executive, who later became a benefactor to The American Prospect. The longtime executive director was a well-respected human rights activist who had worked for Soros, Gara LaMarche. They underwrote some worthy liberal causes and increasingly got involved in electoral politics to help elect Democrats, but radical reform of financial capitalism, not surprisingly, was not high on their list.

Much later, in 2018, the Hewlett Foundation's president, Larry Kramer, a former dean of Stanford Law School, had a kind of epiphany. Neoliberalism was wrecking both a balanced economy and political democracy. Hewlett has been a centrist foundation, moderately liberal in some respects. Kramer persuaded his board to authorize a new initiative on alternatives to neoliberalism. A $50 million commitment was announced in December 2020, "to help develop a new intellectual paradigm to replace neoliberalism—the framework that has dominated our economic and political debates for more than forty years." Much of it went toward establishing new research centers at universities. A grant went to The American Prospect, for which we were grateful.

Kramer's main interest and most of his funding were more at the level of ideas, and less at the level of altering the structures of power in a capitalist economy. In the Foundation's statement announcing the initiative, Kramer is quoted: "Neoliberalism's emphasis on free-market absolutism has outlived its usefulness...We need a new way of thinking about policy, law, and the proper role of government to shift the underlying terms of debate and open up space for solutions that neoliberalism is currently choking off."

During a two-year period, when a key program officer was

Brian Kettenring, a former leader of the community organization ACORN, some funds flowed to some groups that were serious about power as well as ideas. In the world of liberal foundation philanthropy, Hewlett's project was a one-off.

As a journalist whose beat was political economy, I soon got to know everyone of consequence who was working to constrain predatory finance. It was a dedicated and pathetically small group. It included Damon Silvers, who had both a law degree and an MBA from Harvard. He later became a close adviser to Elizabeth Warren. Damon ran a small unit on capital strategies for the AFl-CIO. The idea was that if labor was going to put pressure on management in collective bargaining, one underutilized front could be proxy fights and leverage on the company's stock. Damon became labor's in-house expert on abuses of financial capitalism. Often, when Wall Street was attempting to influence arcane regulations for its own advantage, the witnesses waiting to testify would be a room full of suits and Damon's AFL-CIO colleague, Heather Slavkin.

The biggest of the liberal think tanks, such as the Center on Budget and Policy Priorities (CBPP) and later the Center for American Progress (CAP), a Democracy Alliance favorite, addressed every aspect of economic inequality in America except for the most important one — the overweening political and economic influence of Wall Street. Somehow, the CBPP, respected for its budget analyses, assumed that you could address poverty without addressing wealth. The Center was rewarded for this discretion. It has been a darling of the big foundations and among the largest of the liberal think tanks, with an annual budget of over $40 million. Robert Rubin has been a regular speaker at its fundraising dinners. CAP has been the Clinton Administration in exile.

In short, there is a political economy of influence. The gross imbalance in the funding of the battle of ideas has had real-world impact—on the conventional wisdom, on the mass media, and on Democrats. In 1984, the Democratic nominee for president, Walter Mondale, disastrously bought into several conservative assumptions about the economy. His acceptance speech for the 1984 nomination virtually apologized to the Republicans for Democrats' liberal heresies and accepted conservative conventional wisdom about the economy. There was not a word in it about the injustices of predatory capitalism and how they dragged down the life changes of ordinary people. The speech was heavily influenced by Robert Rubin, who would go on to give bad advice to Presidents Clinton and Obama and failed candidates John Kerry and Hillary Clinton.

"Look at our platform," Mondale declared. "There are no defense cuts that weaken our security; no business taxes that weaken our economy; no laundry lists that raid our Treasury." And he went on to pledge to raise taxes, not to increase benefits to ordinary Americans, but to cut the federal deficit. This fiscal conservatism may have cheered Rubin and his allies on Wall Street, but it did not make for winning politics. Mondale lost 49 states.

———

At the time, there was no Washington think tank on economic policy grounded in the Roosevelt tradition of a managed and regulated form of capitalism. The Brookings Institution, a center-right institution founded in the 1920s with business money and still substantially supported by business, was regularly and mistakenly referred to as a liberal think tank. Brookings received a large grant from Hewlett.

In 1985, several of us began discussions about what it would take to create a genuinely progressive economics think tank. In the early 1980s, there were two fledgling attempts. Ray Marshall, the University of Texas economist who had been Jimmy Carter's labor secretary and his most liberal appointee, attempted to start one, but it never got out of first gear. Historian Gar Alperovitz and antipoverty activist Jeff Faux had launched a somewhat more ambitious and better-focused effort called the Exploratory Project for Economic Alternatives. But it ran on a shoestring. They lacked the funds even to hire research staff.

After a series of conversations in 1985, I joined Faux, Marshall, Robert Reich, Barry Bluestone, and Lester Thurow (two rare tenured dissenting economists, Bluestone at Boston College and Thurow at MIT) to join forces. We agreed that Faux would direct the new think tank, gave it the plain-vanilla name The Economic Policy Institute (EPI), and set about raising money.

The obvious place for seed money — the only place, really — was the labor movement. The project was initially too leftish and untested to win support from mainstream foundations.

The unions were just entering the steep part of what would be a long downward slide, and they knew it. Reagan was relentlessly hostile to unions, beginning with his breaking of the air traffic controllers' strike in 1981, and signaling to private employers that it was open season on unions. Deindustrialization, which Bluestone and Harrison had written about in Working Papers magazine and in subsequent books, was accelerating, at the expense of the major industrial unions.

The Democratic Party was less of an ally than it had once been. The Democratic Leadership Council, a new centrist group headed by Bill Clinton, was lukewarm to unions at best. The larger unions had their own research departments, but much of their work focused on internal matters such as contract negotiations. What they did not have was a credible external think tank researching such crucial topics as widening income inequality or the impact on working people of trade and deregulation.

We met with several union presidents and secured initial commitments of $100,000 each from the UAW, Steelworkers, and AFSCME. The president of AFSCME, Jerry McEntee, then invited other union presidents to a dinner where Faux made his pitch. In addition to the initial three, several other unions came on board with three-year funding commitments. EPI was officially launched in 1986.

From the very beginning, EPI's board and its staff leaders were determined that EPI would not be a propaganda organization but one devoted to unimpeachable research. We did not need embellishment, for the facts were on our side. America's income distribution was growing grotesquely unequal. Deregulation was not delivering its advertised benefits but was creating a new era of unregulated predatory monopolies. Deindustrialization was real, with increasingly catastrophic effects on regional economies. Globalization, far from producing broad economic benefits, served mainly corporate interests. Even EPI did not have the bandwidth for major projects on the role of finance. Its bread and butter was the subject of wages and employment.

Faux's first hire was Larry Mishel, a young labor economist who had worked in the UAW's research department, to be EPI's chief economist. Mishel set about using meticulous research results to debunk what had become conventional wisdom about productivity and earnings. EPI began publishing an encyclopedic annual research volume called "The State of Working America."

In the 1994 edition of The State of Working America, Mishel included a chart that soon became iconic. It shows two lines, beginning in the late 1940s. One is productivity growth. The other is the growth in median wages. Until the 1970s, the lines went up in lockstep as workers reaped the benefits of a growing economy. After 1979, productivity kept growing, but wages flat-lined. Mainstream economists kept trying to find some technical explanation, but over time, EPI won the debate. This was a political economy story about the widening disparity of power between capital and labor, as capital increasingly set the rules.

EPI and the culture of dissenting economists that EPI helped promote went on to win other debates. One was the widespread view that the widening income inequality was the result of new skills demanded in the digital economy. If workers had the requisite skills, they were compensated accordingly. If not, they were part of a large pool of ordinary workers whose skills had been overtaken by the new economy.

The only problem was that the numbers showed nothing of the sort. So careful and thorough was Michel's research that the mainstream eventually conceded that he was right. Widening income inequality reflected an increasing disparity of power, not of skills. Some of the most highly skilled people in the system, Wall Street traders, crashed the system. Others with advanced skills, such as physicians, lost income to financial engineers who took over the medical system.

Of course, from the point of view of the individual, it made sense to acquire skills. Broadly speaking, higher-skilled people had higher earnings. But that was not the controversy. The mainstream economists were trying to blame widening income inequality on a new pattern of demands for skills, and Mishel's research proved the argument wrong.

On a smaller scale than the giant right-wing think tanks, EPI's research department also served as an incubator. It provided a home to several progressive economists who would go on to staff Democratic presidents when they became once again receptive to the message. EPI senior researcher Jared Bernstein became chair of the Biden Council of Economic Advisers.

It was a long, slow slog, but over nearly forty years, EPI gradually had influence on mainstream ideas about the economy. It was increasingly clear that neoliberalism had been an economic failure. But for its sponsors, it had been a great political success, undermining regulated capitalism and dividing Democrats from each other and from their working-class base.

We had a think tank. Now we needed a magazine.

———

Ever since my days at Working Papers, I had been intrigued by the large influence that can be exerted by small magazines. In the 1980s, nearly all of the action was on the right. Through the National Review, William F. Buckley managed to keep alive the kind of free-market conservatism that had been discredited as a practical failure by the Great Depression and the New Deal. Serious conservatives, Buckley liked to say, had been reduced to a remnant. He used his magazine to rebuild a cohort of like-minded intellectuals, to enlarge the remnant, and influence a broader public. Buckley was also a great debater, and for several years, I was the token liberal on his weekly show, Firing Line.

Another influential center-right magazine was The Public Interest quarterly, founded in 1965 by Daniel Bell and Irving Kristol. Bell, an eminent sociologist who called himself "socialist in economics, liberal in politics, and conservative in culture," was a mentor to my friend and co-editor, Paul Starr. At first, Bell's complex liberalism offset the conservatism of Kristol. The early issues of the Public Interest were a rich symposium of pieces by leading intellectuals with diverse viewpoints. But Kristol soon became the quarterly's dominant editor.

By the early 1970s, Bell had left in frustration, and The Public Interest had become the leading journal of neo-conservatism, railing against the supposed failures of Great Society liberalism. Shrewdly, Kristol and his new co-editor Nathan Glazer published some Democrats as well as Republicans, such as Daniel Patrick Moynihan, but the articles emphasized the supposed excesses of the welfare state, feminism, affirmative action, and the need for a tougher foreign policy.

The Public Interest ceased publishing in 2005, when Kristol retired. There was no logical successor, and his work was done. In a farewell piece in the last issue titled "Forty Good Years," Kristol pointed with satisfaction to all the influence his journal had had in resurrecting intellectually serious conservatism. In 1995, his son Bill Kristol founded yet another neo-conservative magazine, The Weekly Standard. The Standard folded in 2018 when it proved too hostile to the ascendant Trumpers. The successive lurches to the far right had overtaken the Kristol family.

Commentary magazine, which had begun in 1945 as the moderately liberal monthly publication of the American Jewish Committee, had become yet another neo-conservative journal under the editorship of Norman Podhoretz. These magazines not only published established intellectuals, they also incubated and mentored younger ones. They were natural outlets for the products of the new wave of right-wing think tanks, and they pushed the entire intellectual dialogue to the right.

Charles Murray, an obscure researcher at the Manhattan Institute, used dubious logic and tortured arithmetic in his efforts to prove that the War on Poverty had caused poverty by coddling the improvident poor. But there was plenty of poverty before LBJ set about reducing it. Murray's 1984 book blaming the poor for bad habits, *Losing Ground*, was lauded in conservative journals. An even more extreme book, *The Bell Curve*, co-authored with the racist Richard Herrnstein, asserted the genetic inferiority of Blacks. Murray went on to be a fellow at the American Enterprise

Institute. He wrote regularly for Commentary, the Public Interest, the National Review, and The New Republic.

In this climate of a conservative upsurge, some of the conventional wisdom about the need for Democrats to move to the center was being articulated by self-described liberals. The Washington Monthly was founded in 1968 by Charles Peters, a generous man and fine editor who had worked in the Peace Corps under Kennedy. I had published a piece on the politics of affirmative action in one of Charley's first issues.

Charley was convinced that liberals needed to move away from their use of activist government and their alliance with trade unionism and become friendlier to business. He published a "Neoliberal Manifesto", making that case. In issue after issue, the Monthly's articles offered variations on this theme. I felt that this view was profoundly wrong, both economically and politically. Why did we need a second Republican Party?

I liked to quote Harry Truman's aphorism, after he rediscovered his inner New Dealer and won in the 1948 election as an economic progressive: "Given the choice between a Republican and a Republican, the voters will pick the Republican every time." Democrats did themselves no favors by imitating Republicans. To the extent that the Monthly was read in Washington as a font of fresh ideas, it did serious damage to the challenge of rebuilding American progressivism.

The word neoliberalism had two different and partially overlapping meanings, which added to the confusion. As used in academia and in Europe, "liberal" meant free-market. Neoliberalism asserted that economic liberalism in its 19th-century sense, meaning the efficiency of free markets, had been correct after all (that was the *neo* part), and that the Great Depression had been a one-off exception. By the 1980s, neoliberalism had become a general ideology of small government, low taxes, deregulation, privatization, and globalization. Thatcher, Reagan, and some revisionist Democrats embraced neoliberalism, especially when it came to deregulating financial markets. I later wrote that neoliberalism had been an economic failure, but a political success for elites.

In Peters' rather different usage, he imagined a new form of liberalism—a *neo*-liberalism—without activist government and strong unions offsetting the political power and economic predations of organized business. Peters was a strong proponent of community-building ideas like national service. His idealized brand of civic liberalism paid little attention to the politics needed to bring it about, or to the disproportionate power of capital. Both versions of neoliberalism were part of the conservative undertow.

Meanwhile, despite the continuing survival of a few liberals in the New Republic (including me as long as Rick Hertzberg was editor), the magazine increasingly expressed the neoconservative views of its owner, Marty Peretz. By 1991, Hertzberg had left the editorship. The new editor was a 28-year-old gay British conservative and favorite of Peretz named Andrew Sullivan. The fact that Sullivan was gay made it hard to pigeonhole him ideologically. Sullivan was an early advocate of same-sex marriage. But on economics and politics, he was an admirer of Margaret Thatcher and Ronald Reagan, and his assignments and his own writing reflected those views. This was fine with Peretz. On issues other than sexuality, the New Republic was now center-right at best.

The far right took full advantage of this shift, since the New Republic still had a reputation as a liberal magazine. When the New Republic echoed a conservative position (cut taxes on rich people, privatize Social Security, end affirmative action), the right delighted in declaring that "even the New Republic" supports it. Liberal refugees from the New Republic of that era joked that the magazine's name should be changed to *Even the New Republic*. Or maybe *The New Republican*.

The New Republic delighted in being contrarian. Whatever the accepted political or policy analysis, the New Republic looked for ways to take the opposite tack. Under Michael Kinsley, a witty and original cynic, contrarianism sometimes produced smart journalism. One of Kinsley's celebrated pieces pointed out that a gaffe is not a mistake but an occasion when a politician inadvertently blurts out the truth.

But under Peretz and Sullivan, contrarianism was invariably directed against liberal ideas, and the New Republic often published material that was just plain wrong. In 1994, on the eve of Clinton's annual State of the Union address, the New Republic ran a cover piece by conservative pamphleteer and Manhattan Institute fellow Betsy McCaughey intended as a takedown of Clinton's health plan, called No Exit. The article was riddled with errors; it was later revealed that Philip Morris lobbyists had helped write the piece.

Meanwhile, the flagship weekly magazine of the left, the venerable Nation, had moved further left. There had been a time when the pages of the Nation, founded in 1865, and the New Republic, founded in 1914, were not all that different from each other, though the Nation was always a shade more radical and the New Republic was more liberal. But now, the Nation was in one of its hard-left moods, while the New Republic had turned right. The chasm between the New Republic and the Nation was wide enough to drive the entire New Deal through. It was time for a magazine of our own.

Chapter 6

Prospects for America

In November 1988, the Democrats lost their third straight presidential election. Unlike Reagan's blowout re-election victory over Mondale in 1984, the contest between Michael Dukakis and George H.W. Bush in 1988 was close and winnable.

For many politicians and commentators, the takeaway from Dukakis's defeat was that Democrats were too liberal. Dukakis was savaged in Republican ads for having sponsored a work release program that allowed a murderer, Willie Horton, to commit armed robbery and rape. Democrats, many critics concluded, needed to be tougher on crime, friendlier to business, more prudent fiscally, and less indulgent of welfare chiselers. This became the formula of the Democratic Leadership Conference, whose leader, Governor Bill Clinton of Arkansas, would be elected president in 1992.

I had the opposite view. Democrats were losing because they had failed to bring the New Deal up to date in a way that might convince working-class voters, who increasingly felt that neither party served their interests. The Democratic Party was already too corporate. Democrats were already moving toward the center, not for principled or strategic reasons but because of the increasing influence of big money on the supposed party of the people.

I had written a book in 1987 called *The Life of the Party*, making the case for a more believably progressive Democratic Party, and detailing the several forces pushing Democrats away from the kind of progressive populism that had elected FDR four times and had built a multiracial coalition under LBJ until he squandered it on Vietnam.

In the Economic Policy Institute, we now had a think tank articulating the case for a more just form of capitalism, not as far-left radicals but as an influence on mainstream debate. Now we needed a magazine. At their best, magazines could hone a public philosophy, cultivate writers and readers, build a community, and influence public debate.

Even before the defeat of Dukakis, Paul Starr, Bob Reich and I began having conversations about starting a magazine. Paul had moved from Harvard's Sociology Department, where he had gotten his Ph.D., to Princeton. I had first met Paul through my wife Sharland in the mid-1970s, when they were both working for Ralph Nader. Paul, while still a graduate student, wrote an important and prescient book sponsored by Nader called *The Discarded Army*, on how the VA was neglecting returning Vietnam Vets. Sharland, meanwhile, co-authored a Nader book criticizing the National Institute of Mental Health, called *The Madness Establishment*. Paul's dissertation became the draft of his 1980 book, *The Social Transformation of American Medicine*, which won the top awards in history and sociology, as well as the Pulitzer Prize. He was a top-quality research scholar who could also write a superb narrative.

After Sharland and I moved to Boston in 1979, we became

socially friendly with the Starr family. I knew Bob Reich from Washington, where he had been the research and policy director at the Federal Trade Commission while I was working at the Senate. Bob had already published three books and was now teaching at Harvard's Kennedy School.

Rick Hertzberg, then a visiting fellow at Harvard, came to some of our meetings. He had his own grand design for a new liberal magazine that he wanted to call TK. The notation "TK" was widely used in journalism as an abbreviation for material To Come later. (TK because TC might be confused with some other notation.) If you were writing a draft of a piece and planned to fill in a few blanks with your next round of reporting, you wrote TK as a notation to yourself and your editor. Calling the whole magazine TK was a sly inside joke.

Rick wrote up a plan for TK, but investment was not forthcoming, so he soon returned to The New Yorker, where he had spent some of his early career. For more than three decades, Rick's weekly essay that opened each issue of the magazine's Talk of the Town section was simply the best thing in journalism.

Paul, Bob, and I originally wanted to call our magazine The New Century, but that trademark turned out to be taken. So we settled on The American Prospect, a name that sounded both forward-looking and patriotic. The question of frequency was to be decided by how much money we could raise. Paul, impressed by the influence of *The Public Interest,* was partial to a quarterly. I was up for more frequent publication if we could raise the money, but I was happy to see our magazine launched as a quarterly.

We wrote a prospectus titled Reclaim a Tradition, as an invitation to writers, founding subscribers, and donors. "We are creating a journal," we began, "about what America is becoming and what it can be." Why another journal? "At their best, journals create a continuing link among a group of writers and their readers. They give shape to evolving movements of ideas." Our objective, we wrote, is to "restore plausibility, sense, and persuasiveness to American liberalism."

We succeed in enlisting several giants of liberal scholarship. Our editorial board included the historian Alan Brinkley, the journalist J. Anthony Lukas, social scientists Christopher Jencks, Arlie Hochschild, and William Julius Wilson, legal scholars Walter Dellinger, Steven Holmes, and Cass Sunstein, and economists Lester Thurow and Alan Blinder. For our board of sponsors, we enlisted an older generation of liberal greats whom we admired: Kenneth Arrow, Daniel Bell, Kenneth Clark, Marian Wright Edelman, John Kenneth Galbraith, Albert Hirschman, and Arthur Schlesinger, Jr., among others.

At a time when liberalism was on the defensive, politically and ideologically, we were their children—the liberal remnant. Bob, Paul, and I were all in our forties. We sent out subscription pitches to everyone we knew and began raising money. We resolved that we would not launch until we had raised on the order of $200,000, enough to publish with a tiny staff for about two years, during which time we hoped to raise more money. Paul agreed to serve as the hands-on editor, with the office located in Princeton.

We went to see Galbraith at his home on Francis Street in Cambridge. "I don't have wealth but I have income," he said, and wrote us a check for $1,000 on the spot. I went to see Irving Howe at Dissent, where I had published several pieces, both as a courtesy to advise that I was trying to start a publication that he might view as a rival, and to solicit his advice about what it was like to run a small magazine. I admired him immensely. Irving could have been three different people. He was a literary scholar of Faulkner and Thomas Hardy, a distinguished Yiddishist best known for his book, *World of our Fathers*, as well as editor of America's leading socialist magazine.

Irving could not have been more friendly. The more magazines, the merrier. The talk turned to raising money. Let me tell you a story, Irving said. I had a friend in college. Every time he met a pretty girl, he asked her to go to bed with him. "You must get your face slapped a lot," I said to him. "I do," my friend replied, "but I also get laid a lot."

That's how you raise money, Irving said. You get rejected, but keep asking. Much later, I learned that the episode had never happened. It was a variant on an old fundraising joke. But the analogy was all too true.

Paul got an introduction through mutual Princeton friends to Max Palevsky, a brilliant and quirky computer engineer-turned-investor-turned-political philanthropist. Max was on the board of Princeton's Institute for Advanced Study. The computer company he had founded, Scientific Data Systems, was sold to Xerox in 1969 for just under one billion dollars. Max, very much a liberal, was the largest single investor in George McGovern's 1972 campaign for president. Neither Paul nor I had any experience raising money, and we were terrible at it.

We arranged a meeting with Max in Princeton. He was supportive of the idea of a new liberal magazine. How much money did we want from him? Paul and I both beat around the bush. Paul went to see Max at his home in Beverly Hills and asked for $100,000. He still did not get a commitment. A few days later Paul called and asked to speak to Max. His wife answered the phone. "You're a lousy closer," she told Paul and passed the phone to Max. Eventually, he sent us a check for $100,000.

I contacted the president of the Joyce Foundation, Craig Kennedy, via mutual friends. Much to my amazement, he agreed to give us a grant of $50,000 a year for three years, plus another $10,000 for start-up expenses. With other small commitments, we now had well over $200,000. We were in business.

We made plans to publish the first issue in early 1990 and began soliciting articles. In addition to Paul and me as co-editors, we invited Deborah Stone, a young political scientist at MIT, to join as senior editor. The entire paid staff was a recent Hampshire College graduate, David Callahan, as managing editor, and one circulation assistant. David went on to be an influential author of books and articles on liberalism and philanthropy.

For a start-up, our first issue was impressive both for the caliber of the writers and the prescience of the articles. The lead piece by Christopher Jencks and Kathryn Edin was titled "The Real Welfare Problem." The piece was contrarian, but not in the New Republic fashion. At the time, conservatives were making a big issue of welfare cheats. Eventually, Bill Clinton would join with Republicans to "end welfare as we know it," in favor of a meager time-limited program.

Jencks and Edin wrote, based on Edin's extensive field work, that a great many welfare recipients indeed cheated. But that was simply because a welfare check provided too little income to live on.

A second featured piece, by our senior editor Deborah Stone, was titled "AIDS and the Moral Economy of Insurance." As Stone wrote, given the financial and underwriting logic of private health insurance, it made perfect sense to deny coverage to gays because they were indeed more likely to contract AIDS. The conclusion was not that the insurers were right—denying health care to people with AIDS was plainly immoral—but that the nation needed the kind of single pool that you get only with national health insurance.

A third piece, by the eminent Black sociologist, William Julius Wilson, was called "Race-Neutral Policies and the Democratic Coalition". At a time when civil rights advocates were pressing for intensified affirmative action, Wilson argued that universal programs that disproportionately benefited poor people, and thus Blacks, were better coalition politics and ultimately better policy.

All three pieces, with minor variations, could have been published yesterday and would still be as relevant. No other publication with a left-liberal view and aimed at a lay audience was specializing in this sort of piece. These articles were wonky, but powerful as narrative and political analysis, and compellingly written.

There is a term that has become current in the past decade—explanatory journalism. It refers to deeply researched and reported narrative articles that also explain how things work. The Prospect has always done this sort of journalism, though with a core point of view. Pure essay can be too facile, and just-the-facts reporting often misses the larger point.

Thanks to our letter-writing campaign, the initial circulation was around 2,500. We started getting noticed. Newsweek wrote a mostly friendly feature about us, but seemed puzzled that we had not joined the chorus of liberals urging a move toward the center. The New Republic marked our launch with a characteristically snarky short item headed More to Read.

In late 1992, after Clinton was elected, I got an anxious call from Paul. He was a fulltime professor and was starting to advise the Clinton transition on health reform. He could not do all that and also conscientiously edit a magazine, even a quarterly.

We had a three-way call with Bob Reich, who proposed that we move the office to Boston and have me take charge as the hands-on editor with a small salary. We found office space in Cambridge on Mt. Auburn Street near Harvard. We had gotten a few other small grants. The magazine was afloat financially, but barely.

Now I was in mostly charge, though once Paul returned from his sabbatical advising Clinton, he continued as co-editor and resumed assigning pieces. In my own assignments, I balanced the articles mostly written by public-intellectual academics that characterized The Prospect's first two years with more pieces by journalists. I brought in my old desk-mate from the Post, William Greider; my friend E.J. Dionne from Commonweal days; John Judis, who had written about politics for The New Republic; the legal scholar Randall Kennedy, whom I knew from Working Papers; and a BusinessWeek colleague who astutely wrote about labor, John Hoerr. At its best, The Prospect featured scholars who could write jargon-free pieces for a broad audience and journalists who could go deeper than the day's headlines.

————

Early in my tenure, I was sitting at my desk when the phone rang. Hello, the voice said, this is Bill Moyers. Hello, I responded, a little startled, never having met the man. I really like your magazine, he continued. Well, you've made my day. I replied. Let me see if I can make your day some more, he went on. You must need money. I couldn't believe what I was hearing.

Moyers explained that due to the sudden death of a close friend who had been the board chairman of a family philanthropy, the Florence and John Schumann Foundation, he had recently been asked to step in as chair and had a lot of money to give away. How much do you need? he asked.

I took a deep breath and came up with the largest number I could think of. In hindsight, I wish I had added a zero. Our budget is $150,000 a year, I told him. We are hoping to have three years' operating expenses in the bank. So about $500,000?, he asked, rounding it up. Uh, yes, I replied. Fine, Moyers said, send me a one-page letter, and I'll send you a check.

This actually happened, just as I've recounted it. The whole call took five minutes. And the check soon arrived, just as promised. I wish I could report that this was the beginning of a beautiful friendship. In fact, it was the beginning of a complex friendship. Ultimately, Moyers gave us more than $15 million, and almost killed the magazine in the process.

But I am getting ahead of the story.

Bob Reich, meanwhile, became Clinton's secretary of labor. The Prospect was well-read at the Clinton White House, including by the President. In one episode cited in Bob Woodward's book, *The Agenda*, Clinton mentions to Reich an exchange that Reich had with Laura Tyson in the Winter 1991 issue of The Prospect. Tyson, then an economist at Berkeley, would soon become chair of Clinton's Council of Economic Advisers.

The question was whether American ownership of multinational corporations mattered. For Reich, if we had highly skilled workers, the world's corporations would beat a path to our door. American corporations were far from patriotic anyway. Tyson's rebuttal was that German, Japanese, French, and South Korean corporations were far more nationalistic than ours, and it did matter whether US-owned corporations survived and thrived. This was a variation of the industrial policy debate. Woodward quotes Clinton, citing The Prospect and telling Reich, "You know what? Laura was right, and you were wrong."

Not only was one of our 3,000 readers the President of the United States, but our editors and writers were among those populating his cabinet. We were barely two years old, and all of a sudden, we were players. The premise that a little magazine could have a big influence seemed vindicated.

Paul and I disagreed politically about just enough things to run an interesting magazine, but without coming to blows. His was more the sensibility of a social scientist. I was more interested in political coalitions and social movements, and assigning more high-level journalists to write deeply reported pieces and essays.

In one exchange in 1991-92 about the differences between liberalism and socialism, we wrote two pieces followed by rejoinders. Paul's view was that the collapse of communism and the turning of Europe's social democrats away from socialism to more liberal policies suggested that liberalism and socialism were two entirely different traditions, and that American liberalism should have nothing to do with socialism. My response was that American liberalism was weak precisely because capitalism was too powerful, and that liberalism would be strengthened by a big dose of social democracy, public ownership, and greater public provision. This kind of informed argument enriched the magazine.

What nearly wrecked our friendship in the early years was a foolish operating principle that required both of us to sign off on a piece before we approved it for publication. One editor and the writer would agree to revisions, and then the other editor would request further changes. This led to protracted wrangling as well as three-way conflicts with the writer and immense wasting of time. A couple of exasperated authors threatened to stop writing for the magazine. Eventually, Paul and I negotiated a simple treaty. The sponsoring editor would have the last word. The other editor could read the draft submission and make comments, but they were only suggestions. We were freed to argue about more consequential matters.

Though Paul and I had friendly intellectual and political disagreements, The Prospect was spared the kind of sectarian and factional infighting that has plagued so much of the left. We liked and respected each other. We were too small to have factions. We were careful in recruiting staff. For the most part, our small staff respected each other and the mission and were grateful to be there.

As The Prospect gained more attention, we were able to raise more money. Both the Ford and MacArthur foundations each gave us multi-year operating grants, allowing us to increase our frequency to six times a year and hire more staff. We moved to larger offices.

In 1997, I created a two-year writing fellowship, in which we would pay a young writer a good salary and provide extensive coaching and exposure. Our first fellow was Josh Marshall, who went on to invent a whole new form of journalism in the web-log, soon shortened to blog, with Talking Points Memo. Early fellows included Ezra Klein and Jamelle Bouie, who both went on to be New York Times columnists. Others were Matt Yglesias, Dana Goldstein, and Nicholas Confessore. The Prospect became known as a great place to launch a career.

We were doing everything such a magazine is supposed to do. We were cultivating a community of progressive intellectuals, academics, and journalists. Our articles were often quoted and had some influence. In retrospect, we might have left it there and had just as much impact and a lot less stress.

We did not have a single angel but had managed to identify several individual donors who each gave us annual six-figure contributions. Each had a different story, but they were all princi-pled liberals. To be a liberal millionaire was an anomaly. They were supporting an ideology and set of policies that ran counter to their own class interests. The right had no such contradictions and had scads of money for their think tanks and magazines.

———

Our angels had one other thing in common. Most were Jews. They were not especially observant Jews, but they all had evidently taken from Judaism a commitment to intellectual inquiry and social compassion. Later, when I began teaching at Brandeis University's Heller School for Social Policy, I was delighted to learn that the school's motto was Knowledge Advancing Social Justice. That could have been the credo of The Prospect. In the 1950s, when every splinter group of the New York left, also heavily Jewish, seemed to be publishing their own small journals, Alfred Kazin got off a marvelous quip. The People of the Book, he said, had become the people of the magazine.

Our six-figure donors were a fascinating lot. In addition to Palevsky, they included Irving Harris, a Chicago-based philanthropist who had made his fortune co-inventing and marketing the Toni Home Permanent. I was introduced to Irving by Adele Simmons, president of the MacArthur Foundation, one of our early benefactors. Irving, a Yale graduate, was not just a savvy businessman but as serious a liberal intellectual as you'd ever encounter. He was incensed by what Republican administrations were doing to the country and wanted a more robust liberalism. Irving was already in his eighties when I met him. His grandson, David Harris, one of the country's leading experts on reducing child poverty, still supports The Prospect.

Alan Dworsky of Cambridge had a niche practice as an investment adviser. Among other clients, he managed part of the Harvard endowment. Alan and I would regularly meet for lunch and talk politics. We'd go to conferences of the Boston Federal Reserve Bank together. I learned a lot from him about financial markets. Alan had two passions—the resurgence of American progressivism and choral music. He and his wife, Suzanne, felt that choral music was an expression of democracy. They regularly sponsored choral concerts at Tanglewood, the summer home of the

Boston Symphony Orchestra. Until his death in 2021, Alan, over the years, gave The Prospect a total of more than $4 million.

Bernard Rapoport lived in Waco, Texas. His father had emigrated from Russia early in the 20th century to San Antonio and supported the family by selling blankets. Bernard, known to one and all as B, considered himself a socialist. He made his millions by creating a life insurance company whose main clients were union health and welfare plans. The company, American Income Life, was headquartered in Waco. B supported a number of progressive causes, including The Prospect, which he considered not quite socialist enough, but supported us anyway.

Another of our large benefactors was Peter Lewis, from Cleveland. He was also in the insurance business, as chairman of Progressive Insurance, the nation's largest auto insurer. Peter was a major backer of a number of liberal causes, including marijuana legalization, and was a regular user himself. He and I also crossed paths at Oberlin, where he was a major donor to the college.

Sidney Harman was an audio engineer who became wealthy as the founder of the Harman Kardon company. In World War II, serving in the Army Signal Corps, he had designed battlefield "sonic deception" systems to trick enemy forces. In an era when Asian companies increasingly dominated consumer electronics, Harman Kardon, later Harmon International, remained a US-owned industry leader. Sidney served as undersecretary of commerce under Clinton, where he was a staunch advocate of industrial policies.

I had never been around very rich people. I met regularly with our benefactors to keep them apprised of what we were doing, solicit their ideas, and ask for another year's donation. Unlike some heads of liberal organizations, schmoozing with wealthy prospective donors did not come naturally to me. But most of these supporters of The Prospect became friends. Each was something of a unique specimen, and there were never enough anomalous wealthy liberals.

We also had one other improbable large donor. One day in 2001, our development director, Amy Keltz, called to tell me that $25,000 had arrived over the transom from someone named Bill Benter. I suggested that she track him down, thank him, and see if he'd agree to meet with me. We met. Eventually, he gave us more than a million dollars. Bill turned out to have a life story out of a novel.

He was a mathematical genius, personally shy and sweet. His company, Acusis, had developed technology to allow doctors to outsource note-taking to English-speaking transcribers in India. A physician would forward a recording by evening, and the next morning, a transcript would be in his or her in-box. This was long before voice-recognition software. Benter made a lot of money by being one of the first to offer this service. But that was not the deeper source of his wealth.

Bill also turned out to be the world's most successful mathematical sports gambler. As a card counter who kept beating the house, he was soon banned from Las Vegas. But operating out of the Jockey Club in Hong Kong, Bill devised formulas that could pick likely win-place-show results based on such variables as the past record of the horse, the jockey, track conditions, prior match-ups, and the weather. With these formulas, he could consistently beat the odds. He used dozens of straws to place bets and made over a billion dollars.

In politics, Bill was a principled liberal. Though not Jewish, his particular passion was peace in the Middle East. He became a friend and a six-figure benefactor of The Prospect, but only for a few years. The newly created Center for American Progress (CAP), the Clinton Administration in exile, got wind of Benter and began courting him. They were a much bigger player than we were. Benter became a major benefactor of theirs, hoping for greater influence, and dropped us. As the saying goes, we were big-footed. But CAP did little for Benter's passion for Middle East peace.

By about 2020, all of our original large donors had died or become inactive. The next generation of liberal billionaires was different. They tended to be from Silicon Valley or Wall Street. They were often liberal on social questions, but had little use for a magazine whose agenda was better economic regulation and more effective unions. The combination of left-leaning cultural issues and right-leaning economic ones would prove lethal for the Democratic Party.

Most of our early group of angel donors did not ask for anything in return other than the satisfaction of helping to rebuild a progressive intellectual community. But there were exceptions.

In the mid-1990s, we expanded our small board of directors beyond Paul, Bob, and me. Thanks to the connections with the Clinton White House, one of them was a man named Hugh Westbrook, who had become a major donor and fundraiser for Democrats. With Paul Starr and Bob Reich both advising the White House, Westbook was under the impression that The Prospect was very close to the Clintons and that helping the magazine would be a favor to the President.

Westbrook was a former Methodist minister interested in ministering to people with life-threatening illnesses. This was at the very dawn of hospice care. Westbrook realized that if hospices could be qualified for Medicare, there was a lot of money to be made. His political contacts helped Westbrook get this done. Once Medicare approval was assured, Westbrook, as an early mover, got rich founding and operating for-profit hospices through his company, Vitas Healthcare. He also became the chairman of the Democratic Senatorial Campaign Committee, working closely with its Senate leader, New Jersey Democrat Robert Torricelli.

This kind of cross-fertilization of political and financial interests epitomized the degradation of the Democratic Party, but I didn't want to be simon-pure and broke. I figured that we could separate church and state. As it turned out, I figured wrong. Westbrook offered us a handsome donation of $500,000 a year, and in return, we made him board chair.

In late 1999, we received a tip that Sen. Torricelli was being investigated by the Justice Department for kickbacks related to his campaign finance activities. We assigned our own investigative piece to run in our April 2000 issue. Given his close relationship with Torricelli, as a courtesy, I notified Westbrook that we would be running the piece. He asked me to see the text of the article. I told him that I could not possibly do that.

A couple of days later, our executive editor, Scott Stossel, mentioned to me that Westbrook had phoned him, asked to see the galleys, and told him that I had okayed the request. I was dumbfounded. We had a board meeting scheduled for the following week. After conferring with Paul, Bob, and other key board members, I called Hugh, asked for his immediate resignation as chair, and requested that he not attend the board meeting.

In my mind, I pictured the cliched image of a $500,000 check with wings. It would not be the last time that the magazine's financial needs would present excruciating choices. Torricelli was never prosecuted but was forced to resign his Senate seat.

———

Bill Moyers had continued to give the magazine six-figure grants. Around the time of the Hugh Westbrook debacle, Moyers came to me with a much riskier proposition. What we really needed was a weekly, he said, specifically a Washington-based weekly. I was extremely skeptical. We costed it out. The subsidy would need to be at least $5 million to $6 million a year, far more than Moyers could cover. All political magazines lost money. Some had a few very large angels. Others had been around long enough to have a large base of subscribers, advertisers, and individual donors. The alternative was to operate on a shoestring but to have influence. At that point, our paid circulation was around 15,000.

After several long conversations and number crunching, we convinced ourselves and each other that a biweekly would be almost as good as a weekly, but less costly. Moyers committed $3 million a year for four years. By the end of the four years, if the magazine had proved its worth, we would have been able to raise enough money from other sources, including expanded paid circulation and paid ads. I never quite believed that, but it was awfully hard to turn down $12 million. Paul, Bob, and our board agreed. Worst case, we'd have four years to adjust.

Moyers took a very hard line on the move to Washington. This presented an awful dilemma for me personally, since I could not easily leave Boston. My wife had died in 1997, our kids were still relatively young, and my mother had relocated from New York to Boston to be near our family. But Moyers was adamant. If we wanted this immense new support, the magazine had to be in Washington. This meant that I had to give up the job of hands-on editor, unless I wanted to move, which I could not.

The demand seemed arbitrary and irrational. The most influential liberal magazines were based in New York, including The Nation, The New Yorker, Dissent, and The New York Review of Books, as well as Commentary, The Public Interest, and National Review on the right, plus Time, Newsweek, BusinessWeek, and Harpers. The Atlantic, among the most respected and influential of monthlies, was based in Boston. With a good Washington

Bureau or a stable of Washington-based writers, you could have all the coverage you needed, regardless of where the home office was. Moyers himself lived on Central Park West in New York, conveniently near his office at WNET. Do as I say, not as I do.

The 19th-century Anglo-American humorist Oliver Herford once wrote, "My wife has a whim of iron." That was Moyers. The Washington demand was capricious, but he wouldn't back down. So I had a terrible dilemma—relinquish leadership of the magazine, move to DC at the expense of my family, or turn down $12 million.

We eventually agreed that I would continue to be a co-editor, but I would hand off day-to-day authority to a new Washington-based executive editor. But who? You need someone like Harold Meyerson, Bill said. Well, how about Harold Meyerson, I responded.

Harold, then the editor of the LA Weekly, had been contributing superb articles to The Prospect since 1996. We met with Harold, offered him a good salary, and he agreed to relocate to DC take the job, with the move set for the summer of 2001. In the meantime, with a much enlarged budget, we set about recruiting staff for what was now a Washington Bureau. It included Josh Marshall, another former writing fellow, Nick Confessore, who later went to the Times, and Josh Green, who went on to write for the Atlantic and Bloomberg. In the meantime, I had the unenviable task of telling the Boston staff, which I had painstakingly built up, that they had to relocate to DC or be laid off.

The first issue produced from Washington turned out to be right after the attacks of September 11, 2001. This was a moment when there was a broad feeling that America would never be the same, that our country would now be subject to almost random terrorist attacks, and that compromises with liberty might be necessary to protect security. We disagreed. Our coverline was "Defending an Open Society." The illustration was vertical red bars evoking both the twin towers and the American flag. Every piece in that issue has been vindicated.

————

We all soon agreed, Harold most of all, that he wasn't cut out to be a manager. Harold and I had an emergency meeting with Moyers, changed Harold's title to editor-at-large, where he could play to his ample strengths as a writer of features and short topical pieces, as well as a great deadline story editor. And we set about recruiting a new executive editor.

We all admired Michael Tomasky, who was then a senior political writer for New York Magazine. Michael, we had heard, was interested in moving to DC. Paul and I had a long conversation with Michael. We bonded, and we offered Michael the job. There was a bit of ambiguity about who was ultimately in charge. Paul continued as co-editor, with prime responsibility for book reviews. I continued to have some assigning prerogatives, with Michael's advice and consent, but Michael could assign what he wanted. His own politics were closer to Paul's than mine, but we all liked and respected each other.

There were too many hands on the steering wheel, though, and after a couple of years, Michael decided to move on. He founded a terrific small journal called Democracy and has served as editor of the New Republic since 2021.

The year 2001 began a long period when I wasn't fully in charge editorially, but was ultimately responsible for keeping the magazine solvent financially. When the large Moyers grant ran out in 2005, we were far from self-sufficient as a biweekly. We reverted to monthly, then to bimonthly.

For early 2006, we planned a 15th Anniversary fundraising Gala to be held in Boston, where I had lots of contacts from my Globe column. One Boston-based Prospect benefactor who had become a friend was Steve Grossman, whose company handled our direct mail. Steve was a stalwart of Jewish and Democratic Party fundraising, having both been influential in the Camp David peace process and chaired the Democratic National Committee. He later ran for governor. Steve knew one and all. His breakfast hangout was the Charles Hotel in Cambridge, where he would greet half the room on the way to his table.

Over one of Steve's power breakfasts, he explained to me how a gala worked. As a draw, you would find someone who would agree to be honored. The honoree would open his or her rolodex and allow you to solicit friends, colleagues, and clients to buy tickets and tables, with the honoree's encouragement. This struck me as a bit cynical, but what did I know? I later wrote a play (never produced) based on the experience, titled "Deeply Touched."

We began meeting to discuss who might agree to be honored. I went Steve one better. Why honor just one person? Why not honor five or six people, all with extensive networks and rolodexes? The challenge for this sort of thing is that the likeliest suspects have already been honored by someone else.

We hit pure gold with one idea. Ted Kennedy was our most celebrated liberal. It would be trite to honor Ted. But nobody had ever thought to honor his wife, Vicky, whom Ted had married in 1992. Vicky was impressive in her own right and was receiving a lot of credit for keeping Ted on the straight and narrow. When Vicky agreed to be honored, that brought with it the entire Kennedy fundraising machine, with Ted as the closing speaker.

We held the Gala in the grand ballroom of Boston's dowager hotel, the Copley Place, and sold about 400 tickets. The Gala was titled Mightier than the Sword: Honoring Liberal Heroes. Organizing the gala, mining the multiple lists of possible donors, pitching ticket sales, and getting all the details right from the cuisine and table assignments to the program had taken about half my time over a six-month period. It was exhausting. The money we brought in, about $300,000 net of expenses, was what we might have gotten from one large check.

———

The big but temporary grants from Moyers proved to be a mixed blessing in more ways than one. In seeking other support to fill what would soon be a huge hole, I was told time and again, "You don't need my money, you have Bill Moyers' money." Now, that money was gone.

One legacy from the Moyers era was a much-expanded paid circulation of around 40,000, which provided about a third of our income. We managed to raise enough foundation money to be barely solvent as a bimonthly.

In 2007, I had become a part-time research fellow at the think tank Demos, supplementing my Prospect salary. The president of Demos, my friend Miles Rapoport, also served on our board, as did other Demos board members, including Stephen Heintz, the president of Rockefeller Brothers Fund. RBF was one of our supporters.

The missions of The Prospect and Demos were almost perfectly aligned, with Demos as a research and advocacy center and The Prospect as a magazine. In 2009, Miles and I came up with the idea of a quasi-merger. The Prospect would serve as an outlet for many Demos policy papers, which we could shape into magazine pieces. Demos would cover some of our costs. Miles was a far better fundraiser than I was.

We would do this on a trial basis, keeping separate but overlapping boards and separate incorporation, in case the arrangement did not work out. We began the formal partnership in 2010, with Miles as chair of both organizations. In the end, it did not work out. We published a lot of great pieces, but Miles and his board concluded that the arrangement was too much of a drain on Demos. That support ended in 2012. Now we faced an even bigger hole.

I contacted all of our alums and asked them to help with an emergency fundraising drive. Dozens of close friends of the magazine sent out all-points alerts. Jonathan Cohn, one of our early executive editors, then at the New Republic, began a blog post with the words, "A member of the family is in trouble." We raised over $100,000 in the first week and hit our emergency target of $500,000 overall.

Now I was back in charge, and under dire circumstances. Because of our budget crunch, I was operating as both editor and publisher. I cut costs and continued raising money. Paul, as co-editor, worked with the business side and continued assigning pieces. I was helped by a terrific new board chair, Mike Stern, a onetime roommate of Paul's at Columbia, where they both worked on the Columbia Spectator during the epic protests of 1968. Mike had gone on to be a journalist, a PhD in literature, a Charles Dickens scholar, and had gotten a law degree. He was now a successful Silicon Valley lawyer. Mike tended to represent start-ups and avoided toxic tech monopolies. He had also been an executive producer on some movies and was savvy about media, and was a lovely human being. I'm not sure we would have survived without Mike.

———

In August of 2017, my wife, Joan, and I were enjoying our usual late-summer routine of spending a few weeks in a rented house in Lenox, MA, where we attended concerts at Tanglewood, summer home of the Boston Symphony Orchestra, and plays at Shakespeare and Company. During the day, we kept up with work.

One morning, I was startled to receive an email from a staffer at the Trump White House. Steve Bannon, Trump's chief political strategist, had read one of my articles criticizing the free trade establishment. As an economic nationalist, he agreed with my arguments and wanted me to come to the White House to brief Trump's senior staff.

This was the very day that Bannon had already gotten in trouble for praising the neo-Nazi rioters at Charlottesville. Maybe he was hoping to change the subject? Or maybe he wanted to go out with a bang. I explained that my wife and I were on vacation and maybe we could meet at the White House after Labor Day, but that I'd be happy to talk with Bannon on the phone.

An hour later, Bannon called. I hit record on my computer. Bannon, one of the nation's savviest media manipulators, did not bother to say whether the conversation was off-the-record, so everything he said could be quoted. In our conversation, he was wildly incautious, including in his comments on Trump. The last words on the recording, after Bannon hung up, are me saying, Holy Fuck.

Bannon, whom I'd never met, greeted me as if we were soul-mates. "It's a great honor to finally track you down," he began. "I've followed your writing for years, and I think you and I are in the same boat when it comes to China. You absolutely nailed it."

Mainly, Bannon wanted to talk about how his boss, President Trump, was at heart a China hawk but didn't quite get it. He criticized the influence of the Wall Street people around Trump, and his own plans for cleaning house at the Department of State. "They're wetting their pants," he said.

I asked Bannon about the connection between his program of economic nationalism and the ugly white nationalism epitomized by the racist violence in Charlottesville and Trump's reluctance to condemn it. Bannon, after all, was the architect of the strategy of using Breitbart to heat up white nationalism and then rely on the radical right as Trump's base and shock troops.

He dismissed the far right as irrelevant and sidestepped his own role in cultivating it: "Ethno-nationalism—it's losers. It's a fringe element. I think the media plays it up too much, and we gotta help crush it." He added, "These guys are a collection of clowns."

Bannon made one other comment that I wish Democratic Party leaders had taken more seriously. "The Democrats," he said, "the longer they talk about identity politics, I got 'em. I want them to talk about racism every day. If the left is focused on race and identity, and we go with economic nationalism, we can crush the Democrats."

I first called our board chair, Mike Stern, to tell him what happened and get his okay to publish. He began by asking, oddly, what state I was in. I considered the question. Shock? Amazement? Euphoria? "No, where are you physically?", he continued, "Which state?"

Massachusetts, I said. Too bad, said Mike, Massachusetts is a two-party consent state. You did not have his consent to record the conversation.

Well, I responded, can you imagine a journalist being convicted for recording Steve Bannon? Mike did a little quick research and found that there had been no successful prosecutions of journalists in Massachusetts for recording sources without their consent. We decided to damn the torpedoes and publish.

The piece appeared the next day on The Prospect's site as "Steve Bannon, Unrepentant." The piece quoted Bannon saying several things bound to infuriate Trump. It quickly got a million page views and was front-page news.

I started getting calls from all the networks to appear live as soon as I could get on a plane. I was not about to decamp for a tour of networks in New York and Washington, and I had some rare leverage to set the terms. I found that the closest broadcast-quality TV studio was in Amherst, about an hour away. I arranged to spend the entire day there and do serial interviews back-to-back well into the evening. I was transported in network limos.

The next day, Trump fired Bannon. I spent another day camped out in Amherst doing more TV interviews. I appreciated Andy Warhol's quip that everyone will be famous for fifteen minutes. My fifteen minutes lasted two days. Donors were always asking about impact. This was impact.

———

Mike Stern and I slowly returned the magazine to solvency. With just enough money in the bank to attract decent candidates, I set about recruiting a new editor. By this time, I was in my mid-seventies. This new editor had to be my successor, with no ambiguity about who was in charge, though I might continue doing some writing. I also planned a large testimonial dinner, marking The Prospect's 30th year, to raise more of a financial cushion. The testimonial would honor my own quasi-retirement and welcome the new editor-in-chief.

And then I got very lucky. I had published several articles by David Dayen. David had begun in film and TV, moved into blogging, and then became a intrepid investigative reporter. His interests overlapped my own, notably in the areas of financial corruption. He had published the definitive book on the mortgage scandals that had crashed the economy in 2008, called *Chain of Title*.

David had never worked as an article editor, but after a couple of long conversations, I decided to take a big risk, and so did David. With the board's consent, I offered him the job. After taking a very close look at our none-too-reassuring balance sheet, he decided to accept, just in time for our 30th anniversary gala in October 2019, which netted over $300,000. I had pitched the gala as a testimonial and called on a lifetime of friends and professional acquaintances to buy tickets and tables. Sherrod Brown was the featured speaker.

Normally, when the founder of an institution steps down, he quietly goes away. The unanimous advice of the personnel experts is that the successor needs to be clearly in charge, without the predecessor deliberately or inadvertently second-guessing and undermining him. This is known as founder's syndrome. But David has had enough self-confidence to keep me around as a senior writer and occasional editor. I respect that he's unambiguously in charge. Not only is the magazine in good hands, but I still get to be part of it. Hosanna.

Before David, senior staffers, with the exception of Harold Meyerson, tended to treat The Prospect as a career pit-stop, like a triple-A baseball club. Stay a few years, learn the trade, write some impressive pieces, and then move on to a bigger publication. Many went to the Times, the Post, The New Republic, and The Atlantic.

David has treated The Prospect as the place where he builds his own career as he builds the magazine, and the result is a major-league publication. I have written for the best editors of my era, including Bill Whitworth of The Atlantic, Bob Silvers and then Emily Greenhouse of The New York Review of Books, and Rick

Hertzberg of The New Republic. As an editor, Dave Dayen is their equal, maybe even better.

David sent me this holiday card in December 2024.

I want to thank you for trusting me to steward this organization that you built. And I continue to marvel at your consistent brilliant output day after day. I'm so glad you've been freed to write; it's a great asset. Have a great holiday and Happy New Year.

David

For the founder of an institution who kept it afloat for 35 years, it doesn't get any better.

Chapter 7

The Political Economy

The mainstream economics profession serves as the ideological department of political conservatism. Standard economics teaches that markets are basically efficient. With minor exceptions, private supply and demand generates the right mix of products and services, at optimal prices. If that is the case, then government meddling can only make things worse. Unlike the private economy, which operates in a pristine world of self-correcting markets, even well-intentioned government initiatives are tainted by politics.

If markets are basically efficient, they are also basically just. People get what they deserve. "Must be" is the favorite verb form of standard economic discourse. If a billionaire takes out massive profits from the economy, it "must be" because he contributed that much to total economic well-being. Conversely, if a nursing home worker makes only minimum wage, it "must be" that this was all she contributed to the total economic product. For these are the outcomes produced by supply and demand. To reach that conclusion, standard economics assumes equal bargaining power on the part of buyer and seller, worker and boss—another unreal fantasy. It assumes no "externalities"—costs or benefits to society not accurately captured in the price of a given transaction.

Entering Oberlin in 1961, I had been eager to study economics. But when I took an introductory course in the fall of my freshman year, I found the assumptions out of touch with the way the economy operated in the real world. In addition to the mistaken premise of market efficiency, the method of inquiry was formalistic and largely detached from history, political power, and complex human motivations. The idiom was all graphs and equations, built on assumptions that were impervious to contradictory evidence. Economics as a discipline seemed to reward students with a facility for advanced math and an incuriosity about actual institutions. I made myself a total pain in the ass to the instructor.

A lot of what I was being taught defied common sense. If markets were basically efficient and self-correcting, why did they deliver periodic great depressions? How could fifteen percent unemployment ever be efficient? If market prices were basically accurate, why did the market price of carbon create catastrophic climate change? If financial markets priced securities accurately, how could the collapse of 2008 have occurred?

The assumption of efficient markets and the use of abstract algebra reinforced each other, since efficient markets can be modeled, while actual history is messy. I found it surprising and appalling that most professional economists focused relentlessly on formal, stylized models and left out history and politics. To the extent that most mainstream economists included politics at all, they did it via a rudimentary disparagement of interest groups as meddling with market prices, typically trade unions or welfare advocates, but not the most powerful interest group of all in a capitalist economy—namely, capitalists.

By translating Candide's premise that this has to be the best of all possible worlds into abstruse math, the systematic mistakes of the discipline were not just an academic problem; they undermined the self-confidence and program strategies of center-left parties. In the 1990s, the folly of deregulation, privatization, and corporate globalization was embraced by American Democrats and European Social Democrats on the advice of their economists. It turned out to be lethal politics.

A free market does not exist in a state of nature. All the basic rules of the economic game—the definition of property rights, the nature of money, the terms of permissible competition—are defined by the state, even in an ostensibly free-market system. The rules set by the state, in turn, are creatures of politics. As the great political economist and historian Karl Polanyi wrote, savoring the irony, "Laissez-faire was planned."

———

As a college freshman skeptical of what I was being taught in introductory economics, I didn't yet appreciate that I had stumbled upon the difference between *economics* as taught in most universities and *political economy*, which adds the realities of institutional legacy and power. I never took another economics course at Oberlin. Instead, I got accepted to spend my junior year at the London School of Economics, where I studied a blend of applied economics, economic history, and comparative economic systems. Spending a year in London and visiting continental Europe also opened my eyes to the fact that different nations with different governing systems and different political histories have different social contracts. Social democracy can be just as efficient as capitalism—sometimes more efficient—but with very different distributive results.

When I returned to Oberlin for my senior year, I asked my

professors if there was a graduate school where I could earn an economics degree that focused on history, institutions, and political power rather than arcane formulas. I was told that I was too late. They used to teach political economy like that; it was known as institutionalism. But all of the top graduate departments were now committed to the more abstract and mathematical approach, unless I wanted to attend one of the few explicitly Marxist departments, or one of the second-tier state universities where something of institutional economics survived.

So I resolved to engage these questions as a political scientist. I went off to Berkeley to study what I learned was called comparative political economy. This was the academic year 1965-1966.

It was not a happy experience, personally or academically. I had thrived at Oberlin in the small atmosphere of a liberal arts college, and Berkeley was immense. My college girlfriend and I had discussed getting married, but decided to go our separate ways, and I missed her. I should add that the constructive radicalism of Oberlin was a lifelong influence on me. Several of my closest friends are classmates from my Oberlin days. All of them have had idealistic careers working for the common betterment. This was also the beginning of the era of militant anti-war protest. I was pulled between my own opposition to the Vietnam War as a liberal and the ultra-radicalism of some of the Berkeley protestors, who sat down on the tracks to block troop trains, provoked riots with cops, and did other acts of civil disobedience.

So I threw myself into my studies and managed to get straight A's in my first semester. But I didn't want to stay at Berkeley. I applied to transfer to Harvard's doctoral program in government and was accepted with a Harvard Prize Fellowship, a four-year tuition-plus-expenses award that made me a member of the prestigious Society of Fellows. My adviser was to be someone named Kissinger.

But by spring, I knew that I didn't want to be in graduate school at all. I can recall the precise moment that pushed me over the edge. I was taking a course at Berkeley called "The Politics of Developing Areas." One of the readings was by a political scientist named Fred W. Riggs, described in his biography as a "towering figure" in the field of comparative public administration.

In the assigned reading, Riggs' main method was to create taxonomies, assigning new names to familiar concepts. For instance, a "rule" was Riggs' name for a government. A "macro-rule" was a national government. An "oli-polar macro-rule" was a federalist government. An *oli-polar macro-rule?* Besides the sloppy mixing of a Greek adjective and a Latin noun, this new pretentious terminology added no useful insight at all. I did not want to spend several years in grad school to grow up to be Fred W. Riggs.

The clarity of journalism and activism beckoned. Besides, all hell was breaking loose in America between the civil rights struggles and the broadening opposition to the war. Four or five more years hiding out in a university, even with the benefit of a draft deferment, seemed to be an eternity. So I took my master's degree and left town. From Berkeley, I went to Washington, as recounted in earlier chapters. After my misadventures at the Washington Post, my work as an investigator for the Senate Banking Committee taught me applied political economy.

———

Contrary to the conceits of orthodox economics, history shows that it is possible to have a society that is both economically dynamic and socially just. The hard part is the politics. As I learned at the Senate Banking Committee, the tension between a decent economy and the power of elites is especially pronounced when speculative finance breaks loose from its regulatory moorings.

Seldom do the political stars align to allow social contracts that optimize both economic efficiency and social justice thanks to activist government. The period that began with Franklin Roosevelt's New Deal was one such time—Cowie's "great exception" to most of economic and political history.

Due to a series of lucky accidents, the US and Europe after World War II had a pretty good blend of managed capitalism and social democracy. The happy accidents included Franklin Roosevelt being the American president. His version of American hegemony, uncharacteristically, called for making the world safe for New Deals everywhere. Another fortuitous convergence was the fact that laissez-faire in Europe had been brought down, ideologically and politically, by the economically disastrous interwar period, whose miseries led directly to Hitler and a second world war.

In 1945, as Europe restored democracy and began rebuilding, there were literally no right-wing parties in contention. The political right had been discredited by fascism and collaboration with the Nazis in occupied countries. The libertarian right had been discredited by the Great Depression. The practical challenge was postwar reconstruction, and this could not be accomplished by private markets; it required substantial state intervention.

The architecture of the postwar global economic system was created at the Bretton Woods conference of 1944. The co-chair of the conference was John Maynard Keynes, who first came to prominence as an adviser to the British delegation to the Versailles peace conference of 1919. There, Keynes warned that the onerous terms being imposed on a defeated Germany would lead to a depressed European economy and a second European war. He was ignored. Keynes quit the peace conference early and went home to write a short, prophetic book, *Economic Consequences of the Peace.*

Twenty-five years later, Keynes became the rare prophet without honor to get a do-over. In 1919, he was an unknown junior adviser to the British government. Now, in 1944, as Lord Keynes, he was the world's most celebrated economist and a senior financial diplomat. Unlike at Versailles, when he was a lone voice against national political leaders, Keynes had a strong ally in Franklin Roosevelt. The two wanted a global financial architecture to make possible a strong postwar recovery safe from the deflationary undertow of private finance.

Traditionally, if a nation used Keynesian-style deficits to increase public investment and social spending, speculators in private financial markets would bet against its currency, forcing the offending outlier nation to relent. FDR in 1933, invoking the Bible, had vowed to banish "the money-changers" from "the temple of our civilization." Bretton Woods achieved that goal internationally by creating a regime of fixed exchange rates—which literally banished money-changing—and by increasing the supply of public capital, first through a new World Bank, later complemented by the Marshall Plan, intended to support a global new deal.

Nothing like this had occurred after World War I. The prime goal of the Allies was to punish Germany, not to promote a recovery. This time, the Allies understood that the best way to prevent a resurgence of fascism and strengthen fragile German democracy was to help Germany recover and anchor it within a prosperous and democratic Europe.

The far-reaching British Labour program of 1945 illustrates the power of fixed exchange rates. Defeating Hitler had cost Britain about one-fourth of its national wealth. Britain emerged from the war with a debt-to-GDP ratio of about 250 percent. Without fixed exchange rates, the government would have had to embrace a perverse program of austerity to reassure private financiers, or the pound sterling would have been crushed. With fixed exchange rates, Britain could go further into debt to finance postwar reconstruction, nationalize industries, and build an expansive welfare state as well. Britain had just one modest devaluation, in 1948.

The actual policies that ensued in most European nations were an amalgam of social democracy and Christian Democracy. In some countries, such as Britain and all of Scandinavia, they were explicitly social democratic. In other nations, such as West Germany and Italy, Christian Democratic parties governed. In practice, they were almost as social democratic as the Social Democrats. In both West Germany and Italy, the Communists were the largest opposition party. To remain in power, the centrist Christian Democrats had to deliver substantial benefits to the working class and embrace a surprisingly left-wing program.

As counterweights to private capital, some social democratic governments have included substantial nationalization of key industries. The British Labour government that took office in July 1945 was probably the most radical durable government elected in a democracy. It nationalized banks, steel, coal, shipyards, railroads —in all about 20 percent of the economy. It also created the West's most explicitly socialistic system of healthcare, the National Health Service, which required the government to nationalize more than 3,000 hospitals.

Others, as in Scandinavia, rely less on nationalized industries than on very strong unions. In general, social democracy prizes an effective labor movement, both to defend worker rights directly and as a mass constituency to elect and re-elect social democratic governments. All of the social democratic parties of the West were founded or co-founded by labor movements.

Through the West, during what the French called the Thirty Glorious Years, the economy not only grew at record peacetime rates. It grew more equal. Mass unemployment had been banished; major nations literally had over-full employment and had to import temporary foreign "guest-workers" to fill job vavancies.

This prodigious economic success was attributed by some to the engine of postwar reconstruction. But nothing comparable occurred after World War I, a period of economic breakdown, because the orthodox rules of the game promoted austerity and precluded broadly based expansion and prosperity.

You might think that the postwar model of a mixed economy was such a practical success that it would endure indefinitely. But it proved to be surprisingly fragile. As long as social democracy is built on top of a basically capitalist economy, capitalists eventually chafe at the restraints. In the first two decades after the war, capitalists seemed resigned to a new order. In the US, Eisenhower didn't try to undo the New Deal. Large corporations bargained with their unions and didn't try to destroy them. In the UK, the conservative governments that succeeded the great Labour government of 1945-51 accepted most of its social reforms.

But over time, capitalists recovered their usual political power. It took only one bad economic decade, the 1970s, caused by random factors such as the OPEC oil price increases, to undermine the credibility of the postwar social compact. The governments that followed, led by Margaret Thatcher and Ronald Reagan, were not like the moderate conservatives of the 1950s. They ferociously worked to reverse several elements of managed capitalism, with notable success. Worse, the center-left parties moved in the direction of the new consensus, leaving no credible champion of working-class voters.

One result was changes in global economic rules that moved away from the Bretton Woods system which had allowed participating nations political space to chart their own course. Universal market rules dominated.

My first big piece for The New Republic in 1983 was on the new Mitterrand government in France. Editor Rick Hertzberg put the piece on the cover with the title, "Liberty, Equality, Technology." The illustration was a takeoff on the French national symbol Marianne, with a robot lying at her feet, a high-speed train in the background, and Mitterrand to her side carrying a boom box and a portable hair dryer. Mitterrand was promoting national industrial policies to make France a technological leader. Would they succeed?

The deeper subject of my reporting was a question that would recur in my future work. Can a nation that strives to be a social democracy withstand the pressures of globalized capitalism? The answer, increasingly, was no—because the system's rules now made it impossible for an outlier nation to chart its own course. This was the opposite of what Franklin Roosevelt had intended for the postwar economic system as World War II was ending.

The British Labour government of 1945 was able to sponsor an expansive left program, sheltered from the deflationary pressure of private capital markets by the Bretton Woods system of fixed exchange rates. But by the time the Mitterrand government of 1981 ventured a similar expansionary program, the postwar Bretton Woods system had collapsed. Neoliberal rules prevailed, and currency values were once again set by private financial markets, as in the 1920s. The money markets began betting heavily against the franc, which crashed. Within a year, Mitterrand had to accept a humiliating reversal of his socialist policies. In the era that followed, global rules were intensified as instruments for enforcing neoliberalism and creating obstacles to progressive national policies. This became the subject of my 2018 book, *Can Democracy Survive Global Capitalism?*

Even in Scandinavia, where social democracy was more deeply entrenched, Social Democratic parties did not govern all of the time. When conservative parties periodically returned to power, they proved highly skilled at weakening the elements of the social democratic model that promoted social solidarity, introducing privatized health and education options, and cheaper unemployment insurance for people who did not get it through their unions. But to appreciate all of these dynamics, you had to study a lot of history and comparative politics, not just economic theorems.

The systematic mistakes of the economics discipline were not just an academic problem; they undermined the self-confidence and program strategies of center-left parties. The trilogy of deregulation, privatization, and corporate globalization was embraced by American Democrats and European Social Democrats in the 1990s on the advice of their economists. By ignoring the impact on these parties' working-class constituents, the policies were disastrous politically. And except for the benefit to financial elites, they proved to be perverse economics.

The policy mischief of mainstream economics was vividly on display when the European Union and the International Monetary Fund (IMF) responded to the Greek economic crisis that began in 2009 by demanding austerity as the perverse cure for an economy already heading for recession because of the larger financial crisis. The social democratic Greek government that came to power in October 2009, led by reformer George Papandreou, found that the outgoing conservative government had faked the books. The actual government deficit was about four times the reported figure.

When Papandreou learned the truth, he dutifully reported it to the European Commission (EC) and the European Central Bank. (ECB) This was the cue for hedge funds to make massive bets against Greek bonds. Instead of taking the other side of those bets and stabilizing the bond market, the ECB and the EC, joined by the IMF, punitively piled on, making austerity demands in exchange for paltry aid that went mainly to bail out banks and bondholders and not to help the real Greek economy. (Imagine if such demands and policies had been imposed on FDR's New Deal during the Great Depression.)

All of this reflected the orthodox economic advice that in a crisis, austerity is needed to reassure investors. Greece needed to be an object lesson in the perils of budget deficits. A handy side effect was that bankers were made whole.

For ordinary Greeks, the result was great human suffering. Greece lost a quarter of its GDP, the greatest economic loss experienced by any national economy in peacetime. I wrote about this and kindred events and policy biases in my 2013 book, *Debtors' Prison: The Politics of Austerity Versus Possibility.*

I began work on *Debtors' Prison* in the aftermath of the 2008 financial collapse because I was curious about the peculiar institution of bankruptcy. In a bankruptcy, a corporation that goes broke is permitted to write off or write down its debts and get a fresh start. But the shareholders lose everything. Except it turns out that sometimes they don't. In the aftermath of the 2008 collapse, the Federal Reserve and the Obama Administration created special programs to bail out major Wall Street banks that were insolvent, without costing their shareholders a nickel or replacing the incumbent management whose reckless speculation had contributed to the collapse.

My research found that double standards in bankruptcy date to the very creation of the institution. My mentor on this project was Harvard Law School's leading scholar on the history of bankruptcy, Professor Bruce Mann. He is married to Elizabeth Warren.

Modern bankruptcy was invented during the reign of Queen Anne in 1706. Before that, people who could not pay their debts simply went to prison. But in the 1680s and 1690s, honest businessmen were devastated by wars and plagues. Sending them to prison, where they had no chance of earning money to repay their debts, would do nothing for creditors and would further sandbag the economy. And so there was agitation for reform.

The Statute of Anne provided that if a businessman went broke, not due to his own improvidence, but due to factors beyond his control, his creditors could meet with a magistrate, agree to a plan that would repay them so many pence in the pound, and then the slate would be wiped clean, and the debtor could resume economic life. But this provision was only for businessmen. Ordinary deadbeats would still rot in prison. Charles Dickens writes about the horror of debtors' prisons in his 1858 novel, *Little Dorrit*, based on the experience of his own father, John Dickens, who went bankrupt and was sent to the notorious Marshalsea Prison.

I meant my title, *Debtors' Prison*, as a metaphor. Ever since the Statute of Anne, the politics of debt collection have been replete with double standards. So has the treatment of entire nations. Ordinarily, creditors rule. That was the norm after World War I, and it destroyed the possibility of economic recovery for Europe. The process after World War II was the great exception. Fully 93 percent of defeated Germany's debt was written off, and repayment of the rest was stretched out over forty years, so Germany could recover.

The treatment of indebted developing countries has followed the norm. Under Chapter 11 of the US bankruptcy code, corporations are permitted to write off debts and start over. But countries are not. The IMF's treatment of heavily indebted third-world countries has been brutal. New credits are extended, but only on terms that require severe austerity, and the new money is used primarily to repay old debts to bankers, not to restore growth. My book's subtitle captures the dynamic: *The Politics of Austerity versus Possibility*. Which brings me back to the case of Greece.

Greece accounted for just two percent of the EU's gross domestic product. Economic help would have been cheap. Instead of punitive austerity and deflation, Greece needed a Keynesian recovery program. But the richer nations of the EU had little sympathy for the poorer ones, and Keynes was out of fashion. So Greece was put through the wringer of an austerity program, while new loans from the IMF and the European Central Bank were used to repay creditors, not to help the Greek economy recover. Greece suffered the most catastrophic decline of GDP, about 26 percent, of any modern country not ravaged by war. All of this was caused by administered austerity, not because of Greek profligacy. But austerity, on terms to benefit creditors, is history's rule more than the exception.

Despite the fact that Keynes had been vindicated twice—first in his prophetic warnings about the consequences of Versailles and again in his successful design of key elements of the expansive post-World War II economic system, Keynes was a profound threat to the core beliefs of mainstream economics, most notably when he published his 1936 masterwork, *The General Theory of Employment, Interest, and Money.*

It was impossible for the mainstream to deny that the Great Depression had happened, or the accuracy of Keynes' core insight that a market economy can reach an equilibrium of supply and demand far below its productive potential, resulting in mass unemployment that feeds on itself. Keynes also had plenty to say on the sheer irrationality of pricing in financial markets, which placed bets on what investors thought other investors believed, not on economic fundamentals. Keynesian economics also pointed to the monopoly power of sellers to set prices, and the perverse tendency of individuals to save during a downturn when the economy needed consumer spending.

These and other insights meant that the market prices set by supply and demand were often wildly wrong and that markets did not self-correct. Keynes, in short, demolished the basic assumptions of classical economics.

But the profession could not have that. So the mainstream revisionists of Keynes came up with an ingenious dodge. In 1933, the Norwegian economist Ragnar Frisch first invented the distinction between *macroeconomics,* meaning the study of the whole economy, and *microeconomics,* meaning the study of individual sectors and the setting of prices. Frisch did not mean that the two aspects of the economy operated according to different principles. But in the late 1930s, the mainstream elevated this distinction to contend that at the micro level of ordinary producer and consumer prices, supply and demand still worked as advertised. But somehow, at the macro level, supply and demand failed to produce an efficient equilibrium. That in turn called for emergency government intervention.

This was plainly nonsense. Either market prices were accurate, or they weren't. But the macro/micro schema allowed the profession to have both a bit of (bowdlerized) Keynes and keep their traditional model, too. Keynes' great radical insights about the deeper dynamics of capitalism were watered down into nothing more than a strategy for smoothing out business cycles. It was all reduced to algebra and taught to generations of students. The emasculated form of Keynes was dubbed the "neoclassical synthesis." Keynes' great protégé Joan Robinson termed this supposed synthesis "Bastard Keynesianism."

The effort to neuter Keynes continued as the first textbooks using Keynesian economics were published. In 1947, an American economist who had studied with Keynes in Cambridge, Lorie Tarshis, published a textbook titled *The Elements of Economics.* Tarshis was no bastard Keynesian. The textbook addressed the broad array of market failures as taught by Keynes himself and the positive role of government, not just during crises.

The text was readily adopted by leading economics departments, including Yale, Brown, Middlebury, and Stanford. But then a red-baiting campaign against Tarshis began, though he was far from a Red. Business groups put pressure on university trustees and department chairs. Soon, the Tarshis textbook was dropped in favor of a far more anodyne textbook by Paul Samuelson, published in 1948, that taught the neoclassical synthesis. The Samuelson book went through nineteen editions and became a best-seller. It was used in the freshman course at Oberlin that turned me against standard economics. Once again, there was a thumb on the scale of the marketplace of ideas, in favor of a model that comforted elites.

———

I was delighted to chance upon another line of Joan Robinson's: "Study economics to avoid being deceived by economists." I used that quote as the epigraph to my second book, and it became a credo. The book, published in 1984, was titled *The Economic Illusion: False Choices Between Prosperity and Social Justice.* In my book, I combined an exploration of different forms of European capitalism with a critique of one of the most fundamental premises of mainstream economics, the idea that greater equality necessarily came at the expense of economic efficiency.

My foil was an economist named Arthur Okun, who had published an influential book in 1975 titled *The Big Tradeoff: Equality and Efficiency.* Revealingly, this was not some right-wing ally of Milton Friedman. Okun, who considered himself a liberal, had been chair of Lyndon Johnson's Council of Economic Advisers. Here was the essence of the travesty of mainstream economics—even liberal economists accepted conservative assumptions.

Okun made his case in two ways. First, he used deductions from first principles. If markets were efficient (which was true by definition), and the government tried to make them more equal, that would sacrifice some efficiency. Conversely, efforts to make them even more ruthlessly efficient would sacrifice some equality. It was a linear trade-off. Okun also used some homespun examples to illustrate his aphorism that "the welfare state redistributes with a leaky bucket." Some government benefits went to people who didn't really need them. And it took expensive bureaucracies to run social welfare programs.

What Okun didn't do was to take a close look at the real world. In fact, there are clear cases where making the economy and the society more equal also makes it more efficient. As I pointed out in *The Economic Illusion*, a good example is free, tax-supported public education. If the education of the next generation were a function of the parents' ability to purchase schooling for their children at market rates, half the population would grow up illiterate. Educating them makes society more productive. So free, tax-supported public education is a gain for both equality and efficiency. How efficient it is in practice depends on the details of how it is carried out, not on prior assumptions.

Some affluent parents could well afford to pay for public schooling. But mean-testing public education would undermine its broad political constituency. That's a political economy argument about why universal social programs tend to be better and what it takes to build and maintain broad coalitions to support them. Rich families are always free to opt out and send their kids to private schools, but well-financed public schools are so good in affluent suburbs that most rich parents stick with the public system.

One can make similar arguments about health care. If low-income people had to succumb to disease because they could not afford to pay the doctor, the society as a whole would be more vulnerable to epidemics. Our jumble of means-tested Medicaid, universal Medicare for the elderly, and partly subsidized employer-provided insurance is far from as efficient as it might be, but that's the result of politics and the influence of interest groups. At least with Medicaid, nobody dies on the street for lack of basic health insurance. Universal health insurance programs, of the sort that most other Western nations have, are both more efficient and more egalitarian—another case where equality and efficiency are on the same side.

Much of *The Economic Illusion* was an inquiry into how some European nations managed to have positive-sum social compacts. This was a consequence of their parliamentary institutions, their history, and their politics.

In Denmark, the economic model is built on an ingenious system of labor market policies backed by unions and employers alike. If you lose your job, you can get a retraining sabbatical that lasts as long as two years and get paid up to 95 percent of your former wage. The Danish government spends an astonishing 3 percent of GDP on these so-called active labor market policies. The US spends less than one-tenth of one percent.

The result of this system is that employers are free to replace workers as needed. Employment security is not tied to the security of a particular job. Danish workers change jobs at Europe's highest rates. The system also assured that Denmark, heavily dependent on exports, also has a very competitive workforce, thanks to the continuous retraining.

Sweden developed a variant of this system, with an even stronger role for unions. It added the concept of a solidarity wage policy, equalizing the wage structure generally via collective bargaining settlements that disproportionately raised wages for the lowest-paid workers. The unions, representing upwards of 90 percent of Swedish workers, took seriously their role as custodians of the larger system. They used their substantial power not to push for the highest wage increases, but to ensure that labor costs stayed closely aligned with Swedish productivity, so that Sweden would remain competitive internationally.

Clearly, there was more than one way to reconcile equality with efficiency, and to optimize both. Okun's lens, by leaving out a knowledge of history or a comparative political economy perspective, totally missed the key material and the real story. He needed to get out of the office.

Reflecting on that book after more than forty years, it occurs to me that some readers might point to Europe's lagging growth rates and conclude that maybe Okun was right all along. However, it wasn't the welfare state that stunted Europe's economic performance; it was the constraints of neoliberal globalism. The Nordic nations that stayed truest to the social democratic course have had both the best income distribution and the best economic performance.

———

I went on to address the failings of standard economics in a major piece for The Atlantic called "The Poverty of Economics." I wrote:

When it is pointed out that high unemployment, or segmented labor markets, or oligopolistic corporations, or national economic-development strategies, or big public sectors, or regulated banks, or protected agricultural markets—or the logic of social organizations in general— suggest a world very far from the textbook picture of perfect competition and self-correcting markets, the economist has essentially two choices. He can turn pamphleteer, as so many economists do, and insist that the world would be a better place if it did conform to the textbooks. (As the Cambridge University economist John Eatwell has said facetiously, "If the world is not like the model, so much the worse for the world.") Or the economist can scrap the formalism, get out of the office, and study the profane world of real institutions.

But too few economists studied the messy real world. Given the norms of the profession, that was not how you got tenure. There were a handful of more heterodox economists, mostly of an older generation. They tended to be disparaged as "popularizers," or as not true practitioners of economics, even though their work often yielded a truer picture of the real economy. Many specialized in economic history, like John Kenneth Galbraith, or in the history of economic ideas, like Robert Heilbroner, both topics that are no longer taught to graduate students at elite universities. The very fact that they wrote graceful prose rather than abstruse equations made them suspect. A tiny handful of younger economists, such as Joseph Stiglitz, Simon Johnson, and Dani Rodrik, skilled at both math and real-world curiosity, could inhabit both worlds.

In my Atlantic piece, I quoted Heilbroner. Economics, he told me, "has become like medieval theology. Before economics can progress, it must abandon its suicidal formalism." But as I wrote, "Mainstream economics is doing nothing of the kind...Thus the economic orthodoxy is reinforced by ideology, by the sociology of the profession, by the politics of who gets published or promoted and whose research gets funded."

Throughout the 1980s, in my own work at the New Republic, the Atlantic, and BusinessWeek, I continued to challenge the conservative brand of economics that was currently ascendant, both its mainstream variant and the far-right version that called itself supply-side economics. In the mid-1990s, I combined my critique into my most important and influential book, *Everything for Sale: The Virtues and Limits of Markets.*

I hadn't set out to write such a book. I just wanted a deeper understanding of where markets worked as advertised, where they did not, and why. In my research for articles, I kept looking for a book that would provide a comprehensive critique of the market model in terms accessible to a lay reader. There was no such volume, so I decided to write it myself. I ended up spending about five years working on the book.

I began by comparing the several assumptions of the economic model with the real world. I contrasted a supermarket with the health care market. A supermarket actually works more or less like the model. There are usually several supermarkets in town, so the consumer is free to shop around. Prices are relatively transparent.

I wrote, "Somehow, at the end of the day, the average consumer's lack of infinite time to go shopping, and less than perfect information about the relative prices of a thousand products in several local stores, exactly allows the supermarket to earn a normal profit." Supermarkets, I added, are also relatively efficient labor markets and capital markets. They pay just enough to attract competent staff and earn just enough to attract capital.

What's true of supermarkets, I pointed out, is true of most consumer goods and services. There is no shortage of restaurants, hotels, barbers, photocopiers, or dry cleaners from which to choose. In all of these realms, the market mechanism mostly works.

But compare the market for ordinary consumer goods with the market for health care, which violates virtually all of the model's assumptions of well-informed open competition with prices freely set by supply and demand. On the supply side, there is no "free entry"—you can't just hang out your shingle as a doctor. That gives doctors market power. On the demand side, consumers do not "shop around" for a hospital based on price. They mostly follow doctors' orders. Much of the time, it's not consumers who pay the bill; it's insurers.

The fact that health care is a far cry from a textbook perfect market sets up a chain of perverse incentives. In ordinary markets, sellers aim to maximize profits by minimizing costs. In health care, the seller's objective is to maximize insurance reimbursements. In the three decades since I wrote *Everything for Sale*, the commercial aspects of healthcare have become even more baroque and impenetrable to consumers. Socialized health care cuts through these knots.

So, the practical question, in assessing the market economy as a whole, is whether more of the economy is like supermarkets or like markets for health care. It is fairly easy to demonstrate that at least half the economy—healthcare, banking, R&D, education, public utilities—does not lend itself to the efficient discipline of private supply and demand. We are in a much messier realm of social investment and public regulation, which is itself vulnerable to political capture. Mainstream economists added to the confusion by advising that even if these sectors could not be perfectly efficient markets, they could become more "marketlike." That also proved to be an illusion.

From this beginning, my book undertook a tour of the real economy. A chapter on labor markets demonstrated that human labor was not like other factors of production. A chapter on money markets explained why banking was anything but self-regulating and the risks of insider conflicts of interest repeating the Great Crash of 1929. This was at a time when free market theory was ascendant, and both parties were competing to deregulate finance. A decade after the book appeared, financial markets duly collapsed.

Another chapter explored and debunked the behavioral assumptions of standard economics. It turned out that actual humans stubbornly refused to behave like the model. They were social beings, not utility-maximizing automatons operating in a social vacuum. They left tips in restaurants in cities they would never visit again, because it seemed the right thing to do. They donated blood, and a famous study by the British sociologist Richard Titmuss demonstrated that blood banks based on voluntary donations were far cleaner and more reliable than commercial ones. The down-and-out fellow who sold his blood was the last person whose blood you'd want to have.

Brits who regularly donated blood were not maximizing their utility in the manner specified by the market model. Many remembered the sacrifices of World War II. They were donating out of social solidarity, a concept foreign to market economics.

From there, I explored different realms of the economy that did not lend themselves to the discipline of perfect markets, and the set of "second best" alternatives and their politics. Deregulation of several industries had begun under President Jimmy Carter in 1978, thanks to the tutelage of his adviser, Fred Kahn. The verdict was now in. In industries that were imperfectly competitive, such as airlines, telephones, and electric utilities, deregulation didn't work. The result was not more price competition and consumer choice. Companies found ways to merge and increase their market power and use complex pricing to deceive consumers.

I also explored the epic case of market failure—the market's tendency to pollute and the need for offsetting health, safety, and environmental regulations. The book concluded with a chapter on the inevitability of politics. Democratic politics will either regulate markets in the broad public interest, as happened during the New Deal era, or commercial forces will overwhelm democratic counterweights and corrupt the economy and the polity. The quest for perfect markets was a dangerous illusion.

The book, published by Knopf, got the front page of the New

York Times Sunday Book Review. In the Washington Post Book World, Suzanne Garment of the conservative American Enterprise Institute generously wrote, "To understand the economic debates that will take place in the next few years, you can't do better than to read Robert Kuttner's spirited book." Robert Heilbroner called it "quite simply the most readable and important book about the economy that I have read in a very long time."

If I were writing *Everything for Sale* today, I would do one thing differently. I wrote the book as a detailed critique of the premise that markets are efficient, as if this were an academic debate that I could win by using good evidence to refute bad theory. I think the book wins that debate. But after nearly thirty more years of witnessing the deepening concentration and corruption of capitalism, and in turn its corruption of democracy, I have a greater appreciation for the fact that the problem isn't "the market." The problem is capitalism as a system.

The first principle of democracy is one citizen, one vote. The first principle of capitalism is one dollar, one vote. Capitalism as a system keeps undermining political efforts to temper its tendency toward extreme inequality and periodic catastrophe. Capitalism encroaches on democracy itself, as wealth translates into power.

Democratic governments regularly tried to keep money in its place. The Tillman Act of 1905, when Teddy Roosevelt was President, banned corporate campaign contributions. The Federal Election Campaigns Act, enacted after Watergate, attempted to strictly regulate political giving. But Supreme Court justices appointed by conservative allies of business overturned both, deeming them violations of corporate free speech.

None of this had anything to do with the question of whether and when markets were efficient. This was about power, pure and simple. Many of the newer inventions of financial capitalists, such as private equity, in which investors made windfall profits by looting the companies they bought with borrowed money, were travesties of market efficiency.

As Polanyi pointed out, capitalism has a relentless tendency to turn everything into a commodity. Karl Marx had made a similar point. But Polanyi, with the benefit of almost another century of economic history, could be far more detailed and more nuanced than Marx.

As Polanyi demonstrated in his masterwork *The Great Transformation* (1944), when markets become "dis-embedded" from society and create severe social dislocations, people eventually revolt. Polanyi saw the catastrophe of World War I, the interwar period, the Great Depression, fascism, and World War II as the logical culmination of market forces overwhelming society—"the utopian endeavor of economic liberalism to set up a self-regulating market system" that began in nineteenth-century England.

Extreme market commodification of everything leads to a popular explosive reaction. Threaten people's basic livelihoods, and many people will give up on democracy in exchange for something that offers security and respect. In the 1920s and 1930s, excess marketization ended with fascism. Something similar produced Donald Trump. This turned out to be more accurate than Marx's picture of the workers of the world uniting. On the contrary, extreme economic dislocations led to ultra-nationalism. Hitler, Trump.

Like Keynes, Polanyi has been vindicated, in this case three times. Once, when he warned that the dislocations that result from extreme commodification lead to fascism, a second time when the containment of hyper-capitalism during the postwar era led to enhanced democracy, and a third time when we repeated the patterns of the 1930s. It was Marx who said that history repeats itself, first as tragedy, then as farce. Under Trump, we have both tragedy and farce.

———

In the nearly half-century since we founded the Economic Policy Institute, the economics profession has moved a little closer to reality. There is more empirical curiosity and less deductive reasoning from axioms and models. Some mainstream economists at major universities now take politics into account.

In 2019, MIT economist David Autor and two colleagues wrote an article in the flagship *American Economic Review* titled "When Work Disappears." The article examined the loss of factory jobs due to trade and the impact on regional economies, on marriage, and on political backlash. This story was well known to journalists, sociologists, and historians. The only thing new was that a mainstream economist was attesting to the reality. That's progress of a sort.

In 2020, Autor and three co-authors published a follow-up article in the *American Economic Review* with the startling title "Importing Political Polarization?: The Electoral Consequences of Rising Trade Exposure." The researchers, using an extensive data set, concluded that areas heavily impacted by free trade and outsourcing populated by the white working class "saw an increasing market share for the Fox News channel (a rightward shift), stronger ideological polarization in campaign contributions (a polarized shift), and a relative rise in the likelihood of electing a Republican to Congress (a rightward shift)." Once again, this was hardly news. What was notable and unusual was a mainstream economist addressing political consequences.

Economists who challenge the reigning paradigm have won

Nobel Prizes. In 2001, Joseph Stiglitz shared a Nobel Prize for his insights about asymmetries in bargaining power, which impeach the standard story of supply and demand. Two Nobel Prizes were awarded to theorists of behavioral economics, which challenge the orthodox model of human motivation: Daniel Kahneman in 2002 and Richard Thaler in 2017. And Angus Deaton, who wrote about "deaths of despair" from suicide, drug addiction, and other perverse behaviors related to economic hardships, won the Nobel Prize in 2015. It was a far cry from the textbook picture of rational homo economicus maximizing his utility.

However, in the economics taught to undergraduates and graduate students, and in the process for winning tenure and publication in the most prestigious journals, the orthodoxy has proved stubbornly resilient. I wrote a feature piece for The Prospect in 2023 based on extensive interviews with economists titled "Is Economics Self-Correcting?" My conclusion was that the profession was making more room for heterodoxy, but less so in classrooms. Journal articles like Autor's were very much the exception, and risky for young economists not yet tenured.

My most interesting interview was with Gabriel Chodorow-Reich, a brilliant young Ph.D. from the Berkeley economics department, now teaching at Harvard. Like others whom I interviewed, he made the point that the increasing use of data is evidence that the profession is becoming less theory-bound and more empirical.

But are these data being used to ask the right questions? Chodorow-Reich and two colleagues wrote a paper on the dynamics of the Greek fiscal crisis and subsequent economic collapse, titled "The Macroeconomics of the Greek Depression," later published in *The American Economic Review*. The paper combines a great deal of data with a "rich estimated dynamic general equilibrium" model and an immense amount of algebra, and is technically unimpeachable. Its broad finding is that external demand, government consumption, and fiscal transfers fueled the pre-2007 Greek boom, while fiscal contraction was implicated in the collapse, with wages and prices falling precipitously.

This is illuminating as far as it goes. What's missing is the *political* story of what drove the perverse fiscal policies that, in turn, deepened the Greek collapse. As we talked, it became clear that Chodorow-Reich knew that part of the story as well as I did. In the article, it is mentioned only in passing. Rather, the Greek case is used mainly to demonstrate virtuosity in the abstract idiom of orthodox economics. I asked him if there was any way of integrating the political-economy story with his elegant technical analysis into a single article that might be accepted in one of the top economics journals. He thought there wasn't.

The United States also experienced a deep recession following the financial collapse of 2008. We were spared the fate of the Greeks because the US could borrow in its own currency and throw money at the banks. But because of the perverse counsel of the orthodox economists advising Obama, the US stopped far short of the kind of recovery spending that would have prevented a prolonged recession. By 2009, when the economy was far from healed, Obama's economists were already recommending a shift to deficit reduction as the prime goal. This backwards policy prolonged high unemployment and slowed recovery. It was another factor in the discrediting of Democrats and the rise of Trump.

———

One personal bonus from having researched and written several serious books about the economy is a part time teaching career. Despite not having a Ph.D. in economics or in any other subject, I was invited to teach graduate students at Brandeis, first as a visiting professor in its business school and then at the Heller School for social policy, a relationship that is approaching twenty years. I find that my teaching nourishes my journalism, and vice versa.

Typically, graduate schools in public policy look at policies in a political vacuum. At Heller, which is far better than most, I bring a political economy approach. How does the constellation of political power set agendas and narrow the realm of the possible? How does the power distribution compel Congress to settle for inefficient policies that then frustrate citizens make the government look bad? Politics is said to the art of the possible. How can we use politics to enlarge what is possible?

Chapter 8

Winning the Arguments, Losing the Politics

In the 1990s and early 2000s, reality demolished the fundamental tenets of market fundamentalism, also known as neoliberalism. Deregulation of several industries did not promote greater efficiency or consumer choice. Mainly, deregulation produced greater concentration and monopoly pricing power, insider enrichment, and financial speculation that ended with the 2008 collapse. The experiment proved once and for all, at great political and economic cost, that markets and their masters cannot be trusted to regulate themselves.

Corporate globalization helped China, but it mostly harmed the United States, which lost industry after industry and ended up with an ever-increasing chronic trade deficit. Globalization did help American corporations and investment bankers, but destroyed the prosperous blue-collar middle class, killing a key constituency of the Democrats.

Deregulation of financial markets had an especially catastrophic impact. As financial engineers created new opaque kinds of securities, conflicts of interest on the part of insiders turned Wall Street from its textbook role as benign supplier of capital to the real economy into a Ponzi scheme. The smart money got out before the collapse even richer; the suckers lost. An insider slogan of the era was IBGYBG. By the time it all comes crashing down, I'll Be Gone, You'll Be Gone.

In the aftermath, the government bailed out the bankers but not the homeowners, millions of whom lost everything. The great recession that followed, on Obama's watch, was prolonged by neoliberal policies of fiscal conservatism, globalism, and weak bank regulation, and undermined what remained of the Democrats' credibility with working families.

Further to the right, supply-side tax cuts did not stimulate growth, much less fulfill the claim that the cuts would pay for themselves with increased revenues. Mainly, they increased deficits, which then led to political pressure for cuts in social spending. Contrary to Charles Murray and company, antipoverty programs did not cause poverty. Reagan's suspension of antitrust enforcement, under Robert Bork, did not promote new competition. Rather, it led to anti-competitive pricing tactics and greater monopoly.

Bork's theory, that the only test of monopoly power that mattered was "consumer welfare"—did prices increase in the short run?—was embraced by economists and legal scholars generally. It led to the de facto termination of antitrust enforcement by Democratic administrations as well as Republican ones. Later, as platform monopolies like Google and Amazon bought out or crushed potential competitors and extracted profits from both rivals and advertisers, weaponizing their surveillance of consumer buying habits, the fact that consumers got some bargains was used as proof that these platforms were not abusive.

It was only when Joe Biden hired Lina Khan to head the Federal Trade Commission that the deeper anti-competitive abuses were exposed, and antitrust was revived—until Trump killed it again. In the meantime, private equity companies, pursuing their model of extractive capitalism, began buying up everything from nursing homes to veterinary practices to trailer parks, jacking up prices and cutting wages. It was another abusive innovation that traditional antitrust didn't reach.

I addressed these issues in my own writing. The Prospect covered them in its articles, and EPI challenged the orthodoxy in its papers. We did this through research and reporting, not polemic.

Why did we keep winning the arguments and losing the politics? Some of it was the deep entrenchment of dominant views, reinforced by the potent alliance between the financial elite and the economics profession. Some of it was simple corruption. The Democratic Party proved to be a feeble opponent of these trends because so much money was to be had if you just went along with the prevailing ideology. Challenging corporate influence was far less rewarding. Central to the problem was the increasing influence of Wall Street Democrats.

The most emblematic and politically damaging of these several neoliberal elements was "free trade," as defined by corporations. By the 1990s, the policy was no longer in the national interest, but it served the corporate interest and the opportunistic alliance of leading Democrats with corporate money men.

Free-trade ideology once aligned with America's economic and security interests. In the era after World War II, open markets were good for domestic industry because the US had emerged from the war as the pre-eminent economy. America had a huge trade surplus based on exports and could be generous about accepting barrier-free imports. Openness to imports also helped anchor Washington's Cold War alliance, as America's military allies earned dollars by sending products to the US.

Not surprisingly, free trade became an article of ideological and diplomatic faith. With America's economic dominance, the US government could overlook the fact that in Japan and much of Western Europe, postwar reconstruction (some of it initiated by the US-sponsored Marshall Plan) was anything but laissez-faire.

The free-trade credo became more contradictory beginning in the 1970s. US markets were open, but others were not. Japan and South Korea used blatantly mercantilist policies that paid lip service to US-sponsored trade doctrine but actually relied on subsidies, quotas, cartels, and close coordination among banks, governments, and industry, all of which violated free-market norms. These strategies helped Japan and South Korea gain market share at US expense in sectors ranging from steel to autos to machine tools, computer chips, and consumer electronics. By 1976, the chronic US trade surplus turned into a deficit that only kept deepening. American manufacturing continued to lose market share and jobs.

Yet in the decades that followed, American business and political leaders intensified their support for hyper-globalization. The US has promoted this ideology globally, and it is codified in the US-sponsored World Trade Organization, established in 1995. The government pursued trade policies seemingly at odds with the national interest because they served corporate interests.

Multinational corporations could profit by manufacturing less at home and offshoring production to low-wage countries. Investment bankers could prosper by underwriting complex global financial deals. American tech firms became the world's standard, even though Apple produced no computers or iPhones domestically. All of this served to displace workers, enrich capitalists, widen America's inequality of wealth and income, and eventually invite the right-wing populist reaction that culminated in the 2016 election of Trump.

I published my first critique in a piece for The New Republic called "The Free Trade Fallacy" in 1983. I continued refining this critique in several books and articles. For most of those years, I was very lonely. One mainstream economist who began criticizing the ideology and practice of hyper-globalization was Dani Rodrik of Harvard's Kennedy School, in his 2010 book, *The Globalization Paradox*, calling on nations to reclaim a measure of economic sovereignty. The early work of Paul Krugman, interestingly enough, criticized claims about the economic benefits of free trade, but when he became a celebrity economist and New York Times columnist, Krugman prudently reverted to the orthodoxy. When Krugman parted company with the Times in 2024, he was liberated to write what he really believed in daily Substack posts, and did some of his best work.

————

The embrace of ultra-globalization and neoliberalism generally was epitomized and reinforced by the presidency of Bill Clinton and his top economic advisers, Robert Rubin and Larry Summers. More than any other president, Republican or Democrat, Clinton also intensified deregulation and prioritized budget balance over social investment. He was no friend of unions.

Clinton had come to national prominence as the moderate governor of a conservative state. As Arkansas governor, Clinton seemed to epitomize a New South, which turned away from racial hatreds in favor of economic progress and alliances with local businesses. Jimmy Carter had been the same sort of southern governor.

But by 2020, the New South was politically defunct. Democratic candidates for governor could no longer get elected with that kind of coalition, in part because neoliberals like Carter and Clinton, once in the White House, presided over policies that destroyed the economic prospects of working-class voters. Republicans were able to rebuild the old-time Dixiecrat coalition of economic elites and beleaguered white working-class voters who blamed their plight on the upward mobility of Blacks.

When Clinton began his campaign for the Democratic presidential nomination in 1991, he was hard to pigeonhole. The famous sign in his campaign headquarters, "The Economy, Stupid," posted by his strategist James Carville, seemed to suggest a campaign that would emphasize pocketbook economics, at a time when ordinary working Americans had been losing ground. But Clinton managed to run to both the left and to the right, especially on social issues. His base was the Democratic Leadership Council (DLC).

The DLC was created after Mondale's blowout defeat in 1984. The organizers were corporate Democrats and southern politicians who viewed the party's liberalism as a political killer. The matchmaker was Al From, a former Congressional staffer for Rep. Gillis Long of Louisiana. As From tells the story in his memoir, he recruited Bill Clinton to chair the DLC and eventually run for president. "I've got a deal for you," he told Clinton. "If you agree to become chairman of the DLC, we'll pay for your travel around the country, we'll work together on an agenda, and I think you'll be president one day and we'll both be important."

From offered Clinton $100,000 a year, a huge raise from his salary of $35,000 as governor of Arkansas. Other DLC leaders included southern senators Chuck Robb of Virginia, Florida's Bob Graham, Tennessee's Jim Sasser and Al Gore, and Georgia's Sam Nunn as the DLC's founding chair. These states still elected moderate Democrats, but Republican opponents regularly tarred them with the liberal reputation of the national Democratic Party. A more centrist national party would presumably be less toxic for southern politicians. The DLC coined the label, New Democrat, to claim the future and disparage bad Old Democrats.

Clinton and the DLC did reposition the national party more to the center in the 1990s, but that didn't save southern Democrats. Moderate Senate Democrats from southern states dwindled from eight in 1996 to three in 2006, two in 2014, and zero in 2018. Not until Georgia narrowly elected two progressives in 2020, relying on a very different ideology and coalition, did Democrats return to the Senate from the deep South.

After Clinton won the 1992 election, he returned the favor to the DLC with a massive fundraising event in December 1992 at Union Station. Some 139 trade associations, lobbyists, law firms, and corporations donated over $3.3 million to the DLC in a single evening, reinforcing the DLC's budget and influence.

The DLC critique called for toning down Democratic support for affirmative action, being tougher on crime, joining Republicans in backing tax cuts and deregulation, embracing globalization, and moving away from the alliance with trade unions. The idea was to reject party "interest groups" and serve the interests of the broad middle class. The interest groups referred to were advocates for Blacks, working families, gays, and the poor. The most powerful interest group of all, Wall Street, got a free pass.

In a DLC manifesto written in 1989, titled "The Politics of Evasion," William Galston and Elaine Kamarck excoriated progressives for the sin of Liberal Fundamentalism. "Since the late 1960s, the public has come to associate liberalism with tax and spending policies that contradict the interests of average families; with welfare policies that foster dependence rather than self-reliance; with softness toward the perpetrators of crime and indifference toward its victims; with ambivalence toward the assertion of American values and interests abroad; and with an adversarial stance toward mainstream moral and cultural values."

That critique seemed telling—until you remembered that both Carter in 1980 and Mondale in 1984 had fled their liberalism as fast as was decently possible, and it didn't save them.

———

Clinton managed to win the 1992 nomination by blurring what he stood for. He had the advantage of running against George H.W. Bush, after 12 years of Republican rule. Bush was a far less effective politician than Reagan. In 1991-92, a mild recession created more headwinds for Bush. The 1992 election had a third-party candidate, H. Ross Perot, offering a mash-up of anti-system themes, including the risk that NAFTA would send jobs to Mexico ("a giant sucking sound"), and an obsession with the national debt as an emblem of the failure of both parties.

There was a disconnect between Perot's program and what was actually troubling voters. Few cared about the national debt. But Perot channeled popular disaffection from politics as usual. Perot himself was a billionaire investor, a fake populist, and a made-for-TV protest candidate whose persona and themes did not add up to a coherent governing program. If that rings a bell, the Perot phenomenon occurred fully 24 years before the fateful election of 2016. Perot prefigured Donald Trump. A fake populist TV billionaire who could actually get elected was an accident waiting to happen.

Perot got 19 percent of the popular vote in a 3-way race, allowing Clinton to be elected with just 43 percent. Clinton's campaign was a jumble of a conspicuous right-wing shift on social issues, initially combined with traditional Democratic pocketbook themes. Clinton, in a characteristically ambiguous promise, pledged to "end welfare as we know it." To the right, that signalled throwing the cheats off the welfare rolls. To the left, it signaled replacing coercive welfare traps with ladders to a better self-suffi-cient life. The calculated ambiguity was pure Clinton.

During the transition, Clinton tacked to the left. In December 1992, he convened an economic summit in Little Rock and invited a number of progressives. I was flattered to be given a brief speaking part and was impressed by Clinton's obvious intellect and knowledge of the issues. My enthusiasm won the dubious honor of being teased by Maureen Dowd in the New York Times.

It was a lesson in the perils of flattery and the temptations of trying to be an insider. My old boss, I.F. Stone, was the better model—to have uncompromised influence as an outsider. My early skepticism of Clinton proved all too accurate.

The Clinton presidency was tricky for The Prospect. Two of the three founders, Bob Reich as labor secretary and Paul Starr as an architect of the administration's health plan, had gone to work for Clinton. I was outside, running the magazine. Soon, however, Bob Reich was marginalized by Clinton's more conservative advis-ers. He left after one term. And Paul returned to Princeton and The Prospect after the health plan failed. We were all free to resume our role as loyal opposition to an increasingly corporate Democratic Party.

———

One conservative veteran of Washington politics who played Clinton like a violin and pushed him further to the right was the Federal Reserve Chair, Alan Greenspan. Clinton had hoped to raise taxes on the rich and spend the money on social programs and economic development. But Greenspan, in his first meeting with Clinton on December 3, 1992, explained that Clinton had it backwards.

As Greenspan told it, the better course was to cut the federal deficit. If Clinton cut the deficit, that would reassure bond markets, lower the cost of credit, and thus increase productive private investment. Greenspan offered Clinton a deal. If Clinton embraced deficit reduction, Greenspan would reassure the bond market by giving the program the Fed's seal of approval.

Clinton, famously, complained that his presidency was being held hostage by "a bunch of fucking bond traders." But he went with the program. In the economics of the Clinton-Greenspan grand bargain, you stimulated the economy not by taxing or borrowing to increase the purchasing power of ordinary people, as Keynesian economics called for. Rather, you increased prosperity via private financial market mechanisms—lower deficits leading to lower interest rates, which in turn would lower capital costs for businesses and consumer credit.

It was standard right-wing economics. The approach meant gutting the more progressive parts of Clinton's program. The Greenspan formula made Clinton even more of a centrist president.

Greenspan's advice proved wrong in every respect. Clinton delivered on his part of the deal. The deficit was cut from 3.7 percent of GDP in 1993 to 2.1 percent in 1995, to just 0.3 percent in 1997. But the bond market did not reciprocate. After Clinton's budget deal in 1993 cut the deficit by $140 billion, interest rates on 30-year mortgages and Treasury bonds actually went up.

Nor did Greenspan deliver on his part of the deal. For Clinton's first four years, the Fed kept short-term rates high as well, because Greenspan himself continued to be overly worried about inflation. So Greenspan's economics were all wrong—both the theory and the execution.

Clinton's other policies were mainly New Democrat. He became a passionate free trader and embraced NAFTA, an unfinished creation of George H.W. Bush. On the social front, Clinton achieved some incremental progress while offending just about everyone with his gays-in-the-military policy of "don't ask, don't tell." Conservatives were outraged, and gays indignantly rejected the premise that they had something to hide. Clinton repeatedly raised the idea of cutting or partly privatizing Social Security as part of a grand bargain on budget balance (a project relentlessly promoted by Robert Rubin), and had to be regularly talked out of it by his political advisers.

Clinton was a good retail politician on the campaign trail but a novice in the ways of Washington. His market-oriented health plan, known as "managed competition", designed by a task force headed by Hillary Clinton, was well to the right of traditional Democratic approaches for comprehensive health coverage. It later became the model for Republican Massachusetts Governor Mitt Romney's plan. Clinton neglected to enlist key congressional leaders in the scheme's complex design, and it died without even coming to a vote.

NAFTA was opposed by about two-thirds of the House Democratic caucus. When NAFTA finally passed, mainly with Republican support, it left a bitterly divided Democratic Party. These failures and splits led to a record loss of 53 Democratic House seats in the 1994 mid-term election, and Republican Newt Gingrich as Speaker.

Having lost his congressional majority, Clinton then moved further to the right, relying on two DCL-affiliated pollster/strategists, Mark Penn and Douglas Schoen. They came up with the strategy known as "triangulation," to put the president above party — his own party, as well as the opposition party.

Over strenuous Democratic opposition, Clinton relied on Republican votes to carry out a right-wing version of his campaign pledge to "end welfare as we know it," The new Temporary

Assistance to Needy Families (TANF) law substituted a stingy, time-limited replacement for Aid to Families with Dependent Children (AFDC) leaving millions of needy people in poverty without providing the promised ladders to a better life through work and child care.

After Clinton opted for TANF, three assistant secretaries of the Department of Health and Human Services resigned in protest. Another former Clinton HHS official, David Ellwood, wrote a piece for The American Prospect titled "Welfare Reform as I Knew It." It was the authoritative account of how to do welfare reform right, Clinton's capitulation, and the serious flaws in the TANF program.

Yet Clinton, with his own political skills, managed to survive these debacles. He even survived the Monica Lewinsky scandal, thanks to Republican overreach and a bungled impeachment attempt. But the sheer ickiness of the Lewinsky mess led Al Gore to distance himself somewhat from Clinton, an awkwardness that contributed to Gore's narrow loss to George W. Bush in 2000.

As I wrote at the time, throughout his presidency and in his influence beyond it, Clinton was the Typhoid Mary of Democratic politics. He survived; those around him got sick.

———

Clinton, belatedly, got his economic recovery, but it was the wrong sort of recovery and it taught the wrong lessons. In his second term, economic growth was propelled by an unsustainable financial bubble, driven by market speculation and borrowing, all supercharged by financial deregulation.

Uncharacteristically, Federal Reserve monetary policy helped to inflate the bubble rather than contain it. The Clinton Administration's pressure on developing countries to open their financial markets to speculative capital inflows led to financial crises in Mexico, Russia, and East Asia. That in turn led the Federal Reserve to flood global financial markets with cheap dollars to bail out investors. The architect of both the speculation and the bailout was Robert Rubin.

When the cheap money policy also led to a 1920s-style stock market bubble, Greenspan kept interest rates low to prevent a market collapse. That only led to more borrowing and more speculation. Ordinarily given to Delphic pronouncements, Greenspan candidly expressed his alarm in a famous 1996 speech warning about "irrational exuberance" in the stock market.

Greenspan knew that financial bubbles are notoriously hard to deflate gently. They tend to expand until they pop. The greater the financial deregulation, the more opportunities there are for debt-financed speculation, just as in the 1920s. The best way to prevent the cycle of bubble and crash is to have well-regulated financial markets, but that was out of fashion in the 1990s.

Greenspan now had three simultaneous crises on his hands, all driven by financial deregulation. Not only was there a currency crisis overseas, but an unregulated hedge fund called Long Term Capital Management (LTCM) had a no-fail trading model advised by three Nobel Prize-winning economists. The model called for placing large bets using money borrowed from different banks.

When the model's economic predictions went badly wrong, and the model failed in the late summer of 1998, it suddenly came out that LTCM had borrowed so much money that its collapse could render most of New York's money center banks insolvent. The Fed had to convene an emergency meeting and strong-arm all the major banks into bailing out LTCM to the tune of $3.625 billion, backed by the Fed. It was a harbinger of the far worse systemic crisis to come in 2008, based on the same kind of speculation.

Greenspan's reliance on very cheap money, combined with anxiety over LTCM, also produced a very volatile stock market. On August 31, 1998, the Dow fell by 513 points. Though economic fundamentals called for a slight increase in interest rates, that would have only spooked markets further. So Greenspan persuaded his Fed colleagues to cut rates by a quarter point.

The tech-heavy NASDAQ rose from about 800 in 1994 to over 5,000 in March 2000, before crashing more than 80 percent when the dot-com and telecom stock bubble burst. This crash was contained, but it was a harbinger of the far more pervasive and damaging collapse of 2008.

At the time, Clinton and the New Democrats claimed credit for several years of growth and job creation. They mistakenly credited the budget balance as the source of the low interest rates and the prosperity. By 2000, the budget was in surplus. But the prosperity was illusory and the policies perverse. The short-lived Clinton boom of the late 1990s was pure bubble prosperity.

Calculations by several independent economists, notably EPI's Dean Baker and Robert Pollin of the University of Massachusetts, showed that at the peak of the stock market bubble in 2000, households held approximately $5.0 trillion in bubble wealth in stocks. This perverse form of stimulus, which translated into an extra $275 to $450 billion of purchasing power, is mostly concentrated in the upper brackets. This analysis was confirmed by two Fed staff economists, Dean Maki and Michael Palumbo.[*]

A related, entirely bogus claim advanced by Clinton and embraced by Al Gore was that the proceeds of the budget surplus

---

[*] Bubble Wealth. Dean Maki and Michael Palumbo, "Disentangling the Wealth Effects," 2001, Available at https://www.federalreserve.gov/econres/feds/disentan gling-the-wealth-effect-a-cohort-analysis-of-household-saving-in-the-1990s.htm

were going into a "lockbox" that would safeguard Social Security. This was just a wishful metaphor for the idea that some future Congress might allocate part of a federal surplus to Social Security. But Social Security funds are not kept in segregated accounts; they are part of the consolidated federal budget. The program's long-term solvency depends on its balance of payroll tax receipts and pension payouts, not some imaginary lockbox.

Clinton's budget surplus, which was projected to continue well into the 21st century, lasted only until 2001 when George W. Bush decided to tap the surplus for an immense tax cut tilted towards the rich. Money that might have gone for Democratic priorities, such as increased public investment and more generous social programs, instead went for tax breaks for millionaires and billionaires. By 2002, the federal budget was back in deficit, to the tune of $157.8 billion. Money markets didn't seem to care. With the connivance of the Fed, interest rates stayed low.

In sum, Clinton's legacy was a set of shibboleths that created bubble prosperity during his own second term, but were toxic for Democrats and ordinary working families over the long term—an embrace of financial deregulation, budget balance, globalism as defined by and for finance, and limited use of the public sector—the opposite of Roosevelt's New Deal. Tragically, these policies would be echoed by those of Barack Obama, despite far more auspicious circumstances for a New Deal revival.

———

The three prime architects of Clinton's economic policies were Greenspan, Robert Rubin, and Rubin's deputy and protégé, Larry Summers. Each contributed to the distancing of the Democrats from their traditional base of working families, a process that contributed to the rise of Trump, who filled the vacuum of progressive populism with racist nationalism.

A co-chairman of Goldman Sachs, Rubin had become influential in the Carter-Mondale years as a donor, and soon mutated into an influential advisor and strategist. He was a prime influence on Mondale's politically disastrous 1984 nomination acceptance speech, calling for tax increases not to expand social programs but to balance the budget.

Rubin became a major donor, fund-raiser, and policy adviser to the Clintons. After his election in 1992, Clinton created a new institution in the office of the president just for Rubin, the National Economic Council, to parallel the National Security Council. Its members would include all members of the cabinet concerned with economic issues. It would be chaired by Rubin, who had direct daily access to the President. In practice, Rubin had more influence than the cabinet.

Rubin used his influence to promote neoliberal policies, above all, corporate globalization and the further deregulation of finance. In Clinton's second term, Rubin became Secretary of the Treasury, leaving the National Economic Council to be led by his protegé and close ally, Larry Summers. When Rubin exited to return to Wall Street in 1999, Summers became Treasury Secretary.

Rubin epitomized the kinds of conflicts of interest facilitated by the Wall Street-Washington revolving door. He was a strong supporter of NAFTA, which required Mexico to open its markets to both American exports and American financial investments. Goldman Sachs, which Rubin left to join Clinton, was a prime underwriter of Mexican bonds both before and immediately after the passage of NAFTA.

Goldman underwrote the privatization of the Mexican national phone company, Telmex, in the late 1980s. After

NAFTA created a gold rush of foreign money into Mexico, enriching Goldman Sachs and its clients and triggering an unsustainable speculative boom followed by a crash, Rubin promoted the bailout of Mexico that made foreign bondholders whole. A little-noticed provision of NAFTA permitted foreign banks to acquire Mexican ones. In 2001, Rubin, back in the private sector, negotiated Citigroup's $12.5 billion acquisition of Mexico's leading bank, Banamex.

As Clinton's adviser in trade negotiations, Rubin's top priority was less a level playing field for American exports than rapid access for US financial capital. In negotiations for China's membership in the World Trade Organization, then-Chinese Prime Minister Zhu Rongji came to Washington in April 1999 to consummate the deal. According to Joseph Stiglitz, former head of Clinton's Council of Economic Advisers, Zhu, a reformer, went home empty-handed because he failed to satisfy the Treasury's conditions on rapid financial market liberalization and on access for foreign banks, which Rubin pushed, over the objections of the State Department and the US Trade Representative.

Rubin also acted to facilitate the growth of private equity by promoting legislation that made it easier for private equity general partners to sell shares to investors, called limited partners. This maneuver allows private equity companies to evade the disclosures to the SEC and investors required of publicly traded companies.

What is now called private equity began in the 1980s. At the time, it had the less flattering moniker of "corporate raids", using leveraged buyouts financed by high-yield "junk bonds." In the early 1990s, the sector was rebranded with the more soothing name, private equity. Since then, private equity has metastasized into a giant player, whose business model is to borrow money and loot the operating companies that it acquires, selling off real estate, extracting dividends, cutting wages and shutting down workers' pension funds.

Rubin's crowning achievement was the repeal of the 1933 Glass-Steagall Act, which had separated largely unregulated and more speculative investment banks like Goldman Sachs from government-supervised and -insured commercial banks like Citi, which play a key role in the nation's monetary policy. Glass-Steagall was designed to prevent the kinds of speculative conflicts of interest that pervaded Wall Street in the 1920s and helped bring about the Great Depression (and reappeared in the 1990s).

Glass-Steagall was steadily weakened by regulatory exceptions under three administrations, going back to George H.W. Bush. The premise was that tearing down the regulatory walls would promote competition. But the effect was to create greater concentration and renewed opportunities for insider enrichment.

Financier Sanford Weill gradually assembled the empire of insurance, commercial-banking, and investment-banking pieces that ultimately became Citigroup, helped by indulgent regulatory policies promoted by Federal Reserve Chairman Alan Greenspan and Rubin. When Congress formally repealed Glass-Steagall in November 1999, the act was termed in some circles the "Citigroup Authorization Act." Rubin had stepped down as Treasury Secretary that July. His new job, announced in late October, was chairman of Citi's executive committee. Rubin's initial annual compensation was around $40 million.

In November 2001, as Enron was collapsing, Rubin phoned Peter Fisher, Bush's undersecretary of the Treasury for domestic finance, and inquired whether it might be a good idea for the Treasury Department to suggest that credit-rating agencies delay a downgrading of Enron's debt. Enron owed Citi about $750 million. Fisher wisely fended off the pressure.

When word of Rubin's lobbying leaked out, the Treasury and

"a source close to Rubin" issued nicely complementary statements, so that Rubin's inquiry was treated by the press as tentative, hypothetical, and above all public-minded. The New York Times published a page-one story on Rubin's role with the misleading headline, "Rubin Relishes Role of Banker as Public Man." The story mentioned Rubin's contacts with the Treasury, then helpfully added that in his conversations with the Treasury, Rubin "spoke as a banker, and also as a former Treasury chief concerned about the risks to the markets." In other words, Rubin was not mainly looking out for Citigroup's interests; he was acting as a public-spirited citizen. You can't buy more tame press coverage than this.

On February 15, 1999, astonishingly, Time magazine published an admiring cover story, featuring Rubin, Greenspan, and Summers, called "The Committee to Save the World." The story described how their policies were working to contain financial crises in East Asia, Mexico, and other countries where financial liberalization and speculation were followed by a crash. The story omitted to mention why the world needed saving. The cause was the hyper-deregulatory policies of the same gang of three.

Among financial regulators, there was one notable opponent of Rubin and Summers. And they got her fired as fast as they could. Clinton had gotten a much more independent official than he bargained for when he appointed a lawyer named Brooksley Born from the establishment firm of Arnold and Porter in 1996 to chair the relatively obscure Commodity Futures Trading Commission (CFTC).

Futures were traditionally contracts to buy or sell farm products or industrial raw materials at a fixed price on a fixed date, so that a buyer or seller could hedge against the risk of unexpected price swings. The small cost of buying the future operated as a kind of insurance. It was a quiet, low-profit corner of the financial system that served a benign purpose. Futures were known as derivatives because they were securities derived from the underlying transaction at one remove.

In the 1980s, Wall Street financial engineers created new kinds of derivatives. You could buy a derivative tied to a mortgage, or a stock, or almost any financial instrument. Financial derivatives became a source of pure speculation for traders and great enrichment for investment banking houses. Because they used borrowed money, the degree of leverage was often far higher than the ratio of equity capital to debt permitted in ordinary financial transactions. When the financial economy collapsed in 2008, the house of cards that derivatives built was heavily implicated.

In 1998, Born began looking closely into financial derivatives and was troubled by what she saw. So-called over-the-counter or customized derivatives fell between the cracks of different categories of regulation. Their details were opaque, and the odds favored the house—the house being the giant investment banks that created them and profited from them. By the late 1990s, the value of custom financial derivatives had grown from almost nothing a decade earlier to over $70 trillion. When the heavily leveraged market for derivatives backing subprime mortgages collapsed a decade later, the failure to regulate financial derivatives was at the center of the mess.

The big banks had managed to fend off any form of derivatives regulation. Their close ally, Alan Greenspan, declared in 1997 that government regulation was "wholly unnecessary" because "private market regulation has been achieving public policy objectives quite effectively and efficiently."

Born disagreed. In 1998, she proposed a "concept paper" to consider whether the regulation of financial derivatives should be strengthened. Wall Street and all its allies in the Clinton Administration all came down on her. In March 1998, Larry Summers phoned Born and said, "I have thirteen bankers in my office, and they all say that if you go forward with this, you will cause the worst financial crisis since World War II."

What caused the worst financial crisis since the Great Depression, of course, was the *failure* to regulate financial derivatives. Born went ahead and issued the concept paper in May 1998, and the sky did not fall.

But by 1999, Rubin and Summers had pushed Born out of office and drafted legislation to make sure that no future official would ever try to regulate financial derivatives. It was titled the Commodity Futures Modernization Act, signed into law in December 2000, just before Clinton left office. Just to be sure, it prohibited regulation of derivatives as either insurance or as securities, and all too aptly, it also barred states from regulating derivatives as gambling.

———

Out of office, Rubin's influence on the Democratic Party only intensified. In 2004, Rubin was serving as a key economic adviser to Democratic nominee John Kerry, and blunted Kerry's more progressive instincts. That April, AFL-CIO president John Sweeney grew concerned that Kerry was getting too much of his economic advice from the Wall Street wing of the Democratic Party. In the general election, Kerry would need the unions.

Sweeney proposed a private meeting, and the candidate invited the labor leader to his Beacon Hill home. Sweeney arrived at the Kerry manse, bringing his policy director, Chris Owens, and Jeff Faux of the Economic Policy Institute. There, seated in the elegant living room, were Robert Rubin and his two longtime lieutenants: investment banker and former Rubin deputy Roger

Altman, and fellow Clinton alum Gene Sperling—now Kerry's key economic advisers.

The group discussed the deficit, taxes, trade, health care, unions, and living standards in a wide-ranging three-hour conversation. The labor people urged the candidate to go after Wal-Mart's low wages. Rubin countered that a lot of people like Wal-Mart's low prices. Kerry eventually announced that the meeting needed to wrap up, because "Bob has to get back to Washington." Rubin responded that, no, he could stay as long as Kerry wanted.

Sweeney and his colleagues were ushered out the door; Rubin, Altman, and Sperling remained. "Wall Street was in the room before we arrived," Faux told me, "and they were there after we left."

When the Democrats took back the House in 2006, incoming Speaker Nancy Pelosi advised the new Democratic caucus that its first two briefings would include one on defense, with three experts of differing views. On the economy, Robert Rubin would be appearing solo.

In the tightly contested 2008 presidential primaries, Rubin managed to stay on very close terms with both Barack Obama and Hillary Clinton. Whichever of them won, Rubin would be a key adviser. When the winner turned out to be Obama, all of his key economic advisers would be Rubin allies or protégés, beginning with Larry Summers in Rubin's old job as chair of the National Economic Council.

In late 2006, I decided to write an authoritative profile on Rubin and his influence for The American Prospect. In reviewing published articles on Rubin going back two decades, I could not find a single feature piece that was, on balance, unflattering. It was a reflection of Rubin's multiple roles and his skill at persuading a docile financial press of his public-mindedness.

I also wrote a long investigative profile of Larry Summers.

What I found was a history of making blunder after blunder, but being protected and promoted by Robert Rubin, right into the presidency of Harvard, where Summers managed to get himself fired. Summers was an even more relentless promoter of reckless financial deregulation than Rubin. He was the point man in the successful campaign to destroy Brooksley Born.

When Rubin became Clinton's top economic official, he saw to it that Summers would be appointed undersecretary of the Treasury for international economic policy. In that powerful post, Summers fought with State and Defense Department officials for control of Russia policy. His secret weapon was the International Monetary Fund, whose assistance Russia urgently needed, as its economy was collapsing. Abrupt price decontrol, executed on January 1, 1992, had led to annual inflation rates of over 2,000 percent. Would the IMF be generous or stingy, and what conditions would be attached? As undersecretary, Summers was the main US liaison with the IMF, and not shy about using that leverage.

The Clinton administration was divided. People who knew the region best argued that Russia should be given time and substantial financial help to convert to a European-style, democratic mixed economy. They were opposed by military hawks who viewed post-Soviet Russia as a continuing geopolitical threat, and by free-market hawks led by Summers, who counseled shock therapy.

Applying free-market theory where it didn't fit, Summers pressured then-premier Boris Yeltsin to privatize state assets as rapidly as possible. So-called voucher privatization was carried out in two waves. First, in 1993-1994, Russian citizens were given vouchers with which to buy shares. Aspiring oligarchs bought up the vouchers, picking up the Russian extractive economy's crown jewels for a song. Insiders at energy giant Gazprom, which was worth at least $40 billion, acquired the company for about $250 million.

In the second wave, in 1995-1996, the Yeltsin government, itself in need of cash, floated a corrupt scheme known as "loans for shares," which delivered the rest of the state-owned economy to oligarchs, who reciprocated with massive campaign contributions for Yeltsin's 1996 re-election. The real economy kept faltering, living standards collapsed, and the result was big political gains for both Communists and nationalists. It was Putin who picked up the pieces.

Summers's advice was also pockmarked by a personal conflict of interest. His close friend and longtime Harvard colleague, Russian-born economist Andrei Shleifer, was head of a Harvard-initiated project in Moscow that held the prime contract with USAID to help with the post-Soviet economic transition. On the side, according to federal prosecutors, Shleifer and his wife were using insider knowledge to make investments. The case was finally settled in 2004, by which time Summers was president of Harvard. Shleifer paid $2 million; Harvard, as directed by Summers, paid $26.5 million. Shleifer continued as a tenured professor, and though Summers' disparagement of women got more publicity, his protection of Shleifer was one of the key factors in faculty pressure for Summers's ouster.

There has been a good deal of commentary about how "campaign finance" undermines political democracy. In the standard account, the liberation of unlimited campaign giving, thanks to two Supreme Court decisions beginning with *Buckley v. Valeo* in 1976, allows a candidate's quest for money, most of it from rich and self-interested donors, to overwhelm the power of votes. Thus does money undermine democracy.

This abstract account is true as a generalization, but it omits the fact that the influence of Wall Street is up close and personal. Figures like Rubin and Summers are not arms-length donors. They are inside the tent. They and their proteges literally took over the making of economic policy, under Clinton and then Obama, distancing the party of the people from the people.

Rubin was also an unfortunate role model for the president himself. One insidious way that conflicts of interest work is that while still in office, you imagine your opportunities once you leave, when you are able to blur your civic post-presidential role with your commercial ventures. This makes an opportunistic president think twice about offending Wall Street. (A rare exception to this pattern was Jimmy Carter, whose long post-presidency was devoted to selfless service. He was a far better post-president than a president.)

After leaving office, Clinton created the Clinton Foundation and the Clinton Global Initiative, multi-million dollar enterprises that allowed the Clintons to blur good works with opportunities to raise money from self-interested donors. At a time when Hillary Clinton was Barack Obama's secretary of state, the Clinton Foundation took gifts from a number of entities seeking to influence the Administration, including the dominant companies providing mercenary soldiers, Blackwater, as well as the governments of Saudi Arabia, the United Arab Emirates, Oman, and even allies, including Germany and Australia. It was an open secret that Hillary Clinton would run for president in 2008.

Bill Clinton took no salary from the foundation, but the cross-fertilization enabled him to command six-figure speaking fees from players seeking to buy influence, as well as other sources of income. When presidential candidate Hillary Clinton in 2016 undermined her own credibility as any kind of progressive by taking fees as high as half a million dollars for speeches on Wall Street, she hadn't noticed the contradiction. It was second nature.

The Clintons' net worth in 2025 was around $100 million.

Clinton also had global influence. In the 1990s, center-left governments in Britain and Germany emulated Clinton's brand of neoliberalism and his alliance with financial elites. Both did lasting damage to their parties, and both profited personally.

In Britain, when Tony Blair became Labour Party Leader in 1994, he copied Clinton's New Democrat tactic and rebranded the Labour Party as New Labour. Blair's party manifesto of 1996, heading into the 1997 general election, was titled "New Labour, New Life for Britain." The idea was to abandon Labour's commitment to democratic socialism, break with the unions, make a closer alliance with the City, Britain's counterpart of Wall Street, and remake Labour as a centrist party.

Blair had a particular hostility to the unions, and not without some reason. In 1979, when the Labour Prime Minister was James Callaghan, the unions faced the problem of severe inflation cutting into the value of their wages. While Callaghan tried to break the spiral of price and wage increases, many workers resorted to wildcat strikes. In the coldest winter in two decades, trash piled up on the frozen streets, corpses could not be buried because of a gravedigger's strike, ambulances refused some calls, and drivers of oil tankers struck for higher pay, causing service stations to close.

In the ensuing election of 1979, frustrated voters elected Thatcher and the Tories by a modest seven points, 44 to 37 percent. But like Trump, Thatcher treated her election as a landslide mandate, ushering in 18 years of hard-right Tory rule. Blair finally ended that, winning a landslide election in 2007. He was determined to weaken what he took to be the trade unions' stranglehold on the Labour Party. He kept most of Thatcher's policies, weakening unions, and doubled down on her deregulation of finance.

When the President of the Trades Union Congress (TUC), John Monks, very much a modernizer who wanted a Scandinavian-type social bargain rather than disabling strikes, Blair was having none of it. Monks told me of his first meeting with the new prime minister at the TUC office. Blair pointed to photos on the wall of the two most recent Labour prime ministers, Harold Wilson and James Callaghan, both of whom had been hurt politically by union strife. "Is that your trophy gallery?" Blair asked. "Well, you're not going to have my head on that wall."

Blair managed to get re-elected twice. He moved Labour to the center. The British income distribution worsened during his tenure. Along the way, he did his best to purge or isolate left-wingers. By the time the Tories regained power in 2010, the Labour Party was a factionalized mess, badly split along personal and ideological lines.

In 2015, an unreconstructed old socialist, Jeremy Corbyn, got elected Labour Party leader. He did so by taking advantage of a change in the rules created by the party leadership in 2014, intended to weaken the unions. The maneuver backfired. Individuals from the far left joined the party to elect Corbyn. This time, the Tories stayed in power for fourteen years.

Through a series of miscalculations, Tory governments also presided over Britain's self-defeating exit from the European Union. In this, they were aided by Labour's Corbyn. As a hard left-ist, Corbyn had long been critical of the EU as too capitalist. Corbyn lost the entirely winnable election of 2019 by equivocating about where he stood on Brexit.

When Labour finally returned to power in 2024, the government under Keir Starmer was hobbled by a badly weakened British economy. One of his principal advisers was Tony Blair.

Blair, meanwhile, had created the non-profit Tony Blair Institute for Global Change, which took contributions from a wide array of governments and corporations, and a parallel for-profit consulting firm. He earned between $5 and $10 million a year. In 2025, his net worth was estimated at $80 million.

In Germany, Social Democratic Chancellor Gerhard Schroeder was elected in 1998, succeeding conservative Helmut Kohl. Schroeder emulated Clinton and Blair by branding his program as the *Neue Mitte*—the New Center.

Schroeder set about with market liberalization for both capital and labor. In December 1999, Schroeder announced changes in the tax law so that banks could sell appreciated stock in corporations without paying capital gains tax. The tax was cut from 54 percent to zero. *Der Spiegel* termed this shift "a type of financial deregulation that Helmut Kohl would never have dared."

After narrowly winning reelection in 2002, Schroeder unveiled a manifesto titled Agenda 2010 for drastic liberalization of Germany's social welfare and labor system—as if these were somehow responsible for the sluggishness that had afflicted Germany since the Federal Republic's costly absorption of the former East Germany.

The reforms were intended to force unemployed workers to take low-wage jobs. One instrument was drastic cuts in unemployment benefits. Before the reforms, long-term unemployed people could collect indefinite benefits of around 55 percent of their prior net income. The benefits were cut and the duration capped at 18 months for most workers. If people refused to take even dismal jobs, they would be cut off.

The reforms also defined a new category known as mini-jobs, which paid well below prevailing wages and received less than full social protections. The result of these reforms was to drastically increase the size of the low-paid workforce, widen income inequality in Germany, and weaken the bargaining power of labor generally.

These policies provoked a split in the Social Democratic party, the SPD. In May 2005, former party chair and finance minister Oskar Lafontaine quit the party and soon spearheaded the creation of a new German party, *Die Linke* (the Left). The Left party was a combination of disaffected Social Democrats and leaders of the former, ostensibly reformed, communist party of East Germany.

The SPD never recovered from the split, which was followed by sixteen years of rule under conservative Angela Merkel. The SPD and *Die Linke* together won a majority of seats in the 2005 election, but such was the bitterness that a coalition was out of the question. Merkel became chancellor with the SPD as junior part-ner. When the SPD finally returned to power in 2021 under Olaf Scholz, the party received just 26 percent of the vote and had to govern in a shaky three-party coalition. The SPD and Scholz suffered a blowout defeat in the elections of February 2025.

Having undermined his party, Schroeder, like Clinton and Blair, made out just fine. Shortly before leaving office, in September 2005, Schroeder approved a $4.7 billion dollar pipe-line deal with the Russian gas giant, Gazprom. In December, he was rewarded with the chairmanship of the venture. His estimated net worth in 2025 was upwards of $200 million.

Clinton was an unfortunate role model, personally and ideo-logically, for other center-left parties. But his most lasting damage was at home. When the Democrats took back the presidency in 2008, they bungled what should have been a Roosevelt moment. The architects of this epic blunder were Clinton's economic team.

Chapter 9

The Tragedy of Obama

In the fall of 2007, I published *The Squandering of America,* warning that the economy was headed for a 1929-style financial collapse. The deregulation that had gutted New Deal safeguards and promoted opaque forms of financial engineering had created the mother of all financial bubbles. The Fed's frantic efforts to prop the economy up with low interest rates only made the bubble bigger. The book's original title was *The Coming Crash,* but the editors at Knopf thought that was a little too risky.

Around the time my book came out, Bear Stearns, the nation's fifth-largest investment bank, was going under. To paraphrase a famous Ernest Hemingway line, the firm went broke "gradually and then suddenly," as creditors and investors fled. Bear had been one of the major issuers of mortgage-backed securities, a highly speculative derivative whose own value depended on subprime mortgages. As it became evident to investors that many subprime mortgages would never be repaid, the value of mortgage-backed securities sagged and then collapsed.

In late 2007, hedge funds sponsored by Bear lost nearly all of their value. As investors deserted Bear, the firm's true financial condition was revealed. It had burned through all of its capital. As Warren Buffett once said, you only learn who is swimming naked when the tide goes out. The Federal Reserve Bank of New York tried to save Bear with an emergency loan, but this was not a crisis of confidence or a shortage of liquidity—Bear was insolvent. So in March 2008, the Fed brokered a shotgun sale of Bear to JPMorgan Chase, at a price of $10 a share, a fraction of the $133 per share valuation of Bear months before the firm unraveled. The proceeds were used to pay off creditors at a few cents on the dollar.

Bear's bust was a preview of things to come. The larger economic collapse, based on similar dynamics that afflicted the entire financial sector, was contained, but only for a few months.

In early 2008, as the economy was tottering, it appeared that Barack Obama could well defeat front-runner Hillary Clinton for the Democratic presidential nomination. I saw a possible rendezvous of man and moment. If the economy did collapse and Obama did win the nomination, he would have a good shot at getting elected, because the collapse would occur on the watch of Republican George W. Bush. And since the collapse was the consequence of free market economics taken to an absurd extreme by Wall Street speculators, an Obama presidency could be the long-deferred chance to restore something like the New Deal.

Obama might also restore a multiracial progressive voting coalition, which had been fragmented ever since Nixon. Given the collapsing economy, many whites were prepared to vote for an impressive Black man who promised a better future. Voters of all races were also attracted to Obama's personal integrity and probity. He had a lovely, attractive family that happened to be

Black. Not a whiff of personal scandal attached to Obama, in welcome contrast to the stench of tawdry affairs that lingered over the last Democratic president, whose long-suffering wife, Hillary, Obama had beaten for the nomination.

In the 2008 election, Obama was elected by a wide margin. He flipped nine states that Bush had won in 2004—Colorado, Florida, Indiana, Iowa, Nevada, New Mexico, North Carolina, Ohio, and Virginia. His party picked up 24 seats in the House and eight seats in the Senate. For a year, the Democrats held the Senate by a 60-40 filibuster-proof majority. It was the first time since 1964 that a Democrat had won the White House with major coattails.

The people had voted for change. Mostly, they didn't get it.

As events turned out, I was right about my first two assumptions—the economy did crash, and Obama did get elected—but I was wrong about who Obama would turn out to be as president. In office, Obama hired the Robert Rubin team, bailed out the banks, and did not pursue fundamental financial reform. He left the rest of the economy in a prolonged recession as he pivoted prematurely to deficit reduction as his paramount goal. In his first mid-term election, in 2010, Democrats in Congress would suffer record losses.

As I thought about the Obama opportunity in early 2008, I had been reading about great transformative presidencies, inspired by the work of the presidential historian James MacGregor Burns. My first thought was that the potential Obama moment would make a terrific magazine piece for The Prospect, so I reached out to another presidential historian whom I knew and admired, Doris Kearns Goodwin, to see if I could persuade her to write the piece.

Doris, however, was busy finishing her book on Teddy Roosevelt. Instead, we recorded a long conversation about Obama's opportunity that was published in The Prospect. And in the course of our conversations, Doris suggested that I write the article myself, or even better, write a short book. She offered to provide ideas and read chapters.

So I decided to take something of a risk. I wrote a book for publication by Labor Day, making some bold assumptions—that Obama would be the Democratic nominee and the next president; and that the economy would crash before the election. If I was right, I might have a best-seller. If I was wrong, we'd have a bonfire. My book was titled *Obama's Challenge*. The subtitle was America's Economic Crisis and the Power of a Transformative Presidency. Talk about the audacity of hope!

I had several extended conversations with Professor Burns, who also offered to read my chapters. Burns, in his 1978 book, *Leadership,* distinguished between transformational leadership and merely transactional leadership. As Burns wrote, contrasting "transactional leaders who thrive on bargaining, accommodating, and manipulating within a given system" with the rare case of "transforming leaders who respond to fundamental human needs and wants, hopes and expectations, and who may transcend and even seek to reconstruct the political system rather than simply to operate within it."

History could well offer Obama the kind of rare opportunity that history offered Roosevelt—to be transformational. As Doris Goodwin put it in our conversation for The Prospect, the greatest presidents used their leadership to transform public understanding of what was necessary and possible, appealing to the nation's deepest ideals as well as mastering the political moment. The abolition of slavery seemed inconceivable in 1860, as did a vastly expanded federal role in the economy in 1932, or the full redemption of civil rights in 1964. But transformational presidents made all of this possible.

By June of 2008, Obama had collected enough delegates to be

assured the nomination. The economy kept teetering. It collapsed right on schedule, the week after Labor Day. The collapse was a larger version of the forces that had brought down Bear Stearns — the largest banks betting the farm on derivative securities that in turn were backed by almost no real capital. This was all perfectly legal and opaque to regulators, thanks to the successful efforts of Robert Rubin and Larry Summers in 1999 to prohibit the regulation of financial derivatives.

When investors began panic-selling, the result was a cascade of collapses. To contain the subprime crisis, in the summer of 2008, the Federal Reserve permitted the government-guaranteed mortgage-purchasing entities, Fannie Mae and Freddie Mac, to buy $200 billion in subprime mortgages. But that only caused Fannie and Freddie to go broke themselves. On September 7, they were nationalized.

The next to fall was the venerable investment bank, Lehman Brothers, a larger player than Bear Stearns. This time, the Fed did not offer an emergency loan, and nobody wanted to buy Lehman. On September 15, Lehman declared bankruptcy, driving the Dow down by more than 500 points. The insurance giant, American International Group, which had bet massively on derivatives, also went under. A day later, Merrill Lynch broke. This time, the Fed and Treasury did broker a government-guaranteed shotgun sale to Bank of America. All of this happened in a single week.

It soon became clear that the strategy of enlisting the biggest banks to acquire failing ones has run its course. By late September, nearly all of the money center banks were themselves insolvent. Were they to close, credit would be choked off, and the entire economy would face Great Depression II.

On September 18, Bush's Treasury Secretary, Hank Paulson, met with senior leaders of Congress. He literally got down on his knees to plead for a $700 billion bailout to recapitalize the banks. All of the economy's credit markets were seizing up, he warned.

Paulson epitomized the conflicts of interest that led to the crash. He was a former CEO of Goldman Sachs. As Treasury Secretary, he had successfully promoted a change in SEC rules on bank capital that facilitated the extreme leverage that worsened the crash but allowed Goldman to get even richer along the way. In begging for the bailout, was he speaking for the Treasury or for Goldman? Was there a difference?

Wall Street's policy dominance would continue under Obama, whose policies were run by protégés of Robert Rubin, another former CEO of Goldman. No wonder ordinary people crushed by the financial collapse and the ensuing deep recession perceived that America had a single political party, the Goldman Party, whose interests were not theirs.

Paulson's proposed bailout was to be coordinated with emergency Federal Reserve lines of credit, running well into the trillions. The Fed chairman, Ben Bernanke, a Republican Bush appointee, was a student of the Great Depression. He was well aware of the perils of not acting. So the Fed created new lending "facilities" out of thin air, going far beyond its statutory authority.

The election was now less than two months away. In these conversations and hearings, some of which were public, both presidential nominees participated. Obama was plainly more impressive, with a better grasp of the issues, than his Republican rival, Sen. John McCain. President Bush barely participated. Eventually, in early October, Congress did pass the $700 bailout, creating the Troubled Asset Relief Program (TARP) to shovel money out to the banks. The "troubled assets"—a polite euphemism for securities that were largely worthless in the marketplace—would be taken onto the government's books, in exchange for cash.

As a condition of their support, the Democrats insisted on

creating a special Congressional Oversight Panel to be the TARP's watchdog. To chair the panel, Senate Democratic leader Harry Reid selected a Harvard law professor expert on bankruptcy named Elizabeth Warren. As her deputy, House Speaker Nancy Pelosi chose the AFL-CIO's specialist on capital markets, Damon Silvers. Both were intimately familiar with the games bankers played. After the election, as the incoming Obama Administration took charge of the TARP and the bailout of the big banks on remarkably generous terms, Warren and Silvers would function as Obama's progressive loyal opposition.

Warren invited me to join the oversight panel's senior staff, but as much as I admired her, I decided that I was more useful as a journalist. We stayed in close touch.

———

Until early 2008, when the magnitude of the financial damage became clear, Obama had not expected to be a president whose main challenge was managing an economic collapse. Obama had come to prominence as a racial healer and a critic of the Iraq War. In the keynote speech that made him a national figure, at the 2004 Democratic National Convention, Obama famously declared:

"The pundits like to slice-and-dice our country into Red States and Blue States; Red States for Republicans, Blue States for Democrats. But I've got news for them. We worship an awesome God in the Blue States, and we don't like federal agents poking around our libraries in the Red States. We coach Little League in the Blue States and have gay friends in the Red States. There are patriots who opposed the war in Iraq and patriots who supported it. We are one people, all of us pledging allegiance to the stars and stripes, all of us defending the United States of America."

At that point, Obama was not even a US senator—his own election was that fall—but the speech marked him as someone special. His 2006 book, *The Audacity of Hope*, written in anticipation of a presidential race, contained some nervy words on the loaded subject of race, suggesting a leader capable of unusual empathy and rare capacity to reframe how America thought—a transformative leader:

> *"I imagine the white Southerner who growing up heard his dad talk about niggers this and niggers that but who has struck up a friendship with the black guys at the office and is trying to teach his own son different, who thinks discrimination is wrong but doesn't see why the son of a black doctor should get admitted into law school ahead of his son. Or the former Black Panther who decided to go into real estate, bought a few buildings in the neighborhood, and is just as tired of the drug dealers in front of his buildings as he is of the bankers who won't give him a loan to expand his business."*

As late as May 2008, Obama's campaign had just two economic policy staffers plus some occasional outside counsel from Paul Volcker, who did not like the massive financial engineering that had invited a crash. One of the staffers was a little-known academic economist named Austan Goolsbee, who Obama knew from the University of Chicago. The other was a Georgetown Law professor, Daniel Tarullo, who was the campaign's sole expert on how financial markets worked, and a well-informed critic of deregulation and market manipulation.

Obama had his first opportunity to deliver a major speech on the economy on March 27, at Cooper Union in New York. The symbolism of time and place was powerful. Bear Stearns had just gone under. Cooper Union was the place where George Washington had taken his first oath of office. It was the site of Lincoln's celebrated address of February 1860 on slavery.

Obama had asked Tarullo to draft the speech. The two had met early in Obama's Senate term, and Tarullo volunteered as soon as Obama declared for the presidency. The speech was the topic of extensive staff brainstorming at Obama's Chicago headquarters, but the subject matter proved too complex for other staffers, so Tarullo's draft emerged largely unscathed except for grace notes added by the candidate.

Obama declared,

"Under Republican and Democratic administrations, we've failed to guard against practices that all too often rewarded financial manipulation instead of productivity and sound business practice. We let the special interests put their thumbs on the economic scales. The result has been a distorted market that creates bubbles instead of steady, sustainable growth; a market that favors Wall Street over Main Street, but ends up hurting both."

This was a pointed critique of Clinton as well as Bush. It was far tougher than anything Hillary Clinton had to say about the economy—not surprisingly, since her husband had been the architect of these policies. Obama added: "Unfortunately, instead of establishing a 21st century regulatory framework, we simply dismantled the old one, aided by a legal but corrupt bargain in which campaign money all too often shaped policy and watered down oversight." He added, "This was not the invisible hand at work. Instead, it was the hand of industry lobbyists tilting the playing field in Washington, as well as an accounting industry that had developed powerful conflicts of interest and a financial sector that had fueled over-investment."

His proposed remedies were well-informed and far-reaching.

"The large, complex institutions that dominate the financial land-scape don't fit into categories created decades ago," he said. "We need to regulate institutions for what they do, not what they are."

This speech marked Obama as a president who would be a Roosevelt-style explainer and radical reformer who welcomed a battle with Wall Street. This would be in drastic contrast to the bipartisan captivity to Wall Street personified by Rubin and Paulson.

But this stance was short-lived. In June, when it was clear that Obama would be the nominee and that the economy was in for a very rough time, his donors and other financial advisors suggested it was time for him to bring in the A-team. This turned out to be the same Clinton team that had created the policies that produced the crash. It was a stunning turnabout and a testament to the power of elites. Obama's warning about lobbyists tilting the playing field proved to be a sadly apt description of his own admin-istration.

On June 7, as I was just finishing my book, my heart sank when I saw the list of Obama's new senior economic advisors. Nominally, the campaign's director of economic policy would be Jason Furman, 37, a junior aide to Robert Rubin. In practice, Rubin would be pulling the strings. Rubin and his allies succeeded in installing Rubin's longtime number two, Larry Summers, who eventually became Obama's top economic policy official as head of the National Economic Council. During the campaign, Summers took charge of the economics team's weekly phone calls, with Furman in the junior role of recording secretary.

After Summers left office in 2001, the ubiquitous Robert Rubin, who also served on the seven-member Harvard Corpora-tion, succeeded in installing Summers as president of Harvard in 2003. After a series of blunders, Summers was forced out in 2006. While at Harvard, he also made windfall profits moonlighting on

Wall Street. The hedge fund D.E. Shaw paid Summers $5.2 million for about a day of work a week. Goldman Sachs paid Summers $135,000 for a single speech. The Wall Street Journal editorialized acidly, "That must have been some stemwinder."

Another Clinton veteran with close personal ties to Rubin was Tim Geithner as Secretary of the Treasury. Geithner's most recent job had been President of the New York Federal Reserve Bank. He was selected by a panel headed by Republican arch-conservative private equity billionaire Peter G. Peterson. The press release from the New York Fed announcing Geithner's appointment noted that Peterson had been advised by Robert Rubin. Geithner had previously served as an undersecretary of the Treasury from 1998 to 2001 under Rubin and Summers. Geithner's views were anything but insurgent. It was a close-knit, like-minded club.

Other Rubinistas included Michael Froman, who became Obama's top official on trade, and the Office of Management and Budget Director Peter Orszag. Froman was an unreconstructed corporate globalist, and Orszag a balanced-budget man. After leaving government, both got plum jobs in the financial industry thanks to Rubin's patronage. Froman had been Rubin's chief of staff at the Clinton Treasury. After leaving government, he followed Rubin to Citigroup as the head of emerging markets. Rubin got Orszag a job at Citi as a managing director and vice chair in charge of investment banking.

For his chief of staff, Obama selected Rahm Emanuel, whose entire revolving-door career had been marked by conflicts of interest. He had been a major fundraiser for the Chicago Daley machine and one of Bill Clinton's chief money men in the 1992 campaign. He then used his political contacts to seek his own fortune on Wall Street. Bruce Wasserstein, former head of Lehman Brothers and a Clinton ally, set Emanuel up in the Chicago office of his boutique investment banking firm, Wasserstein Perella. There, Emanuel did several deals drawing on his political contacts. After two and a half years, he had made about $18 million and decided to run for Congress in a safe Democratic seat. He raised more money from Wall Street than any other House Democrat.

In 2005, having served just two terms, he was put in charge of the Democratic Congressional Campaign Committee. His strategy was to recruit center-right New Democrats candidates who could raise lots of Wall Street money. He arranged to double the size of the House Financial Services Committee, to fill it with dozens more Democrats who would do the bidding of big finance. In 2009, when committee chair Barney Frank, a progressive, was working on what would become the Dodd-Frank financial reform bill, Frank could not count on a majority of his own committee.

When Obama named Emanuel as his chief of staff, the idea was to get someone who really knew Congress. But Emanuel knew Congress in the most corrupt way. The whole senior team was committed to defending the financial status quo. It was as if Franklin Roosevelt got elected and turned economic policy over to Herbert Hoover's advisers.

The only outliers were Jared Bernstein, formerly of EPI, who was given the title of the vice-president's chief economist, and University of California economist Christina Romer as chair of the Council of Economic Advisers, the panel that had been demoted in influence after Clinton had created the National Economic Council for Rubin. Bernstein sat in on some of the meetings where real decisions were made. Romer emerged as a sometime foil to Summers, calling for a much larger economic stimulus than Summers recommended. Summers prevailed.

The group quickly isolated Daniel Tarullo, whose tough views of regulation were at odds with theirs. As a consolation prize, he was packed off to the Federal Reserve, where Obama appointed him as one of seven governors serving under Rubin ally Ben Bernanke, who would be reappointed by Obama in 2013.

The Rubin team even managed to marginalize Paul Volcker, who had volunteered to help Obama early, formally endorsed him in January 2008, and who knew more about the dynamics of the financial collapse and its connection to financial engineering than any of them. Volcker was named to head something called the President's Economic Recovery Advisory Board. It had no budget, no staff, and didn't even meet until late May 2009. Volcker was excluded from all the serious meetings. Paul Volcker was too left-wing for Obama's economic team.

In sum, Obama had the makings of a transformative president, especially when it came to race and to some extent foreign policy. But on economics, the most important test of his presidency, he was thoroughly captured by the old guard. In Burns's terms, his leadership was purely transactional.

Why? To some extent, this was insecurity. Economics was not a topic he knew well. He deferred to the supposed experts. He also did not want to risk a wider collapse, and propping up the big banks was the course of least resistance. There are those who believe that Obama was averse to triggering the "angry Black man" trope, though anger directed at the bankers on behalf of the common man and woman, FDR style, would likely have been welcomed.

In early 2010, I published a book titled *A Presidency in Peril* on Obama's first year, warning that Obama was on the wrong track and that he would likely pay the price at the polls and in his legacy. It was a sequel to my earlier book, *Obama's Challenge*, which was the first book published on the new administration. *Obama's Challenge* was even the best-seller that I had hoped for, but that was small comfort. The message of the book was ignored by the one reader who mattered.

———

Obama had three big decisions to make. Would the bailout for the big banks be conditioned on fundamental reform of a speculative financial system that had caused the collapse? Would there be relief for the millions of homeowners who had been tricked into taking out subprime loans and who then lost everything in the crash? And would there be a program of stimulus and public investment at a sufficient scale to get America out of a recession fast? Advised by Rubin's team, Obama went the wrong way on all three. We are still paying the price.

The first big decision was whether to clean out the big banks that had profited from creating the speculative instruments that caused the crash — or just bail them out. Summers, Geithner, and company advised that cleaning out the biggest banks would be too risky. In the end, there was no regime change at any of the major money center banks. A decade after the collapse, they were bigger and with a more concentrated market share than before.

The two major players who opposed the Summers-Geithner strategy were Elizabeth Warren, as chair of the Congressional Oversight Panel, and a holdover Republican appointee, Sheila Bair, who chaired the Federal Deposit Insurance Corporation. Bair, a former staffer to Republican Senator Robert Dole, was a far tougher regulator than any of Obama's appointees. Warren and Bair had one other thing in common. They both had a deep under-standing of bankruptcy.

As Warren later told me, when the crisis was unfolding in the fall of 2008, she used it as a kind of rolling case study for her law school class on bankruptcy. When a company goes bankrupt, shareholders lose everything. Other creditors may get paid off at so many cents on the dollar, depending on which assets remain. There is often a struggle over whether present management keeps their jobs while the company is reorganized—this is known as debtor in possession. Or, if the bankruptcy judge finds that the executives were culpable for running the company into the ground, new management will be brought in by a receiver. And if the remains are just beyond salvation, what's left of the company will be broken up and sold off.

Warren was of the view that the executives of the major banks that had caused the crash should lose their jobs, and that some should face criminal prosecution. She was also a severe critic of the phenomenon known as "too big to fail"—if a bank was large enough, no matter how reckless its behavior, the government would just have to bail it out. This functioned as a perverse incentive and an unfair competitive advantage. The biggest banks took the biggest risks, and they should be broken up.

Sheila Bair, the holdover chair of the FDIC, had a similar view and a lot of practical experience. The FDIC tends to be the toughest of the several bank regulatory agencies because its trust funds are tapped to pay insured depositors if a bank fails. In the run-up to the 2008 collapse, several FDIC-insured banks did go broke.

Bair presided over a well-established FDIC practice known as resolution. FDIC auditors assess the bank's assets and liabilities; current management is fired, depositors are made whole, and the FDIC takes over operation of the bank until the healthy parts can be sold to another bank.

In July 2008, Bair acted to seize an insolvent $32 billion mortgage lender, IndyMac, which had bet heavily on subprime and was now $6 billion underwater. In taking over the bank, Bair devised an ingenious plan to help the 60,000 homeowners with IndyMac mortgages avert foreclosure and loss of their homes. She offered them refinancing. She could do this because the FDIC was the temporary owner of the bank. Bair offered this approach as a model to the incoming Obama Treasury. They were not interested; their priority was bailing out banks, not saving homeowners.

Toward the end of 2008, during the Bush-Obama transition, Bair took over an even bigger failed bank, the $307 billion Washington Mutual, known as WaMu, which had invested heavily in subprime mortgages. Private equity firms had invested heavily in WaMu. Bair followed the usual resolution procedure. She found a buyer for WaMu's remains, JPMorgan Chase, but only after WaMu's executives were fired, its shareholders lost everything, and its bondholders took a partial hit. There was no cost to taxpayers. This is just the way capitalism is supposed to work. The risk of loss deters excessive risk.

Geithner was incensed. He pressured other bank regulators and the Fed to lobby Bair to declare WaMu as "systemically significant," which would qualify it for the no-cost bailout that Citi had gotten. But Bair hung tough. She earned further Geithner enmity when she blocked a proposed sweetheart deal that would have given Citi control of the failed Wachovia bank, sticking the FDIC with a big share of the losses.

A straw man in the debate about how to treat the big banks was "nationalization." To hear Geithner and Summers, those who wanted to break up the big banks were proposing to nationalize them. This was nonsense. Nobody was proposing permanent government ownership. Rather, the idea, modeled on the well-established FDIC resolution process, was that the government would take the big insolvent Wall Street banks into temporary receivership, do an honest accounting, oust incumbent management, and decide how much TARP money to put into the deal. The healthy part of the bank would be sold off, either as a new free-standing bank or as a merger. A bonus was that the biggest and most corrupt banks would be broken up.

This approach horrified Summers and Geithner. They argued

that it would be too disruptive to the financial system. In truth, it would be disruptive mainly to their cozy Wall Street cronies. On the other side of the argument were knowledgeable outside economists, including Joseph Stiglitz, Simon Johnson, Nouriel Rubini, as well as Paul Volcker, Sheila Bair, and Elizabeth Warren.

In my writing, I weighed in against the Summers-Geithner approach of bailing out without cleaning out the banks. I argued the case with Summers in person at the White House. But they controlled the government, and they prevailed. Thus was a rare moment for profound structural reform lost.

———

While Geithner and Summers were allowing the biggest banks to survive intact, with no replacement of senior executives nor losses to shareholders, they were selling out homeowners. At the insistence of progressive Democrats in Congress, the TARP program included $50 billion to refinance mortgages for homeowners. Much of this was never used.

In the subprime scam, mortgage bankers offered homeowners a deal that seemed too good to be true. And it was. The mortgage would carry a very low interest rate for the first two or three years, and then the rate would triple or quadruple. Often, there would be hidden penalties against refinancing.

The mortgages, in turn, would be sold to a large investment bank, which could package them into a mortgage-backed security, often disguising the true risk. These might be repackaged into an even more opaque "collateralized debt obligation." Complicit rating agencies would bless the security with a triple-A rating, allowing these securities to be bought by life insurance companies or pension funds as sound investments. The entire scheme unwound when many homeowners with subprime mortgages were unable to meet their payments, and their homes went into foreclosure. The value of the securities, in turn, collapsed.

Subprime mortgages were target-marketed in Black communities. A great many homeowners duped by the subprime scam were Black homeowners who had conventional mortgages. A mortgage banker would persuade them to refinance their mortgage with a new subprime loan that would allow them to take out equity. When the introductory rate reset to a much higher rate, they fell behind in their payments.

As large numbers of homes went into foreclosure, the value of surrounding homes fell as well. Many homeowners with conventional mortgages who were current on their payments also lost homes because the lender could call in a mortgage on the grounds that the collateral was now worth less than the mortgage loan against it.

For Sheila Bair, Elizabeth Warren, and their allies in Congress, a priority was saving homeowners. For Geithner and company, the priority was keeping the big banks and their executives intact. As the Geithner Treasury implemented the part of the TARP program intended to help underwrite mortgage refinancing, Treasury turned the program from straightforward refinancing, a tried-and-true practice, into an invented category cooked up with the bankers called "loan modification." The goal was to cost the banks as little as possible. The result was to help far fewer homeowners than Congress intended.

Geithner, assisted by the banks, created two convoluted programs for mortgage relief. The largest of these was the Home Affordable Modification Program or HAMP, unveiled by the Treasury in February 2009. Unlike a true refinancing program, like the Roosevelt era Homeowners Loan Corporation, which saved about one homeowner in five during the Great Depression, HAMP kept the mortgage intact and kept the bank in charge. The exact terms of the modification—how much of a reduction in monthly payments—were up to the bank. The principal owed was rarely reduced, and the application process was a nightmare. The banks kept moving the goalposts.

According to a comprehensive report by the Government Accountability Office, after the program concluded, out of 1.74 million homeowners who received loan modifications, only 300,830 included any reduction in principal owed. In the meantime, during the same decade, some six million Americans lost their homes to foreclosure. Of the $50 billion that Congress earmarked for homeowner relief under the TARP, about $20 billion was never spent.

The results of the subprime crisis, the ensuing collapse, and the failed mortgage relief were especially devastating for Black homeowners. In 2007, on the eve of the crash, the Black homeownership rate had slowly risen to 46.5 percent, thanks to the good work of Community Development Financial Institutions like Chicago's Shorebank and the regulatory carrots and sticks of the Community Reinvestment Act. After the collapse and the Great Recession that followed, the Black homeownership rate had fallen to 41.7 in 2016, below its rate prior to enactment of the 1968 Fair Housing Act.

The Obama Administration's failure to promote a broad recovery, coupled with its coddling of the big banks, allowed the right-wing to promote a Big Lie—the claim that the housing collapse had been a consequence of well-intentioned but misguided efforts by liberals to extend homeownership to minority owners who couldn't really afford it. This was a big lie in two distinct respects.

The first lie was that the rising Black homeownership rate had anything to do with subprime. It did not. The vast majority of Black homeowners had conventional or FHA-insured mortgages. The fact that more moderate-income households were qualified to become owners reflected the careful effort of community development bankers. Until the financial collapse dragged down the value of housing in general, Black default and foreclosure rates were comparable to white rates.

The second big lie was that subprime mortgages were created by liberal do-gooders so that more marginally qualified minority buyers could acquire homes. The investment banks that invented subprime loans and their local loan originators were interested in making a quick buck, not in promoting Black homeownership as a social goal. On the contrary, responsible community bankers knew just how toxic subprime loans were and avoided them.

But despite these realities, the myth that Black homeowners had caused the collapse became a right-wing talking point. On February 19, 2009, commentator Rick Santelli, speaking live on CNBC from the floor of the Chicago Mercantile Exchange, called for a new Tea Party protest movement. "The government is promoting bad behavior," he thundered. He angrily challenged Obama, "Why don't you put up a website to have people vote on the internet as a referendum to see if we really want to subsidize the losers' mortgages?" Santelli declared, "We're thinking of having a Chicago Tea Party in July. All you capitalists that want to show up to Lake Michigan, I'm gonna start organizing."

You could not imagine a better example of fake populism than a CBNC commentator calling for a revolt from the floor of a financial exchange. But because of the perception that Obama was in bed with the bankers, Santelli was able conflate bailing out the banks (which Obama did) with helping distressed homeowners (which Obama mostly did not do).

Santelli's own moment of fame was brief. He never did much organizing, but the call for a new Tea Party took off, and conservatives within days held dozens of Tea Party rallies across the country, subsidized by the billionaire Koch Brothers. Tea Party activists went to work in the 2010 midterms to defeat Democrats. A few years later, they became part of Trump's MAGA army.

While Obama left the details of financial reform to Rubin's team, he had one personal priority: universal healthcare. He spent a lot of his own energy and political capital on what became the Affordable Care Act. But he didn't quite have the votes to enact true universal health coverage. Instead, the ACA was a complex plan to subsidize insurance for the uninsured, using private insurance companies. It was a variant on the failed Bill Clinton plan and the one that Republican Mitt Romney succeeded in enacting for Massachusetts. Nationally, the uninsured were only about 15 percent of the population, mostly lower-income, and the ACA could cover only about half of them.

Progressives were not happy. As their price for supporting the legislation, they came up with the idea of a "public option." Uninsured people could opt for subsidized insurance with a private carrier, or they could choose to join Medicare. A giant lobbying coalition called HCAN, standing for Health Care Action Now, was assembled to push for the legislation, on the condition that it include a public option. The hope was that more efficient public insurance would gradually crowd out less efficient private insurance.

But Obama's deal with the insurance industry was that the ACA would give them a lot more customers. Predictably, the industry went all out to kill the public option, and won allies among key Democrats in Congress. Obama had to advise the HCAN coalition that the public option did not have the votes. They deliberated and decided to support the legislation anyway.

In March 2010, the ACA did pass, squeaking through the House by a vote of 219-212, with dozens of Democrats defecting. Along the way, it consumed a huge amount of Obama's personal attention, to the detriment of more pressing concerns such as the financial collapse and its aftermath.

If the ACA split Democrats in Congress, it would soon have a more disastrous electoral effect. The budget hawks whom Obama had appointed to OMB, already anxious about rising deficits, insisted that the measure indicate how the large subsidies would be paid for. The legislation provided that it would be substantially financed by unspecified future "savings" in Medicare. This gave the Tea Party narrative one more talking point: Your Medicare will be cut to finance insurance for the undeserving poor.

The third great policy question facing the new administration was the scale and design of the stimulus program. By the winter of 2008-2009, the economy was facing a depression. GDP growth had turned negative. During 2009, the unemployment rate steadily rose to 9.9 percent.

In late January 2009, after extensive internal debate during the transition, the Obama Administration sent Congress the American Recovery and Reinvestment Act (ARRA). The cost was about $787 billion. Christina Romer, chair of the Council of Economic Advisers, and a much more proficient technical economist than Summers, calculated that the economy needed a stimulus of about $1.8 trillion. Summers felt that the figure was far too high. He directed Romer not even to mention that number to Obama, and in the end, Summers prevailed.

Some of the argument turned on optics—how much would seem too much to the media—and some of it turned on one's theoretical assumptions about the economy. As a Keynesian, Romer was calculating the shortfall of aggregate demand in the economy, as people lost jobs, causing private investment to fall, leading more people to lose jobs and depressing total demand still further. The faster the government could make up that gap, the quicker the private economy could return to its full productive potential, and the stimulus would eventually pay for itself and more. There was no risk of the increased public deficits leading to higher interest rates.

Summers had a more pre-Keynesian view, and his side of the debate echoed the prevailing assumption of the Clinton years. Restoring demand mattered, but the paramount need was to restore confidence in the money markets. Too big an increase in the deficit would spook the bond market. This argument did not fit the current situation, since the bond market was functioning at all only because the Fed was flooding it with liquid cash at zero short-term interest rates.

In the end, Obama made a political judgment about how large a stimulus felt about right. At the final meeting on the size of the stimulus, Obama listened to all the arguments, then directed his chief of staff, Rahm Emanuel, to report out a number. That turned out to be at the low end of the debate.

But as 2009 wore on and the unemployment rate kept rising, it was clear that the $787 billion of the Recovery Act was too meager. The spending was spread out over four years. Once you netted out deep cuts in spending by state and local governments, which were not allowed to run current budgets, the net stimulus was only about half of one percent of GDP per year.

Democrats in Congress began promoting a second stimulus. The White House used its influence to resist. Despite Obama's opposition, on December 16, House Speaker Nancy Pelosi got the House to pass a supplemental stimulus of $154 billion, emphasizing job creation. Obama and his advisers succeeded in having the measure die in the Senate.

By then, Summers and the rest of the inner circle were

convinced that the recovery was well on track and that it was time to appease the bond market by pivoting to deficit reduction as the Administration's main economic policy. Barely 15 months into the most severe economic collapse since the Great Depression and with unemployment still around 10 percent, this was an astounding decision for a Democratic administration.

Even worse, Obama decided to go along with a scheme that had been promoted by ultra-decifit hawks. The idea was to compel Congress to agree on a package of tax increases and/or spending cuts to reduce the deficit over a fixed schedule. If they could not agree, an automatic formula would do it for them. This later came to be known as the sequester. It was nothing short of astonishing that a Democratic president, with a working majority in Congress and an economy far from a durable recovery, would advocate such a Herbert Hoover-style scheme. At the time Obama appointed the commission, the unemployment rate was 9.3 percent.

The concept, long promoted by Rubin and his right-wing Republican friend, Peter G. Peterson, was turned into reality with the creation by executive order of the bipartisan Bowles-Simpson Commission, headed by a corporate Democrat, Erskine Bowles, and a retired Republican Senator, Alan Simpson. The Commission came up with a complex plan for deficit cuts totaling $4 trillion over a decade. The required supermajority of commissioners did not approve it, but the commission gave the approach broad currency. In the budget agreement of 2012, Obama signed off on a similar a sequester formula requiring automatic deficit cuts over a decade regardless of the needs of the economy.

———

When the Senate's most effective liberal, Ted Kennedy, succumbed to brain cancer in August 2009, the Democrats nominated an inept candidate in state Attorney General Martha Coakley. In the special election of January 2010, she lost to Republican Scott Brown, a pseudo-populist in the Tea Party/Trump mold. It was a harbinger of much worse to come.

Despite branding 2010 as Recovery Summer, the actual recovery was far behind schedule, and the voters felt it. In the 2010 midterms, the Democrats suffered a blowout loss. In the House, they lost a record 63 seats, breaking Bill Clinton's earlier record loss of 56 seats in 1994. In the Senate, they lost six seats. With Republicans now controlling the House and Democrats reduced to a bare majority in the Senate, Obama was now forced to be a narrowly transactional president for his remaining six years.

Newly elected presidents often lose House and Senate seats in their first mid-term elections, especially if their performance is disappointing. The great exception, not surprisingly, was Franklin Roosevelt, who gained 9 seats in the House and 9 in the Senate in 1934, producing 2- to-1 majorities in both chambers. FDR, unlike Obama, used them well.

Obama got very lucky in the 2012 presidential election, facing a Republican nominee, Mitt Romney, who was far from a populist. Obama managed to win re-election with 51 percent of the popular vote, a narrower margin than in 2008. Democrats made some modest gains in Congress but failed to take back the House. And though Congress had passed the Dodd-Frank financial reform act in July 2010, while Democrats still had a strong majority in Congress, Obama's appointees at the Treasury were far from robust in their enforcement of it. With the biggest banks more powerful than ever, many of the old abuses continued, and new ones arose with the proliferation of private equity.

Summers, like Rubin, benefited from the revolving door between his senior government posts and his personal enrichment on Wall Street, though at a smaller scale. The last full public disclosure of Summers's income showed that Harvard paid him just under $600,000 as a university professor in 2008. In that same year, he was paid $5.2 million by the private equity firm D.E. Shaw, where he was a managing director, plus $2.7 million in speaking gigs. So Wall Street paid him nearly ten times what Harvard did. After leaving the Obama administration in 2011, Summers returned to Shaw and Harvard. Liberating Wall Street was not just in his heart, but in his wallet.

When Summers became president, he virtually took over Harvard's endowment from the university's very well-compensated money managers. This was an astonishing act of hubris; as brilliant as Summers is, money management is a whole other skill set than macroeconomist and part-time hedge fund trader. Summers insisted on betting not just endowment funds, but Harvard's working capital, over the objections of both the money managers and the university's finance office.

One trade Summers personally directed was based on his assumption that interest rates would rise as the economy strengthened. When the economy began cratering in 2006-2007, and interest rates fell, Harvard had to spend half a billion dollars to buy back underwater securities that were likely to decline further. The endowment had consistently beaten the market in the years when it was managed by professionals. Summers's mistake cost the university $1.8 billion and led to severe budget cuts.

The survival of Summers is emblematic of which economists have influence, and why. Time after time, from promoting premature privatization of Russian state assets, to demanding deregulation of credit derivatives, to low-balling the stimulus needed after the 2008 collapse (that Summers's own policies had caused), to bailing out the biggest and most corrupt banks rather than cleaning them out, his advice has proven disastrous. Summers also played the role of dog in the manger and publicly attacked the stimulus program that Joe Biden sponsored in 2021 and 2022 as too large, providing talking points to Republicans.

In fact, Biden's stimulus was about right, while Summers's version was too low. Thanks to the Biden stimulus program, the COVID recession was reversed in just a few months, the fastest recovery from a severe recession on record. The mild uptick in inflation, contrary to Summers, was the result mainly of supply shocks, not overheated demand.

And yet, despite these serial policy blunders, Summers' reputation as an economist was intact. It was more prestigious than ever. He was treated as a seer. At the time that he was disgraced by the public disclosure of his extensive emails with Jeffrey Epstein seeking Epstein's advice on how to bed a colleague three decades Summers' junior, Summers' positions included the following: OpenAI, Board of Directors; Bloomberg, columnist. New York Times, Contributing Opinion Writer; Center for American Progress, Distinguished Senior Fellow; Peterson Institute for International Economics, Vice-Chair of the Board of Directors; Yale Budget Lab, Advisory Board.

With the Epstein disclosures, Summers was fired or permitted to resign from all of these. Which raises the question of why an economist who made one disastrous policy error after another retained such prestige. The answer, I think, is that as long as an economist with the views of Larry Summers is a senior adviser to Democrats and is published as a leading commentator, the American oligarchy has nothing to fear.

In the aftermath of the Epstein affair, the executive committee of the American Economic Association (AEA) ordered a lifetime ban on Summers attending events, contributing to journals, refereeing articles, or participating in any other way. They kick you out of the AEA for being a sexual creep, not for being chronically and arrogantly wrong on economic issues.

————

Summers's nemesis was Elizabeth Warren. When Summers launched a campaign in 2015 to persuade Obama to appoint him to chair the Federal Reserve as a career-capper, it was Warren who organized her Senate Democratic colleagues to make sure it would never happen. As chair of the Congressional Oversight Panel, Warren had stayed on good personal terms with Obama despite being a relentless critic of Geithner and Summers. With no help from the Administration, and over the objection of corporate Democrats in Congress, she managed to get her pet idea enacted as part of the Dodd-Frank bill, the Consumer Financial Protection Bureau (CFPB).

Once Dodd-Frank passed, Warren tried to persuade Obama to appoint her to chair the new bureau. But the most he would do was name her acting chair to help set up the CFPB.

At that point, I took Elizabeth to lunch at the old Casablanca restaurant at Harvard Square, now long gone. After pleasantries, I came right to the point. The CFPB was a great achievement, I said, "But you have a much bigger stage to play on." She needed to run for the Senate in 2012 and take back the Kennedy seat from Scott Brown. She looked at me as if I'd suggested that she take a rocket to Mars, but by the end of lunch, she said she'd think about it.

I introduced Elizabeth to my friend Shanti Fry, one of the most effective progressive fundraisers in Massachusetts. The two met, and Shanti became Elizabeth's finance co-chair. In the fall election of 2012, Warren beat Brown, 54 to 46 percent. She has been re-elected twice by landslide margins.

Elizabeth Warren's view of how to be a progressive Democrat stood in contrast to that of the entire Obama presidency, and she only got better at the politics with time. By 2016, Warren was the de facto leader of the progressive wing of the Democratic Party in Congress.

In the Democratic primaries for the presidential nomination, Hillary Clinton once again was the overwhelming favorite. But she was nearly upset by an avowed socialist, Sen. Bernie Sanders of Vermont. Sanders ended up winning 23 primaries, to Clinton's 34. He captured 43 percent of the popular vote.

The Sanders campaign, and the voice of Elizabeth Warren, demonstrated that there was a hunger among Democrats for progressive populism. The failure of the Obama presidency to carry it out, and the even less populist campaign of Hillary Clinton, left the field to Donald Trump to get elected by defining an ethno-nationalist right-wing populism.

In sifting over the entrails of the 2016 election, some commentators blamed Clinton's email fiasco, the eleventh-hour intervention of FBI Director James Comey faulting Clinton for poor judgment, her failure to campaign much in key swing states like Michigan, Pennsylvania, and Wisconsin, and the question of whether Americans were ready to vote for any woman. All of these were factors. But her lack of a compelling pocketbook message, at a time when more and more Americans were losing ground in the seventh year of a prolonged downturn, mattered at least as much as any of that.

Clinton's biggest blunder was thinking that by going left on social issues, such as transgender bathroom rights, she could compensate for her alliance with Wall Street. The combination proved toxic with working-class voters. Clinton left the popular anger for Trump to channel. Astonishingly, she even lost a majority of white women. Had she been elected, Clinton would have been the third Wall Street Democratic president in a row.

Chapter 10

*The Trump Cult and
the Biden Interlude*

As the economy stopped delivering for working people, it took only the right candidate to come to power on a narrative of right-wing populism. That reaction was delayed for decades because the Republican Party kept nominating candidates who were far from populist. The Republican winners—both Bushes—were corporate Republicans. The Republican losers, George H. W Bush running for re-election in 1992, Bob Dole in 1996, John McCain in 2008, and Mitt Romney in 2012, did not have a populist bone in their bodies. The Tea Party reaction of 2014, which anticipated Donald Trump, was a challenge to both mainstream parties.

It required an unusually gifted demagogue in Donald Trump to put it all together. By 2016, the slogan Make America Great Again resonated because downwardly mobile white men remembered an America when a working-class man could bring home a paycheck sufficient to support a family; when wives could keep house and raise kids rather than having to work; when there was lifetime employment with good pensions and health benefits for most white men. Strong economies, in turn, produced strong communities. Offspring could either follow a father into decently paid trades or afford to attend free public universities. America back then truly *was* Great—for ordinary white people.

By the early 21st century, it had all turned to shit. Empty factories in turn meant empty downtowns and ravaged communities. Available jobs were pretty much limited to working at the local Walmart or as a security guard, at a fraction of breadwinner wages. It all produced shame and anger. This is not just mythology of a vanished golden age. It is the lived experience of tens of millions of Americans, who were sitting ducks for a right-wing demagogue.

Trump channeled this resentment. He was consistently under-rated as a politician. He combined economic nationalism with ethno-nationalism, using dog-whistle language for explicit racists. Let me repeat what Steve Bannon told me in our famous conversation: "The Democrats, the longer they talk about identity politics, I got 'em. I want them to talk about racism every day. If the left is focused on race and identity, and we go with economic national-ism, we can crush the Democrats." He was right.

In Trump's narrative, other nations were taking unfair advantage of the United States. Favored minorities and coddled immigrants were taking advantage of patriotic white people. He alone could fix it. In this narrative, his tutor was Bannon. But Trump also drew on his long success as a TV entertainer, a real estate dealmaker, and a bully.

As a TV personality, his trademark was firing people. When he managed to snag the Republican nomination in 2016 by violating the usual courtesies of politics and insulting the rest of the Republican field, he seemed to be articulating the rage that a lot of ordinary Americans felt. He might be a billionaire, not unlike the billionaires who fired a lot of his working-class supporters, but he seemed to be speaking for them. In Hillary Clinton, he drew the perfect opponent.

The two candidates whom Trump beat, Hillary Clinton and Kamala Harris, were both women. Some of that reflected misogyny. They were also weak candidates, especially on the pocketbook issues where Democrats had been failing to deliver. The one candidate who beat Trump was Joe Biden, a white male.

———

The abrupt shift from Obama to Trump in 2016 was an unthinkable shock. I have faulted Obama for bungling a potential Roosevelt moment when it came to the economy and the perverse rule of Wall Street, but he was a leader of eloquence and idealism, as well as a man of personal dignity and probity. Obama signaled that America just might, at long last, be dealing constructively with race. He called on Americans to be their best.

Trump called on Americans to be their worst. His signature was a malignant narcissism and a relentless compulsion for retribution. He violated ordinary norms of decency with a vulgarity that was inconceivable in a President of the United States. Many of his otherwise inexplicable policies turned out to be about his personal enrichment.

When Richard Nixon attempted to destroy an effective opposition party with the Watergate break-in, followed by a cover-up, and the "Saturday Night Massacre" dismissing officials who followed the law, the rule of law held. The Supreme Court ruled 9-0 that Nixon had to turn over incriminating tapes. In the impeachment that followed, Republicans deserted Nixon, and he was compelled to resign. Those of us who lived through that ordeal could reassure ourselves that the system worked.

But when Trump tried to stage what amounted to a coup in

order to stay in office, the system barely survived, and Trump was never held to account. The fact that Biden managed to take office was due mainly to the courage of a handful of Republican officials. By the time Trump became president a second time, the institutions of democracy and the rule of law were even weaker.

According to most insider accounts, Trump had not expected to win in 2016. In part, he ran because he thought the campaign would be good for his brand. His transition team was rudimentary and chaotic, and he soon had a falling out with his transition director, former New Jersey Governor Chris Christie, leaving his transition process even more makeshift.

Several of Trump's policies in his first term were horrific, as was his use of the presidency for personal gain. He banned migration from six Muslim-majority countries. He withdrew from the Paris Agreement on Climate Change and appointed climate deniers to several key posts. He withdrew the US from the nuclear agreement with Iran. Trump's de facto political entente with Vladimir Putin led directly to Putin's war on Ukraine.

His obsession with Mexico and the partial construction of a wall on the southern US border, in turn, led him to pressure Republicans in Congress to kill carefully negotiated bipartisan legislation called Comprehensive Immigration Reform. The compromise plan allowed a path to citizenship for "Dreamers" who had been brought to America as young children, and for other long-term undocumented residents who had stayed out of trouble. In exchange, there would be a serious crackdown on illegal immigration, including sanctions against employers who hired people in the country illegally. Trump killed the legislation because he preferred having an election issue to pillory liberals rather than solving the problem.

At the time, it was hard to imagine that there would be much worse to come. But compared to his second term, none of the policies of Trump's first term were irreversible. And while there were attacks on the "deep state," Trump did not get around to systematically destroying the state until his second term. Government functioned. His relative unfamiliarity with the machinery of government led him to appoint several more orthodox conservatives to senior posts, who, for a time, functioned as a check on his recklessness. Trump could say disgusting things, like terming impoverished African nations "shithole countries," but it was not until his second term that he abolished USAID.

Despite his bravado and pseudo populism and his embrace of a racist brand of nationalism, in many ways Trump was a conventional corporate Republican. Among the major policies of Trump's first term were the Tax Cuts and Jobs Act, enacted in December 2017, which drastically cut taxes for the upper brackets and increased the national debt by an estimated $5 trillion. The legislation was written over a two-week period with no hearings or markup sessions. The Act cut income taxes, estate taxes, and capital gains taxes, and the corporate tax rate was changed from a tiered tax rate ranging from 15% to as high as 39% depending on taxable income to a flat 21%. About half of all the benefits went to the top one percent. To pay for some of the costs and to punish taxpayers in blue states with generous services and high taxes, the new law capped the usually unlimited deduction for state and local taxes at $10,000.

In the year after the tax cut became effective, corporations spent more than a trillion dollars buying back their own stock, an action that does nothing to improve the economy but pumps up the value of their shares to enrich executives and save on taxes. Trump's personal corruption and the corruption of the corporate economy fed on each other. That's one reason why many corporate executives put off by Trump's coarseness were happy to look the other way.

A few of Trump's policies even made sense. After Trump initially tried to kill the Affordable Care Act and failed, he succeeded in killing the ACA's individual mandate, which required uninsured people to either buy insurance or pay a penalty. The mandate reflected a concern that some people would try to save money by waiting to purchase insurance until they got sick, shrinking the pool of healthy insured people to the detriment of the system. Ironically, Obama had originally opposed the individual mandate and criticized Hillary Clinton for supporting it. After Trump successfully got the mandate repealed, it turned out to have little impact.

Trump also pursued a relatively sensible China policy, one that was far more strategic than the China policy of his second term. Trump's top trade official, an experienced and competent expert named Robert Lighthizer, who had first worked for Ronald Reagan, devised a tariff of 25 percent on most Chinese exports, as a rough offset to the impact of China's illegal subsidies and dumping of exports below the cost of production. This was far more coherent than the wild, impulsive swings in Trump's China tariffs in his second term and his disregard of national security concerns to reward cronies.

As part of his animus against Mexico, Trump vowed to repeal NAFTA. But House Democrats, who were also critics of NAFTA, ended up playing a major role in designing the successor to NAFTA, the US-Mexico-Canada Agreement of 2018 (USMCA). Among the more progressive provisions of USMCA were provisions allowing the enforcement of the right of Mexican workers to unionize, and a much tighter definition of North American content that entitled tariff-free imports into one of the three participating countries.

And after initially denying the seriousness of COVID, Trump sponsored Operation Warp Speed, which accelerated the development of vaccines. He did it in such a way that allowed vaccine-makers to reap windfall profits with taxpayer funding, but the vaccines worked. In his second term he appointed a notorious anti-vax crackpot as Secretary of HHS.

Trump was also lucky in that the Federal Reserve, still dealing with the aftermath of the 2008 collapse and the long recession that followed, was keeping interest rates low. This was done both to stimulate the recovery and to recapitalize the banks. So Trump could boast a relatively healthy economy.

Jerome Powell, auditioning for appointment as Fed Chair, persuaded Trump that he would keep interest rates low. Trump named him chair in 2018. As the economy strengthened, the Fed raised rates. It cut rates again during the COVID recession, but this lasted only until the COVID supply shocks spiked inflation. Powell then presided over several rate hikes. Far from being a Trump loyalist, Powell turned out to be a conventional monetary conservative. The Fed, to Trump's outrage, remained one of the few independent power centers that Trump couldn't control. In his second term, Trump tried to illegally fire Powell, then to prosecute him on fake charges.

Trump's top economic advisers, Treasury Secretary Steve Mnuchin and Chair of the National Economic Council Gary Cohn, were both from Goldman Sachs, an unfortunate pattern that dates back to Bill Clinton. Yet they functioned as counterweights to Trump's extreme economic nationalism, and the repeated conflicts between the Wall Street men and the economic nationalists like Peter Navarro and Steve Bannon slowed Trump down. There was not the slavish personal loyalty and sycophancy that characterized his second term.

Many top officials were veterans of the George W. Bush Administration. There were very few fringe figures of the RFK, Jr. or Pete Hegseth variety in senior posts. Other appointments were a disgrace in their own terms, such as Education Secretary Betsy DeVos, whose main passion was for-profit voucher schools financed by public money. Like several other top appointees, DeVos, whose family was heavily invested in voucher schools, was a flagrant case of conflicts of interest.

The senior military men in his cabinet were also forces for restraint. For Secretary of Defense, Trump selected Jim Mattis, a retired four-star Marine Corps general. Mattis had served as Commander of the US Central Command and had commanded forces in the Gulf War, the Iraq War, and the War in Afghanistan. Mattis had also held senior posts in NATO. Trump liked Mattis's nickname, Mad Dog. The appointment violated the norm that the Defense Secretary be a civilian.

Trump expected absolute loyalty, but as a professional military man, Mattis objected to many of Trump's screwball policies. Mattis supported the traditional Atlantic Alliance, backed the Iran nuclear deal, and resisted Trump's abrupt troop withdrawals in Syria and Afghanistan. He especially objected to Trump's plans to use the military for domestic policing. Mattis resigned in late 2018 over Syria policy, the first Secretary of Defense ever to resign in protest. There followed Mattis's strong rebuke of Trump's handling of civil unrest at Lafayette Square in 2020, published in a long article in The Atlantic, where Mattis called Trump a threat to the Constitution.

In that same episode, on June 1, 2020, Gen Mark Milley, chairman of the Joint Chiefs of Staff, had reluctantly dressed in combat fatigues and stood with Trump after Black Lives Matter protestors had been cleared from the square. Milley resisted Trump's efforts to bring in active-duty military troops, but he was appalled that he had succumbed to the symbolism. He went back to his office and wrote a letter of resignation: "I can no longer faithfully support and execute your orders as Chairman of the

Joint Chiefs of Staff. It is my belief that you were doing great and irreparable harm to my country. I believe that you have made a concerted effort over time to politicize the United States military."

By appointing Pete Hegseth Secretary of Defense in his second term, Trump assured himself that he would never get this kind of impertinence. In the end, Trump's own behavior did serious damage to the rule of law, most egregiously with his attempted coup of January 6, 2021. But for most of his first term, the adults in the room were sources of restraint. They included several former generals, including the House Chief of Staff John Kelly, Mattis, national security adviser H. R. McMaster, as well as Rex Tillerson, Trump's first Secretary of State.

It took almost until the end of his term for Trump to break loose from his more mainstream handlers and to figure out how to abuse executive power in dictatorial fashion. In a harbinger of what was to come, Russell Vought served as OMB director for Trump's last two years.

In his second term, Trump realized that if you want absolute loyalty in top officials, one strategy is appoint people who are completely incompetent and unfit to serve. They will be entirely reliant on you. If they destroy the institutions they lead, deliberately or inadvertently, so much the better.

The fascists of the 1930s—Hitler, Mussolini, and Franco—did not try to destroy the state. They strengthened it and turned it to their ends. Most dictators love public works. The state as an engine of economic development and recovery, via both rearmament and public works, was a big part of the fascist appeal. Mussolini famously made the trains run on time. Hitler built the autobahn and expanded Germany's welfare state. Combined with Hitler's rearmament, those policies delivered the prosperity that the Allies denied Germany after World War I. The *Reich*, a term of pride, referred to both the efficient German state and German territorial expansion.

Trump, by contrast, would destroy the state. But there is a method in Trump's madness. As the political scientists Stephen Hanson and Jeffrey Kopstein point out in their 2024 book, *The Assault on the State*, written before Trump's second term, the modern state is essentially rationalist and professionalized, the opposite of Trump's ultra-personalist rule, which they call "patrimonial," following a distinction first made by the great social scientist Max Weber. If you have dictatorial aspirations and your method is ad hoc dealmaking, the institutions of the rational administrative state, demonized as the "deep state," are an obstacle and a nuisance. In the Trump era, the opposite of FDR liberalism is not libertarian in the sense of Friedrich Hayek or Milton Friedman; it is personalist power.

Until the last days of his first presidency, when Trump tried to hold onto power by an attempted coup, Trump's administration, in spite of itself, mostly abided by the norms of electoral democracy. In the 2018 midterm election, Democrats were able to flip 41 Republican House seats. There was some voter suppression, especially in states governed by Republicans—eligible people being purged from the rolls, a reduction of polling places in Black neighborhoods leading to long lines, attempted intimidation of voters and election workers, and threats of criminal charges of fraud. But these were not enough to change the outcome in most districts.

Democrats who were appalled by the 2016 election of Trump had gotten serious about organizing, beginning with the epic women's marches of January 2017, the creation of Indivisible, and other groups such as Run for Something. The result was a massive increase in Democratic turnout in 2018, much of it among young voters, who supported Democrats by a margin of about 2 to 1. The

Democrats' success in taking back the House drastically slowed Trump's momentum. In a mid-term election, there is no opposition leader at the top of the ticket. The success of 2018 was built on local organizing and local candidates, and Trump as a national nemesis. The Democratic momentum continued into 2020, despite Biden being a lackluster candidate. Democrats not only ousted Trump but also kept the House and took back the Senate.

In the razor-thin 2020 contest, it was improbable that Trump, becoming more and more of a dictator, could not find a way to steal the election or otherwise prevent Biden from taking office. It was not for lack of trying. But as late as 2020, there were still relatively principled Republicans who resented Trump's bullying and still had some regard for American democracy. Two were Georgia's secretary of state, Brad Raffensperger, a Republican who was fine with using various techniques to suppress Democrats' ability to vote, but once the ballots were in was personally offended by Trump's explicit demand that he steal precisely 11,780 votes so that Trump could carry Georgia. Another was Vice President Mike Pence, who was appalled by the invasion of the Capitol and the attempted coup of January 6 and rejected Trump's direct order not to certify the electoral count. One can't imagine Trump's current Vice President, J.D. Vance, making such a principled stance. Then, out of office for four years, Trump had time to nurse grievances and systematically plan a far more autocratic second term.

———

After he became President, Joe Biden turned out to be more of an economic populist than almost anyone anticipated, after a long career as the most conventional of Democrats. There were several reasons for Biden's shift away from neoliberalism to a set of policies more like FDR's. One was that neoliberalism had palpably failed ordinary people. To beat right-wing populism, Democrats needed an authentic populism that stood up for regular Americans against the wealth and power of oligarchs.

The second reason was the COVID epidemic and the sharp recession that followed. The government needed to spend a lot of money fast, or the recession that began in late 2019 would turn into a depression. Even Trump understood that. The first of several stimulus laws enacted between 2020 and 2023 that ultimately spent over six trillion dollars was the $2.2 trillion bipartisan CARES Act (Coronavirus Aid, Relief, and Economic Security), which included direct cash payments and enhanced unemployment benefits as well as more generous subsidies for health coverage. The bill passed the Senate unanimously and the House by voice vote and was signed by President Trump on March 27, 2020. Democrats played a major role in its design. This was classic Keynesian stimulus.

The third reason why Biden moved left was that the party base was in a progressive mood. Biden was able to win the Democratic nomination only because the two candidates to his left, Elizabeth Warren and Bernie Sanders, divided the progressive vote. Had only one been in the race, he or she could well have been the nominee. Until the South Carolina primary, where the Biden endorsement by the powerful local Black Congressman, James Clyburn, created a bandwagon effect for that primary and the other southern ones to come, Biden's feckless campaign had lost primary after primary, and he was all but counted out.

When Biden's wins in the southern Super Tuesday primaries of March 2020 made his nomination all but inevitable, Elizabeth Warren endorsed him in early April. That created a bond in which Biden relied heavily on Warren for both policy and personnel. The Biden administration turned out to be surprisingly like a Warren administration. But as I wrote, this created an anomaly—the soul of Elizabeth Warren in the persona of Joe Biden.

The COVID-19 recession continued to influence his actions as president. Rather like FDR, Biden was further left as a president than he had been as a candidate. He sponsored several key pieces of stimulus, supply chain, and industrial policy measures, totaling over $4 trillion. He would have spent even more had he not lost control of Congress in 2023. Having observed the effect of the too-slow recovery under Obama and its political effects, Biden resolved that the risks of going too small were far worse than the risks of going big.

Despite the bipartisan CARES Act signed by Trump, on Inauguration Day 2021, the unemployment rate was still an elevated 6.3 percent, more than 2.8 percentage points higher than before COVID. But at this point, the Republicans, wanting Biden to fail, went into vehement opposition.

Biden's $1.9 trillion American Recovery Plan Act (ARPA) was passed in March 2021 on straight party-line votes, 219-212 in the House and 50-49 in the Senate. It included some startlingly radical measures. What amounted to a family allowance for parents gave families $3,000 a year for each child under age 18, plus an extra $600 per child under age 6. There was no income test. It cut the child poverty rate nearly in half.

These and other measures dramatically shortened the COVID recession. The unemployment rate plummeted from 14.7 percent in April 2020 to just 3.7 percent by early 2022. It was the fastest recovery from a severe recession on record. In the 2022 midterm elections, which pundits predicted would be a blowout defeat for the Democrats, Biden managed to beat the usual jinx of a new president's first midterm election. The Democrats actually gained one net seat in the Senate, and lost only nine in the House, far better than Obama's mid-term loss of 63 in 2010 or Clinton's loss of 56 in 1994.

But in a very closely divided House, a loss of even nine seats was sufficient to turn control over to the Republicans. Two nominal Senate Democrats, Kirsten Sinema of Arizona and Joe Manchin of West Virginia, stopped voting for any more spending. That blocked any serious policy-making in Biden's second two years. Even so, the momentum of the big stimulus and industrial policies of the first two years was sufficient to keep the recovery well on track.

In the four years of the Biden presidency, the economy created a record 16.6 million net jobs, including 775,000 production jobs, a reversal of a long-term decline in factory work. The median wage went up, though only slightly. Real GDP growth adjusted for inflation averaged 3.2 percent. Unemployment stayed below 4 percent. It was an outstanding economic record—far better than either Clinton's or Obama's, Democratic presidents who were both re-elected. Biden also went out of his way to identify with unions.

Despite all this, it was Trump, not Biden, who won a second term. There has been a great deal of commentary about why the Democrats fell short and what they should do now. Here is my own view. The biggest problem was Biden—not Biden's policies, which were fine, but Biden personally. He was too old, and increasingly too frail. He was barely robust enough to govern, much less to seek a second term that would have him in office until age 86. This became increasingly and painfully evident.

Even before his lapses became so palpable in mid-2024 that other party leaders forced him to step aside in favor of Kamala Harris, Biden was a feeble spokesman for his own successes. There are countless examples, well before his catastrophic debate with Donald Trump. Here is just one.

Biden and his publicists made a very big deal of the fact that he was the most explicitly pro-union president ever. Biden forged a close alliance with Shawn Fain, the charismatic leader of the UAW, who had taken an immense risk by calling a strike against all of the big three automakers at once and winning big.

On a carefully planned appearance on September 27, 2023, during the UAW strike, Biden became the first president to walk a picket line. He appeared before a very friendly audience of UAW members, with Fain. The UAW president was full of fire and fight. Biden, who spoke only briefly and mildly to tepid applause, sounded as if he had overdosed on Xanax. I remember wishing that Fain, rather than Biden, was running for president.

———

In 2020, Biden had said that he expected to be a bridge to a new generation of Democrats. Many took that to mean he would only serve one term. I wrote repeatedly that if Biden stepped down at the end of his term in 2024, he would be remembered as the greatest one-term president in American history.

Suppose that Biden had announced after the surprisingly good midterm outcome in 2022 that he would not run again. This would leave him as a lame duck. But with Republicans controlling the House, he was pretty much a lame duck anyway. Had Biden acted to open up the process, there would have been the usual process of primaries in early 2024, and an open convention to pick a nominee.

I don't know who that nominee might have been, but the nominee would have had a lot more legitimacy and enthusiasm than Kamala Harris, who became the nominee by default in July

2024, less than four months before the election. I don't think the fact that she was a Black woman and a sitting vice president would have scared other candidates out of the race. She ran a weak campaign for the nomination in 2020, and she did not improve with age. In an open set of primary contests, I doubt Harris would have been chosen. If by some chance Harris did win the nomination, she would have earned it.

In the context of Biden's belated announcement on July 21, 2024, that he would not be running for re-election and his endorsement of Harris, there were some who called for an open nominating process. But that was a complete non-starter. It was far too late in the election season.

The Democratic National Committee soon made Harris's nomination official. For about three weeks, there was relief and euphoria among Democratic ranks—relief that Biden had finally stepped aside, euphoria that the younger and more vigorous Harris would now be the unifying candidate. People who should have known better were in wishful denial of what a dismal candidate Harris had been in 2020.

Harris was now running as the Democratic nominee for president only because Biden had made a cynical deal with South Carolina's powerful Congressman James Clyburn: Endorse me, and I will appoint a Black woman to the Supreme Court and put a Black woman on the ticket as my running mate. Kamala Harris was who there was. In return, Clyburn gave an endorsement speech that made Biden sound like the second coming of Lincoln.

The euphoria about Biden stepping aside in favor of Harris lasted only through the Democratic National Convention of late August. Harris reveled in the party unity and won wide acclaim for naming Minnesota Governor Tim Walz as her running mate.

But Harris' campaign went downhill from there. In the actual campaign, Harris was a weak campaigner and a profusion of mixed messages. Two weeks before the election, polls of undecided voters yielded comment after comment to the effect that people didn't know what Harris stood for. These were not "low information voters," but voters who were paying attention.

Weirdly, Harris campaigned with Mark Cuban, a billionaire part-owner of the Dallas Mavericks and a heavy investor in crypto. In ostensibly campaigning for Harris, Cuban felt free to criticize some of her program, including her proposal to tax a portion of unrealized capital gains.

Harris herself repeatedly sent mixed messages. In one major speech on the economy, attempting to reassure both progressives and wealthy donors, Harris said she would tax the rich but not as much as Biden would have.

Being the sitting vice president of an unpopular president, Harris was in an awkward position when it came to any criticism of Biden. She repeatedly ducked the question of what she would do differently than Biden had done, saying vaguely that she would go beyond what he had achieved. At a time when too many Americans felt bleak about their own prospects, she spoke about a politics of joy.

Beyond the personal weaknesses of Biden and then of Harris as candidates, there were several structural problems. One was severe divisions within the Democratic Party. Despite Biden's populist measures, the power of big money in Democratic fundraising was immense. That repeatedly led to mixed economic messages.

A second division was over Israel. Younger Democrats, even younger Jews, were appalled at what increasingly looked like a genocide in Gaza. Under Biden, the United States was giving Israel billions of dollars of military aid every year, but Biden refused to condition that aid in any meaningful way on Israel's behavior. Prime Minister Netanyahu, needing to keep the war going in order to hold together his coalition, rally public support, and stay out of jail, played Biden for a fool.

Biden belonged to a generation that viewed Israel as the good guys, by definition—a heroic nation built on the ashes of the Holocaust. It's not clear how much of Biden's reluctance to contain Netanyahu stemmed from his own long history of being reflexively pro-Israel right or wrong, and how much was his fear of offending pro-Israel donors, always a powerful force in the Democratic Party. Very likely, it was both.

What is clear is that Biden's refusal to condemn Israeli barbarism in Gaza, or to use his ample leverage against Netanyahu, cost him dearly in support among America's young. The destruction of Gaza also led to actions at several universities that began as protests against Israel's barbarous assaults against civilians but were soon captured by more militant pro-Palestinian groups. The press began describing them as "pro-Palestinian." Some radicals at the protests insisted that all Jewish students, even all Jews, were Zionist apologists for the destruction of Gaza until proven otherwise. On the other side of the argument, criticism of the Israeli government or Israeli policy got conflated with antisemitism, a stance that was useful to Netanyahu and the Israel lobby.

Antisemitism, always smoldering, became a genuine concern. In fact, as Philip Roth liked to observe, the safest haven for Jews has not been Israel; it has been America. Ironically, the very universities charged with antisemitism are places where both faculty and student bodies have been disproportionately Jewish, and Jews have been able to thrive, pursuing studies and careers in peace.

If there is an upsurge in antisemitism and a new assertion of the old slander that the Jewish tribe is guilty of dual loyalty, the source of the new antisemitism, more than anyone else, is

Netanyahu. His ethnic cleansing and sheer barbarism in Gaza are at odds with Jewish moral teaching and grotesque in light of the Jewish historical experience. Most American Jews have condemned it. Those who defend it provide grist for real anti-semites.

All of this was a gift for the right. Trump, who had been in bed with antisemites when that was convenient, started posing as a defender of the Jews. His allies in Congress began savaging university presidents for not doing enough to protect Jewish students and faculty. Congressional hearings led by Republicans, even before Trump returned to the presidency, forced the ouster of several university presidents and badly divided university trustees and the broader Jewish community. This entire mess gave Trump a head start on the policies that he pursued in office, in which he used the alleged failure of major universities to protect Jews as a pretext for trying to destroy universities financially.

———

Joe Biden did a good job, given the hand he was dealt. Most of his appointments were excellent, and he began the process of re-regulating predatory capitalism. His appointments of Lina Khan to chair the FTC and Jonathan Kanter as head of the Justice Department's Antitrust Division resurrected antitrust enforcement as a long-sidelined mechanism to deal with abuses by platform monopolies. His appointment of Gary Gensler to chair the SEC was the most assertive Wall Street watchdog in decades. Other strong appointments, such as Sarah Bloom Raskin to the Federal Reserve, could not be made because corporate Democrats in the Senate blocked them. I praised Biden for his efforts in my 2023 book, *Going Big: FDR's Legacy and Biden's New Deal.*

But his own frailty fatally detracted from the relative success of his policies. And given the long-term deterioration of living standards and life prospects, especially among the young, two years was simply not enough to fundamentally change that trajectory. Nor was it long enough to make more than a start on the reregulation of capitalism.

Despite Biden's remarkable success in shortening the COVID recession, life for working families looked pretty much the way it has looked for the past few decades. Typical incomes are not enough to build a life, and there are fewer reliable careers and more gigs.

Housing prices, both rental and home ownership, are ever further out of reach. The homeownership rate among young adults continues to decline. More young adults are doubling up or moving back in with their parents. College loans take an ever-higher toll. Childcare often costs more than rent. Even with Obamacare, decent health insurance is unaffordable, leading many people to stay in jobs they'd rather leave, because the employer happens to provide good health insurance. Good pensions are a thing of the past.

In two years of economic recovery from the COVID Recession, Biden was simply not able to change those fundamental realities for most working people. And even though most of the increased inflation of 2021-2023 was the result of supply chain shocks or corporate monopoly pricing power and not macroeconomic overheating, the high price of eggs became a handy symbol for the fact that too many people could not afford a life, and Biden took the fall. All that said, a more effective candidate than Biden or Harris might well have defeated Trump in 2024, precisely by addressing those issues.

As the 2024 election approached, there was an ongoing argument between Biden and many of his political strategists about whether Biden, looking forward to a re-election campaign, should boast about his accomplishments. With his impressive record on job creation and economic growth, it was only natural that Biden would want to trumpet his achievements. But as campaign aides and independent Democratic strategists kept pointing out, for the most part, these very real achievements did not make much difference in people's life prospects. Even worse, by suggesting that the economy was good, Biden made the Democrats sound like the party of the status quo, when most voters were unhappy with the status quo.

One result was that millions of voters who might have supported Biden or Harris in 2024 just stayed home. They saw little that inspired them to vote. There was an astonishing falloff in Democratic turnout, especially given that the stakes were a second Trump term. About 81.28 million people voted for Joe Biden in 2020. But only just over 75 million people voted for Kamala Harris in 2024, in a lower turnout election. Some 12 million people who voted for Biden in 2020 did not vote at all in 2024. A much smaller number switched their votes from Biden in 2020 to Trump in 2024.

A very revealing survey conducted by the Democratic pollster Celinda Lake in mid-2025 found that a large majority of these disaffected nonvoters hold progressive views on the economy. Forty-nine percent said they would have voted for Kamala Harris, compared to just 25 percent for Donald Trump, had they voted at all. But they were not motivated to vote for Harris because they found her views on key pocketbook issues too feeble.

What leaders did these 2024 nonvoters admire? The top two in the poll were Bernie Sanders, approved by 78 percent, and AOC, with 67 percent. These 2024 nonvoters have a split-screen view of the Democrats. In principle, said 39 percent, "They are more for the people and will fight for all Americans." But at the same time, 24 percent said "they are weak and won't stand up for Americans."

When the poll asked what issues would make them more likely to vote in 2026, the top four were secure health insurance, making the rich pay their fair share of taxes while keeping taxes on working families affordable, the cost of living, and affordable housing.

In battleground states, 77 percent of 2020 Biden voters who stayed home in 2024 felt that the nation's top problem was the top 1 percent taking too much at the expense of everyone else, but only 13 percent of such voters felt the main problems were government spending too much, out-of-control immigration, or "wokeness."

Lake concluded that Democrats in 2026 should "offer a populist economic alternative to Trump's current economics that benefits wealthy corporations and wealthy political donors. Fight for working families, and offer specifics."

––––––––

In the aftermath of Biden's defeat in 2024, there was a lot of handwringing about the damaged Democratic "brand" and arguing about whether Democrats could cure their ills by moving to the center or to the left. In July 2025, a widely-quoted Wall Street Journal poll showed that Democrats as a party had an even lower favorability rating than Trump. It was not clear whether this perception reflected unhappiness with Democratic positions, the fact that Democratic positions were a muddle, or the failure of Democrats in Congress to contain Trump.

But all this turned out to be a premature burial. The Democratic brand was tarnished only until the voters got a closer look at Trump's increasingly bizarre behavior, as enabled by Republican control of government. In the 2025 off-year elections, the Democratic brand performed just fine, as Democrats of all ideological stripes did astonishingly well, in both blue states and red ones. These elections all signaled a repudiation of Trump.

In a December special election to fill a vacant House seat in a deep red Tennessee district, there was a 13-point swing in favor of the Democrat. Republican Matt Van Epps beat Democrat Aftyn Behn by nine points, compared to Trump carrying the district by 22 points over Kamala Harris in 2024. In the other special House elections of 2025, Democrats did even better. There was a 23-point pro-Democrat swing in the special election in FL-01, 17 points in AZ-07, 16 points in FL-06, and 16 points in VA-11. The Tennessee election, the smallest of these swings, was an unusually high-turnout special election where Republican funders went all in. If anything like these shifts were repeated in 2026, Democrats would pick up 30 to 40 House seats.

In surprising and improbable places, Democrats picked up down-ballot offices, including innumerable school boards and local commissions. They won two public service commission seats on the five-member state commission in Georgia, picked up state legislature seats in Mississippi, held on to a crucial Supreme Court seat in Wisconsin, as well as three in Pennsylvania.

The Democrats' gubernatorial victories of November 2024 were even more striking. In New Jersey, Mikie Sherrill, a Member of Congress who represented affluent suburbs, was not a great candidate. Her Republican opponent, Jack Ciattarelli, was a feisty campaigner, comfortable with working-class audiences. Right up until election day, pundits expected a cliffhanger. Yet Sherrill blew Ciattarelli away by a margin of 14.4 points, the best performance for a New Jersey Democratic nominee since 1989.

Ciattrarelli made the catastrophic error of associating himself with Trump. Not long before the election, Trump announced that he was suspending all funding on the Gateway rail tunnel, a $14 billion public works project more than two decades in the making. Trump's rationale was to punish New York. Somehow, it escaped Trump's notice that the tunnel, under the Hudson River, connected New York with New Jersey. Even if Trump missed that, New Jersey voters didn't.

In Virginia, a swing state with a termed-out incumbent Republican governor, Democrat Abigail Spanberger did even better, defeating her opponent by more than 15 points. Trump's massive layoffs of federal workers, many of whom live in Northern Virginia, were fatal to the Republicans. Democrats gained 13 seats in the Virginia House of Delegates, increasing their majority from 51 seats to 64 seats in the 100-member chamber. This pickup gave the party its largest Virginia House majority in four decades.

Though Spanberger and Sherill were nominally centrist Democrats, both campaigned on the high cost of living. And it is hard to address the problem of affordability without bumping into the power of the oligarchy and the need to regulate and tax capitalism. Once in office, Sherill declared an emergency and froze utility rates.

To that extent, the oft-heard argument about whether Democrats in 2026 and 2028 should run more to the left or more to the center is misleading, in several respects. The narrative that unifies Democrats is about addressing the cost of living. That has to be a basically progressive message with progressive remedies.

Secondly, if you dig deep into the push for Democrats to move to the center, much of it is based on self-interest rather than principled argument. Most of the centrists are corporate-backed. PACs created by the crypto industry poured money into Democratic primaries to defeat progressives who supported financial regulation. AIPAC and affiliated pro-Israel PACS spent vast sums to defeat Democrats who had the temerity to criticize Netanyahu's annihilation of Gaza. The point was not that progressives were unelectable in a general election but that they were critical of these powerful special interest groups.

The left-versus-center debate conflates two very distinct questions—left on pocketbook issues (yes) or left on cultural issues (no). As I've suggested in previous chapters, when ordinary Americans stopped believing in Democrats on pocketbook issues, the right could fill the vacuum with social and cultural issues. As long as times were generally good, the reckoning could be delayed. The financial collapse of 2008 and the prolonged recession that followed served as the coup de grace. All it took was a figure like Trump to channel and narrate it.

The biggest flashpoints were race, immigration, and the Democrats' embrace of what was easily ridiculed as "wokeism"— not just defensible affirmative action for Blacks, women, and sexual minorities but policing of language. In the 2024 campaign, Trump's TV spot, played over and over again at sporting events, captured the Democrats' vulnerability perfectly. It shows a stereotypical transgender person. The tagline: "Kamala is for they/them, Trump is for us."

The Democrats carry a particular burden because arguments about how far to take compensatory justice for minorities, and which minorities, are carried out largely within the Democratic Party. The strain becomes that much harder when Democrats are not delivering economically. Many liberals bent over backwards to be politically correct by accepting the demands of cultural radicals. Embracing a politics of gesture was far easier than seriously contesting the power of Wall Street. This was a mistake,

At The American Prospect, I won't use the term *Latinx*. I wondered if I would be cancelled by the language police. The word was coined by non-binary Hispanics, a minority within a minority, because it is gender-neutral while ordinary Spanish words ending in "o" or "a" are masculine or feminine. The cultural left then demanded that the neologism be extended to cover all Hispanics, and well-meaning liberals generally complied.

The word violates the Spanish language, which does not use the terminal "x." While many Anglo liberals dutifully shifted to *Latinx*, the vast majority of native Spanish speakers thought the coinage was ridiculous and stuck with Latino. To Hispanics, who increased their vote for Trump in 2024, the use of *Latinx* did not suggest solidarity, but ignorance and condescension. Happily, many Latino voters deserted the Republicans in 2025 over more consequential issues.

I've also refused to declare my pronouns. At Brandeis, where I teach, this has made me something of an outlier. Nor do we declare pronouns at The Prospect. I find the logic perverse. Why should we out someone who may still be sorting out their gender identity? We don't declare our religion or our national origin in email signatures, so why our gender? Virtue-signaling is a form of cheap grace.

Emphasis on wokeness is also a misplaced political priority. As the late Todd Gitlin astutely wrote in his 1995 book *The Twilight of Common Dreams*, "While the Right has been busy taking the White House...the Left has been marching on the English department."

Will Marshall, the founder and president of the Progressive Policy Institute, the think tank of the centrist Democratic Leadership Council (DLC), wrote a withering critique in which he said, "Over the last two decades, progressive activists have introduced lots of sententious words and euphemisms into the US political lexicon. Examples include microaggression, intersectionality, cisgender, BIPOC, Latinx, "the unhoused" (that is, the homeless), returning citizens (ex-convicts), and "pregnant persons" (formerly "women"). For those not up to speed on the latest academic conceits and ideological fads, including non-college voters streaming out of the Democratic Party, progressives might as well be speaking Esperanto."

Fair enough. But the DLC contributes to this exodus by getting agitated about wokeism while largely ignoring the economic plight of those same working-class voters. Progressives earn some room to extend rights to minorities only when they keep delivering economically. Even without silly linguistic excesses, this is a challenging politics.

As long as the economy boomed and unions were strong, the belated extension of civil and economic rights to Blacks and then to women did not fatally undermine white working-class support for Democrats. As late as the election of 2008, large numbers of working-class white men were still willing to vote for Barack Obama, on the premise that he would be more attentive to their needs than the failed Republican Administration of George W. Bush, or Obama's opponent, John McCain. They were mostly wrong. As the economy stopped delivering for working people and Democratic presidents were complicit, it took only the right candidate to come to power on a narrative of right-wing populism.

The extension of full citizenship to groups that Louis Brandeis called despised minorities was always going to be politically tricky for Democrats. If you tried to tell a working-class white guy, whose living standards and life prospects had fallen relative to his parents or even grandparents, that he was "privileged," you would be laughed out of town, and you would certainly not get his vote. But compared to racial minorities, especially to the descendants of slaves, white men, on average, *are* privileged. Yet those averages conceal over-privileged white billionaires and displaced white factory workers.

Class is a far more powerful unifying frame than race, if only Democrats would talk about class. But talking about class would smoke out much of the party's reliance on billionaires who tend to be liberal on social issues but no different from Republicans when it comes to policies that serve the very rich.

Trump keeps being revealed as a phony populist, as well as a vindictive narcissist, and a complete crackpot on the issues. All this clearly gives the Democrats an opportunity. It does not guarantee that they will take it.

Chapter 11

The Road from Here

This memoir has recounted how the decent society of my young adulthood was taken from us beginning in the 1970s, and my own role in the ongoing struggle to get it back. Two Trump administrations seemingly put that project even further out of reach.

In this concluding chapter, I'd like to offer some hope, but without illusions. Given how quickly and impulsively Trump can devise new ploys, it is risky to base an assessment on the state of play at any moment, because things can change in a matter of days, if not hours.

As of this writing, there are some reasons for optimism. Trump's public support keeps sinking. His policies are not lifting the economy. The more he tells voters to trust him rather than their own lived experience, the more credibility he loses. His failed foreign policy is a gift to America's adversaries. He is more flagrantly out of his mind. He can't even get through a carefully scripted speech. His narcissism and vulgarity keep reaching new lows as he desperately looks for things to name after himself.

Three of his most outrageous overreaches backfired spectacularly —his threat to take Greenland by military force; his attempt to take over the Federal Reserve; and his occupation of Minneapolis by ICE. In each episode, large numbers of Republicans publicly objected. All of this, in turn, gives Republicans more reason, as well as more permission, to break with Trump.

As we go to press, Wall Street is still riding the private equity boom and a stock market that has risen several times the rate of GDP. But much of the grass-roots Republican Party is rooted in small business, which is hurt in multiple ways. Tariffs increase the costs of inputs. Small business is disproportionately reliant on the Affordable Care Act to cover employees. Business depends on government contracts and research grants that Trump has strangled. Rising electricity costs harm businesses that actually produce things, as opposed to those that make wagers with other people's money and extract wealth. Meanwhile, there are several signs of financial bubbles, whether in a dangerously concentrated stock market, or crypto, or AI—all portending a possible election-year financial crash.

The economy's growth is primarily a boom by and for the wealthy. Wages have stagnated. GDP growth is close to jobless. Inflation is well above the Fed's annual target of 2 percent, and it hits hardest where ordinary people feel it - in electric bills, health costs, and the grocery store. The Iran War only compounds the economic damage.

From his own crypto brand, $TRUMP, to a foreign policy that is often best understood in terms of real estate deals, Trump's main goal for his presidency is to further enrich himself. At a time when the ability of regular Americans to afford a decent life is emerging as a top public issue, Trump's corruption is not wearing well.

Other Republicans are already treating him as a lame duck. In late December, at the annual conference of Turning Point USA,

Erika Kirk, the widow of the murdered Turning Point founder Charlie Kirk, formally endorsed J.D. Vance as the Republican candidate in 2028. The rest of the conference displayed open splits in the MAGA movement, with podcaster Ben Shapiro attacking MAGA media rivals, calling them "fraudsters and grifters". He singled out Tucker Carlson for conducting a friendly interview with Nick Fuentes, a Holocaust denier.

Trump himself, the one figure who has united the unwieldy MAGA coalition, was conspicuous by his absence. J.D. Vance, Trump's putative successor, is not popular with other Republican elected officials. As the race for the succession intensifies, potential rivals will pile on to undermine Vance. All of this will further fragment the Republican coalition.

The same ideological splits on display at the Turning Point conference are destroying the premier right-wing idea factory, the Heritage Foundation. The Foundation's Trumpian president, Kevin Roberts, a key architect of Project 2025, has supported the same white nationalist antisemite Nick Fuentes. A number of Heritage trustees resigned in protest, and more than a dozen have moved over to a new think tank created by former Vice President Pence, called Advancing American Freedom, which aims to displace Heritage. These schisms will only deepen.

———

Meanwhile, more Republican legislators have been openly defying the White House. House Speaker Mike Johnson, working closely with Trump, could not prevent defecting Republicans from joining Democrats to pass a law compelling the Justice Department to release the complete Epstein files. By slow-walking the release, the Department managed to keep Epstein's connection with Trump in the headlines for several more weeks.

Epstein, in addition to underscoring Trump's well-documented long history as a sexual predator, damaged Trump in one other respect. Epstein epitomized the impunity that has long characterized Trump, his associates, and those whom he pardoned. The revulsion against Epstein, on multiple grounds, splashes back onto Trump.

Former Rep. Marjorie Taylor Greene of Georgia has made clear that a key factor that led her to break with Trump was his behavior toward women. Likewise, Rep. Nancy Mace of South Carolina, a survivor of sexual abuse, and former Republican Representatives Martha McSally of Arizona and Barbara Comstock of Virginia.

Among the most telling of the Republican breaks with Trump was the refusal of Indiana GOP legislators to accede to Trump's demands for a gerrymandered redistricting. They were plainly offended, both by the crudeness and by the arm-twisting. In the end, it became clear that they viewed distancing themselves from Trump as a political plus, as Trump has grown increasingly toxic in Middle America. The Indiana legislators who defied Trump were quintessential Main Street Republicans, just like former Indiana Governor Mike Pence, who was personally offended by Trump's demand in 2020 that he help steal the election.

When half the Republicans in the Indiana legislature rebel, Trump's threat to sponsor primary opponents rings hollow. Just as power feeds on itself, so does impotence.

The larger gerrymander ploy has also backfired. Officials in three other states have refused to go along with it, and the Texas redistricting of five seats stimulated a counter-redistricting of five seats in California. In Texas, Republicans may well have cut their margins too close, dangerously diluting likely Republican voters. All of the five gerrymandered seats have heavily Hispanic populations, a demographic group that broke heavily for Trump in 2020 and just as heavily deserted him in 2024. Democrats could flip two or three of the five gerrymandered seats in 2026.

Government by retribution is also backfiring politically. Trump decided to punish Colorado in multiple ways as punishment for that state's refusal to honor Trump's demand to pardon former election official Tina Peters, who is serving a prison term for tampering with voting machines. Trump used the first veto of his second term to deny federal funds for a pipeline to bring clean water to Colorado's eastern plains, an area that votes heavily Republican. This came on top of moves to cut off transportation money, relocate the military's Space Command, dismantle a leading weather research center, and block disaster relief funding for Colorado counties that suffered fire and storm damage to their electrical grids. In these and other cases of government by retribution, voters will be inclined to fault not just Trump but local and national Republicans who failed to stop him.

———

Ultimately, three major factors will restrain Trump, or not—defecting Republicans, electoral gains by Democrats, and courts. And all three are related—to each other and to an increasingly aroused citizenry.

Trump's budget has put Republicans on the losing side of a highly salient voter issue—their health. At least 22 million Americans suffered massive health insurance price increases as of January 1, when the Affordable Care Act subsidies expired. As the 2026 election comes more into focus, we can count on more Republicans to vote with Democrats to restore health care funding and to reverse Trump on other issues dear to their constituents. The more that Republicans in Congress feel the need to vote against Trump, the more the process feeds on itself, and the more he is weakened politically.

By late January, Republicans in Congress had defied Trump and worked with Democrats to restore innumerable funding cuts that they had previously approved in Trump's "Big Beautiful" budget for fiscal year 2026. Trump's budget cut scientific funding from $198 billion to to $154 billion —a drop of 22 percent. The Senate Appropriations Committee voted to restore spending to $188 billion, a cut of only 4 percent, for research in key agencies such as NSF, NASA, EPA, the Department of Energy, the National Oceanic and Atmospheric Administration (NOAA), and the National Institute of Standards and Technology (NIST).

The broad revulsion against ICE tactics in Minnesota also put some spine in the Democrats. In contrast to their earlier capitulation in the jousting over terms for reopening the government, Democrats stuck together. They demanded concrete limitations on ICE behavior as a condition of funding the Department of Homeland Security.

Trump's bizarre claims on Greenland stimulated more defections and more pointed ones. It was plainly insane, and leading Republicans began saying so. North Carolina Senator Thom Tillis called it beyond stupid. "It's great for Putin, Xi, and other adversaries who want to see NATO divided." Though Tillis is not running for re-election, several other Republicans who are staying in Congress added their voices.

Trump's imposition of punitive tariffs on leading European allies that are resisting his move on Greenland only further undermined his tariff case before the Supreme Court. These tariffs, relying on the International Economic Emergency Powers Act, plainly have nothing to do with economics. On February 20, the Supreme Court ruled, 6-3, that Trump has exceeded his executive authority in ordering a crazy quilt of impulsive tariffs.

Trump's increasingly unhinged campaign against Federal Reserve Chair Jerome ("Jay") Powell also backfired spectacularly. Trump began by trying to pressure Powell into resigning prematurely. When that didn't work, Trump planned an early designation of a successor. Then in January, the Justice Department announced subpoenas, prologue to a criminal investigation.

At that, the normally circumspect Powell went on the offensive, making a statement that declared: "The threat of criminal charges is a consequence of the Federal Reserve setting interest rates based on our best assessment of what will serve the public, rather than following the preferences of the President. This is about whether the Fed will be able to continue to set interest rates based on evidence and economic conditions—or whether instead monetary policy will be directed by political pressure or intimidation."

Powell's stand produced an outpouring of support from Republicans. It increased the likelihood that Powell, whose term as a Fed governor continues until 2028, would remain after his term as Chair expires in May, thus leaving Trump further away from a controlling majority. What's telling is that Powell was behaving as an ordinary corporate Republican, but one who refused to be cowed. It remains to be seen how much crazier Trump gets before more Republicans decide that enough is enough.

At several episodes during 2025 and early 2026, Trump's bizarre behavior and claims to govern as an outright dictator began to look like they might be an inflection point that would lead to his isolation and downfall. At each point, it didn't quite happen. A majority of elected Republicans continued to behave as if their fates were linked to his. Yet that moment inescapably seems to be getting closer.

———

Based on projections from 2025 off-year results, 2026 should be a wave election of epic proportions. The Republican strategy is to offset their own unpopularity by undermining a free and fair election in multiple respects.

The first of these efforts is to give the Justice Department control of all elections. The Department could then disqualify large numbers of voters in blue states as well as red ones, and use other tactics to suppress actual voting and to intimidate local and state election officials by threatening them with criminal prosecutions on bogus charges of fraud.

This strategy began in March 2025, with a Trump executive order that attempted to federalize elections and added other unconstitutional requirements. The order directed the Election Assistance Commission (EAC) to require voters to show proof of citizenship when they register and to rescind all previous certifications of voting equipment and demand new equipment.

This order was blocked by lower courts, and the Supreme Court has not intervened. The Constitution unambiguously gives control of election administration to the states, except where Congress expressly delegates some authority to the executive branch, as in the case of enforcement of the Voting Rights Act or administration of the 1993 National Voter Registration Act, otherwise known as the motor voter law.

Both measures were intended to enhance voting. Trump has sought to turn both laws their opposites, using the Civil Rights Division of the Justice Department to suppress voting. The Justice Department has made demands to at least forty states for their voter files.

The Civil Rights Division, now staffed by people expert in voter suppression, has elaborate plans to run these voter files against commercial databases that purport to show deaths, address changes, double registrations, etc., but that are filled with inaccuracies. This process then becomes the basis for federal purges of accurate state voter files, and for federal prosecutions of state officials who resist.

So far, in places where states resisted, lower courts have blocked all of these orders. However, Indiana and Wyoming have already handed over confidential data to the Justice Department, and 11 other states led by Republicans have said they will cooperate. We can expect a kind of trench warfare, where the Justice Department makes unconstitutional demands, some states and cities resist, while others collaborate, and the courts arbitrate. The Department could then disqualify large numbers of voters in blue states as well as red ones. If we are fortunate, 2026 will be like 2020. Suppression will depress some voting and change a small number of outcomes, but not the overall wave. The activation of large numbers of citizens to monitor voting will also help. In early March, plans were announced for a Democracy Summer, modeled on the Mississippi Freedom Summer of 1964. Students from hundreds of universities will be trained over the summer to work as election monitors in November.

On February 1, Democrat Taylor Rehmet, a machinist, won a seat by 14 points in a special election to the Texas state Senate, in a deep-red district that Trump had carried by 17 points. Polls showed that many of his voters were Republicans fed up with Trump's divisiveness. And that means the Republican strategy of targeting and suppressing likely Democratic votes won't save them.

The basic health of the electoral system even in a red state was shown even more emphatically when James Talarico won his primary for the Democratic Senate nomination on March 4. In two counties, Republicans had tried to confuse primary voters by changing the precincts in which they were allowed to vote. Even so, Democratic votes increased.

The Roberts Court has been terrible on civil rights. Beginning with *Shelby County v. Holder* in 2013, which ended Justice Department pre-clearance of voting changes in jurisdictions with histories of racial discrimination, Roberts seems determined to nullify the 1965 Voting Rights Act. In late 2025, the Court upheld the Texas redistricting plan, whose authors explicitly admitted their intent to dilute the power of minority voting. The Court is on track in *Louisiana v Calais* to overrule the creation of districts intended to provide for the representation of underrepresented minorities. If Republican legislatures in all of the deep south take full advantage of the expected ruling and carry out racial gerrymandering, this could reduce the number of Black Democratic representatives in the House by as many as 19, though not in time for the 2026 election.

One of Roberts's worst decisions in the well-named 2024 case, *Trump v. United States*, granted a president almost unlimited impunity from criminal prosecution for supposedly official actions. Yet even this high court may be running out of patience with Trump's claims of dictatorial power.

Oral argument in two key cases signaled that forthcoming decisions will likely overrule Trump's claims to be able to fire Federal Reserve governors with fixed terms, and his use of emergency economic powers to turn tariffs on and off on a whim. Most close observers of the court believe that the justices will also reject Trump's claim that he can revise the meaning of birthright citizenship, as explicitly defined in the 14th Amendment and repeatedly upheld by courts over a century and a half.

Each of these key decisions is self-executing. Following a decision by the courts tossing out Trump's "emergency" tariffs, importers and retailers would simply stop paying them. It is not practical for Customs officials or the IRS to go after them, one at a time, especially in violation of a Supreme Court ruling. Likewise, when the Court, in a preliminary ruling, refused to suspend

Federal Reserve Governor Lisa Cook, Trump could not declare her seat vacant. And if the Court upholds birthright citizenship, there would be no way for Trump to order federal agencies to review tens of millions of cases, one at a time.

Of recent Supreme Court decisions, the most important one both in its own right and as a harbinger is the December 23 ruling in *Trump v. Illinois,* in which a 6-3 majority left in place lower-court rulings barring Trump from deploying federalized National Guard troops in and around Chicago in response to anti-ICE protests. Equally notable in the Chicago case is the fact that three conservatives, Chief Justice Roberts, Amy Coney Barrett, and Brett Kavanaugh, sided with the Court's three liberals. On New Year's Day, Trump announced that he would be pulling the small contingent of National Guard troops from Chicago, Los Angeles, and Portland—deferring to the Supreme Court.

At this writing, there are 368 active cases where litigation has challenged administration actions in the lower courts, and 149 cases where courts have enjoined illegal executive action. In some of these cases, the Supreme Court has relied on its "shadow docket" to grant the administration temporary relief from lower-court orders. In other cases, like the Illinois ruling on the use of the National Guard, the high court has allowed lower-court prohibitions stand. In early January, a three-judge panel from the Court of Appeals for the First Circuit permanently enjoined the federal government from cutting funding to public health research at universities and research institutions across the country. This will cause billions of dollars to flow, unless the Supreme Court sides with the administration. In March, the US Court of Appeals for the Second Circuit supported lower courts in enjoining Trump's attempts to withhold duly approved funds for New York's trans-Hudson Gateway Tunnel.

On New Year's Eve, Chief Justice Roberts released an annual

Report on the Federal Judiciary, obliquely but unmistakably criticizing threats to our independent courts and signaling to Trump to back off. He began by quoting Thomas Paine, pointedly noting that Paine was a "recent immigrant." He segued from Paine to the Declaration of Independence, adding that "The Declaration charged that George III 'has made Judges dependent on his Will alone, for the tenure of their offices, and the amount and payment of their salaries.' The Constitution corrected this flaw, granting life tenure and salary protection to safeguard the independence of federal judges and ensure their ability to serve as a counter-majoritarian check on the political branches. This arrangement, now in place for 236 years, has served the country well." Politely, Roberts was saying: No Kings.

In general, the Roberts Court has been friendly to the "unitary executive" doctrine. But that means one thing in the context of debates about the independent power of regulatory agencies. It means something else when a particular executive with dictatorial designs is stark raving mad.

———

Thus far, I have offered a relatively hopeful account of what could unfold in the coming months and years. One can also imagine a much more alarming scenario. Trump and his minions could succeed in disrupting the 2026 elections to the point of effectively nullifying them. While this is possible, I don't think it is likely.

Trump could also turn to violence, either intensified state violence on the part of ICE, which in turn would promote more resistance and more arrests, or street violence on the part of private shock troops, as he attempted on January 6, 2021. MAGA extremists have threatened violence against federal judges and members of Congress. Violence also includes reckless wars, which then become the pretext for domestic crackdowns.

Trump could try to further weaponize the Justice Department against his political opponents. Thus far, Trump has failed in his more outlandish efforts. Grand juries twice refused to indict New York Attorney General Letitia James on bogus charges of mortgage fraud. A judge also dismissed the Justice Department's effort, as ordered by Trump, to prosecute former FBI director James Comey.

The effort by Bill Pulte, Trump's head of the Federal Housing and Finance Agency, to comb through mortgage records to find technical violations as the basis for prosecuting James and other officials, including Lisa Cooke and California Senator Adam Schiff, also backfired. At this writing, Pulte is himself now the object of an investigation for abusing his office.

The occupation of Minneapolis and attempted prosecution of Governor Tim Walz and Mayor Jacob Frey combined the weaponization of the Justice Department the use of government violence to trigger local responses and thus justify more official thuggery. It brought America closer to civil war. These and similar conflicts will be in courts that are increasingly losing patience with Trump. In early March, after escalating criticisms from Republican as well as Democratic legislators, Trump abruptly fired DHS Secretary Kristi Noem. Republican unease with the political consequences of a range of policies from tariffs to ICE raids to the Iran war is only increasing.

In sum, though Trump is increasingly on the defensive. it's far too soon to proclaim that "democracy held." Even if we have a relatively normal election in 2026, and even if Democrats take back one or both houses of Congress, Trump will still be president for two more years after that, with all of the awesome power that comes with the presidency—and he doesn't seem to be getting saner with time.

Trump's strategy when a ploy fails is to continue his attempted pattern of shock and awe by changing the subject. If the occupation of Minnesota fails, rehash old grievances of a stolen 2020 election by illegally seizing Georgia voting records. If a Greenland invasion is off, invade some other nation. Trump's relative success at bringing about policy change without full regime change in Venezuela has become an unfortunate model for him. As this book goes to press, Trump's rationale for his vastly more complex Iran War is changing by the day, as the impact of the war keeps widening. The only clear winners so far are Russia and China. The economic impact of the war compounds a damaged economy weakened by rising joblessness and inflation, both the results of other Trump policies.

Iran proved far more resilient than Trump imagined and was able to wreak havoc against US assets and allies in the Gulf, using cheap and easily replenished weapons, notably drones and naval mines. At this writing, Trump was torn between wishful denial and serious consideration of exit options.

The best option -- and it's not that good -- was some kind of deal for a cease fire, in which the U.S. and Israel stop the attacks on Iran and give up on regime change, and Iran allows the Strait of Hormuz to re-open and stops targeting Gulf allies of the U.S. But Iran may not trust Trump enough to accept such a deal. Trump, meanwhile, was sending new assault vessels to the region. All this portended escalating pressure for more troops, prolonged quagmire, and increased global risks.

As this book was going to press, Trump was fixated on legislation known as the SAVE America Act, as a desperation ploy to steal the 2026 midterm elections. The legislation would require proof of citizenship to register, photo ID to vote, and would drastically limit mail in voting. The bill passed the House, but Senate Majority Leader John Thune made it clear that he did not have the 60 votes needed to override a Democratic filibuster.

Trump countered by pressing Republican senators to end the filibuster and increasing pressure on Thune. Trump wrote increasingly hysterical midnights posts, and vowed to veto all other legislation until Congress passed the SAVE Act. But at least four Republicans will not vote to abolish the filibuster--Mitch McConnell and Rand Paul of Kentucky, Susan Collins of Maine, and Lisa Murkowski of Alaska.

However, assuming that SAVE fails, Trump will be back with other schemes. This is a man, after all, who tried and nearly succeed in staging a coup to stay in office on January 6, 2021.

In my darkest moments, I imagine Trump concluding that the world just doesn't appreciate him, so he might as well blow up the world. Singer-songwriter Randy Newman anticipated Trump by several decades in his 1972 parody song, *Political Science* ("They all hate us anyhow, so let's drop the big one now.")

If we can avert the worst, the MAGA interlude could crash and burn so thoroughly that a credible opposition could come to power. Whether that occurs depends not just on a Republican crack-up and more resolute courts, but on whether Democrats and progressives can offer a vision that is inspiring without engaging in magical thinking.

Throughout 2025, many critics pointed to a fatal Democratic gerontocracy. The incipient senility of Joe Biden was not unique. An entire generation of Democratic leaders, such as Nancy Pelosi (82 when she gave up her House leadership post in early 2023) and Chuck Schumer (still Senate Democratic leader at 75), signaled a party out of touch with the young. The proof was the sickening falloff in participation by voters under 30 in 2024, helping to elect Trump.

And then, in November, New Yorkers elected as their mayor a 34-year-old democratic socialist, Zohran Mamdani. The success of Mamdani suggested not just that a progressive can get elected—this is New York after all—but that a leader who blends inspiration with a genuine connection to the common people can rally large numbers of the young and serve as an antidote to cynicism. Mamdani's campaign catalyzed organizing, and the organizing will continue. Some of his policy proposals will succeed, and some are stretches, but his administration revives the promise of competent, activist government serving regular people rather than billionaires.

A classic political-science finding is that Americans tend to be philosophical conservatives but operational liberals. Mamdani doesn't have a monopoly on articulating the concerns of working families in a way that motivates nonvoters to become voters who support Democrats. Kitchen-table economics can also work for candidates who don't describe themselves as socialists. But to succeed, sooner or later, they will run into the political power of capitalists—and become operational progressives, even in spite of themselves.

The point is not that it's easy to create more leaders who blend the idealism and political brilliance of Mamdani's cookie-cutter style. Andrew Cuomo proved that when he tried to copy Mamdani by dressing casually and walking around the city. The point is that Mandami can inspire more young people to get into politics, both as activists and as candidates, to work for a democratic revival.

———

To appreciate just how extensive the repairs will need to be, let's make some optimistic assumptions. Let's assume that democracy holds long enough for the Democrats to take back Congress and the presidency. Let's further assume that Trump's most destructive impulses are restrained by the courts and Congress. Let's go even further and assume that a pragmatic and persuasive progressive is the next president and brings with him a working majority in both houses. Note that such a president would be a far more forceful and effective spokesman for his own agenda than Joe Biden was.

Even so, the post-Trump challenges will be pervasive under the best of circumstances. They include: repairing the damage to the government; revitalizing democracy; repairing US credibility in the world. The most difficult of all is restoring an economy of broad prosperity and possibility, because of deep structural shifts that date back through several presidencies.

What will it take to restore basic functions of normal government? Project 2025 was a detailed blueprint for destroying affirmative government. At this writing, the civil service has been cut by at least 330,000 positions or about 17 percent, but that understates the damage. A great many of the best people have taken early retirements or buyouts. These agencies can be rebuilt, but some of the institutional memory is lost forever. This is especially true of the enforcement agencies tasked with keeping capitalism tolerably honest, such as the SEC, whose enforcement activities were deliberately crippled.

In principle, the FDA and the Centers for Disease Control could be restored to sanity in relatively short order, but time has been lost. Getting vaccine research and production back on track will take months if not years. Many of the talented and dedicated professionals who opted for public health careers will think twice before going to work for the government. There will be long-term damage to research that had been underwritten by NIH, NSF, and to entire research units at universities.

On the other hand, the history of the New Deal suggests that new agencies can get up to speed fairly quickly. World War II is also a model. The United States went from having almost no war production in 1940 to having the world's mightiest war production machine by 1942. The needs of war production also stimulated a profusion of new inventions. More recently, new agencies such as the Consumer Financial Protection Bureau had quick learning curves, and the revived Federal Trade Commission under Biden appointee Lina Khan, who virtually reinvented antitrust, was bringing new cases within months.

Yet some damage may be irreparable. One of Biden's most important initiatives was the effort to increase US capacity in several categories of renewable energy, such as solar and wind. By destroying these, Trump not only sets back this progress on climate and clean energy but also undermines the creation of domestic capacity. This comes at a critical point in the life of the planet. As Bill McKibben has observed, technological solutions to the impending climate catastrophe are at hand. "The solar cell was invented in 1954, and it took from then until 2022 to install the first terawatt worth of solar power on this planet," McKibben has written. "It took two years to get the second."

By the early 2020s, the cost of producing energy from the sun dropped below the cost of using fossil fuels. By 2024, less than half of the electric power in the US was generated from fossil fuels. Trump has been doing his best to reverse that progress. There needs to be a lot of public investment in the grid so that it can accommodate intermittent sources of electric power, such as wind and solar. This has also been cut by Trump.

All this is not just a matter of what is "clean" or what is cost-effective. In the race to save a habitable planet, every year counts. When the history of the climate catastophe is written a hundred years from now, assuming that civilization survives, the story will either be that we got very lucky and just barely accomplished a rendezvous between inventing and installing new technology and averting the worst; or that we missed the rendezvous by a few decades, leading to massive cumulative and permanent effects, such as ruined coastal cities, uninhabitable contintents, droughts and famines. Eight years of Trump will have made a significant difference. Of all of Trump's irreversible effects, this one is potentially the worst.

————

Assuming that we have tolerably fair elections in 2026 and 2028, the work of repairing democracy only begins. Returning the Justice Department to its purpose of monitoring and assuring fair elections is the easy part. Much of the deeper damage to democracy is below the water line.

One core problem is the substitution of money for citizenship. If the role of billionaire money in corrupting democracy is ever to be contained, it will be necessary to re-regulate campaign finance. Efforts by Congress to limit the role of large donations following the Watergate scandal were undermined by the Supreme Court almost from the outset. New efforts would surely be struck down as violations of speech by the current high court, which is even more right-wing than the court that overturned key parts of the post-Watergate regulatory regime in *Buckley v. Valeo* in 1976. Subsequent decisions, such as the 2010 *Citizens United* ruling, allowing effectively unlimited donations by corporations (as fictitious people) and permitted anonymous "dark money", gutted all limits.

Court rulings have had a similarly lethal impact on civil rights enforcement. For more than half a century, courts accepted affirmative action as entirely reasonable compensation for the four-hundred-year history of slavery and segregation, and affirmative action was widely used by private employers as well as all levels of education. But in 2023, the high court outlawed not just excessive DEI but affirmative action itself, in its ruling in *Students for Fair Admissions v. Harvard* and *v. University of North Carolina*, holding that race-conscious affirmative action in college admissions (and presumably affirmative action generally) is unconstitutional reverse discrimination. Progressive policymakers can either resort to subterfuge, such as class-based affirmation, or take on the broader issue of the right-wing lock on the courts.

If we assume that Trump is succeeded by a progressive Democratic administration in January 2029, Trump still has more than two more years to appoint federal judges, creating an even more partisan judiciary. A new administration would be seriously stymied by the courts on all fronts.

It is possible to enlarge the Supreme Court or add term limits for justices by statute. A constitutional amendment is not required. Some might contend that revising the Supreme Court would amount to a constitutional crisis, but we are already in a constitutional crisis. At this writing, the Roberts Court has already rolled back much of the post-1937 conception of the role of government, trampling well-settled precedent and invoking an ever-shifting conception of "originalism" whenever that proved convenient.

———

It will take a concerted effort to restore civil rights enforcement, and here the courts are also central. On his first day in office, Trump issued a series of executive orders ending all DEI programs. This policy has become a cover for hobbling basic civil rights that have nothing to do with affirmative action or DEI.

On February 21 2025, Trump fired the chairman of the Joint Chiefs of Staff, Charles Q. Brown. Gen. Brown, a four-star Air

Force general, was only the second Black officer to chair the Joint Chiefs, the first being Colin Powell.

Brown began his distinguished 40-year Air Force career in 1984 as a fighter pilot. He logged over 3,000 flight hours, including 130 hours in combat. He then commanded the Pacific Air Forces, the Air Forces Central Command, and the Air Force Weapons School, as well as the 8th Fighter Wing and the 31st Fighter Wing. But Defense Secretary Pete Hegseth flatly suggested that Brown was promoted because of his race. "Was it because of his skin color? Or his skill? We'll never know, but always doubt."

Any Black or female public official is at risk of being fired as a presumed diversity hire, and even more at risk if they work in any program having to do with civil rights. All federal agencies have civil rights offices that enforce basic laws against discrimination. If they are doing their jobs, they can't avoid talking about race and gender.

Trump's initial series of executive orders even revoked President Lyndon Johnson's Executive Order 11246 of 1965, which was the origin of the federal government's affirmative action efforts. As Johnson put it in a celebrated commencement address at Howard University in June 1965, "You do not take a person who, for years, has been hobbled by chains and liberate him, bring him up to the starting line of a race and then say, 'you are free to compete with all the others,' and still justly believe that you have been completely fair."

The sociologist Mark Granovetter wrote a famous research study in 1973 called "The Strength of Weak Ties," on how most people actually get jobs. It systematically confirmed what everyone intuitively knew: You got jobs through informal networking. Somebody knew somebody's cousin, or a neighbor heard that such-and-such an employer was hiring. These informal networks simply excluded Blacks because they always had.

Very gradually, thanks to affirmative outreach requirements, racial and gender patterns in the labor force became more integrated, though Blacks and women are still underrepresented relative to their skill levels in many occupations, especially in supervisory and executive positions. The fact that these patterns vary widely among different corporations, depending on the recruitment efforts that they make, is evidence that discrimination persists among some employers.

Under the Civil Rights Act of 1964, someone who believes they are the subject of discrimination in hiring, promotion, work assignments, sexual harassment, or other such grievances begins by filing a complaint with the Equal Employment Opportunity Commission. If EEOC investigators or attorneys find that the complaint has merit, that can lead to a settlement or litigation.

In 2024, the commission won nearly $700 million in monetary damages, benefiting some 21,000 claimants. The commission filed 88,531 new charges in 2024. This work has ground to a halt, except for actions against alleged reverse discrimination.

The Department of Education has an Office for Civil Rights that normally investigates thousands of complaints. Since Trump took office, that process has ground to a halt. The only new cases opened by the office's attorneys have been directed at such Trump priorities as getting rid of gender-neutral bathrooms, banning transgender athletes from women's sports, and pursuing alleged antisemitism.

Another prime target is enforcement of nondiscrimination in housing. Despite the Fair Housing Act of 1968, study after study has demonstrated that discrimination in the sale or rental of housing has persisted. The 1968 act itself requires all federal agencies to "administer their programs" in a manner "affirmatively to further the purposes of" the Fair Housing Act. Trump ordered a reduction in force at HUD's Office of Fair Housing and Equal Opportunity by 76 percent.

Meanwhile, pressed by the administration, major corporations have scrapped DEI programs and affirmative action commitments. They include Accenture, Amazon, Boeing, Citigroup, Deloitte, Disney, Ford, Goldman Sachs, Google, Lowe's, McDonald's, Meta, Molson Coors, Paramount, PepsiCo, PwC, Target, and Walmart. Many of these companies are not just getting rid of exaggerated DEI language, but ending entire human resource programs aimed at recruiting and promoting applicants from underrepresented groups.

Trump's strategy of punishing blue states and destroying habitats where liberals tend to work blends with his perverse distortion of civil rights principles. This poisonous mix came together in the announcement on March 7, 2025, that Columbia University would lose $400 million in previously committed federal grants because of its alleged failure to protect Jewish students from antisemitic harassment. Similar treatment of other universities followed, and several agreed to settlements. Giving in to Trump's blackmail only increased his demands.

The Columbia order created a standard made up out of whole cloth, defining the university's previous actions to protect Jewish students as inadequate. Given the free speech and assembly rights of the First Amendment, it's not at all clear what the university authorities should have done. There is no instance where the Trump administration has shone a similar spotlight on the actions of universities for failing to protect the rights of Blacks, Hispanics, women, or sexual minorities.

This is the same Donald Trump who said of the Charlottesville marauders, whose slogan was "Jews will not replace us," that there were "very fine people on both sides," even after antisemitic marchers deliberately crashed a car into a group of peaceful protesters, killing one. Trump also pardoned the January 6th insurrectionists, who included several members of the anti-semitic Proud Boys and other explicit antisemites who follow QAnon.

Trump is a defender of Jews against supposed antisemitism when that's useful to attack liberal universities, and an ally of the most explicit and vicious antisemites when that happens to be convenient for him. Should it ever become expedient, Trump will turn on the Jews.

A Democratic administration could restore basic civil rights enforcement. But in the absence of reform of the courts, anything remotely resembling affirmative action would still be held to be unconstitutional.

———

One of the most important bolsters of democracy is a free and independent press. Unlike outright totalitarian regimes, such as Nazi Germany or Putin's Russia, Trump's incipient dictatorship has coexisted with relentless press exposés of his lies, power grabs, and blunders. Trump has had mixed success in undermining a free press, including bungled attempts to restrict media access to only friendly journalists.

His greatest success has come from using the business interests of media magnates as leverage to destroy the critical independence of their media properties. Jeff Bezos, who defended the independence of the Washington Post during Trump's first term, has joined the legions of Trump sycophants, eviscerating the independence of the Post's editorial page and turning much of its commentary into a MAGA echo chamber. CBS News, the proud home of Edward R. Murrow and of Sixty Minutes, is now run by a Trump stooge and censor, Bari Weiss. Even so, in mid-January, White House Press Secrertary Karoline Leavitt warned CBS's newly appointed anchor Tony Dokoupil not to edit the tape of a recent interview with Trump. He agreed. She added, quoting Trump, "If it's not out in full, we'll sue your ass off."

The New York Times has often resorted to self-censorship and a spurious attempt at the appearance of even-handedness. Ironically, the conservative Wall Street Journal editorial page, depending on the issue, sometimes delivers withering criticism of Trump.

Brendan Carr, Trump's censorious head of the F.C.C., has repeatedly threatened broadcast media for the sin of accurate coverage of Trump, and has pressured their corporate owners. In mid-March, he warned, "Broadcasters that are running hoaxes and news distortions - also known as the fake news - have a chance now to correct course before their license renewals come up. The law is clear. Broadcasters must operate in the public interest, and they will lose their licenses if they do not."

Trump has also tried to starve public media into submission, shutting down the Corporation for Public Broadcasting and threatening to have the FCC pull broadcast licenses. National Public Radio is as feisty as ever. The larger public radio stations have increased their income from listeners and from underwriting, suffering minor layoffs. The major damage is to smaller public radio stations with smaller listenership to draw on, many of them the only comprehensive source of news in Trump country.

Trump and his allies have also made intermittent attempts to destroy independent media with defamation suits. Even if newspapers ultimately won in court, they could literally go broke paying legal fees. In 2016, right-wing billionaire Peter Thiel succeeded in shutting down Gawker News by funding multiple libel suits. (Gawker was a thoroughly scurrilous site, but the strategy is available against more reputable outlets.)

There has also been talk of having Congress enact an official secrets act, which would place reporters and publishers at personal and financial risk for publishing classified material. Supreme Court Justice Clarence Thomas has suggested overturning *Times v. Sullivan*, the 1964 court decision that protects the press from defamation suits by public figures except in proven cases of "reckless disregard for the truth" or "actual malice."

Trump and a weaponized IRS could also go after progressive media and advocacy organizations that are tax-exempt nonprofits, as well as their funders. As I wrote in a 2024 article for The Prospect titled "The Left's Fragile Foundations," much of the progressive infrastructure is organized as 501 c 3 institutions, so that they can receive foundation grants and tax-deductible donations from individuals. Such organizations are supposed to be nonpartisan. The Trump IRS has not yet mounted a major crackdown, but some foundations have already begun trimming their funding of quasi-political groups, for fear that they could lose their own tax exemptions.

As the co-founder of an independent nonprofit magazine, I believe that smaller media are crucial in holding power accountable. Lately, quite apart from the added assaults of Trump, legacy media have not been doing well. With the exception of the three national newspapers, The New York Times, The Washington Post, and the Wall Street Journal, newspapers are losing ad revenue to Google and losing paid readers to websites and Substacks.

Regional papers, especially those that cover state capitals, are in particular distress. Their problems have been compounded by the takeover of thousands of papers by private equity companies, whose strategy is to cut staff to the bone, the better to extract profits. When a state capital or county seat becomes a news desert, with little if any probing or investigative coverage, democracy suffers. Citizens lack a sense of what is going on, corruption flourishes, and the public further loses confidence in government.

Though there is no substitute for a good regional daily paper, to some extent, new forms of media can fill the gap. While legacy media, with their costly business models and dependence on ads, are suffering, publications like The Prospect can be lean but investigative and fearless. To protect against a weaponized IRS and intimidated foundations, The Prospect is moving toward 100 percent reader-funding. Substacks are also filling the gap, often scooping the big dailies with deeply reported expert explainer pieces.

There is also some hopeful news as the social medium formerly known as Twitter implodes, and the social media fad begins to become passé. Social media has been toxic for democracy. At its worst, it spreads lies in the national discourse and promotes vicious bullying locally. At its most harmless, social media offers a way of staying in touch with old friends or of exchanging cat videos. Social media also promotes texting and creates a learned incapacity in the young for face-to-face communication.

One of the best reforms of the past year has been the banning of smartphones in classrooms. After objecting, most students find actual communication, as opposed to texting, to be satisfying. It's too soon to dismiss social media as yesterday's fad, but the cool kids may be abandoning it.

———

What of Trump's foreign policy? A successor administration could restore a benign role for the US in the world, but some of the damage will be irrevocable. Trump has done everything possible to help Vladimir Putin and undermine the Atlantic Alliance with other democracies. By the end of Trump's term, it would take a miracle for Ukraine not to be a Russian satellite, and for Russia not to be threatening other near neighbors. While Trump has talked a good game on China, his actual policies have helped China gain more leadership in more industries and technologies at the US's expense. Trump's gratuitous conflicts with India have removed one possible counterweight.

While China, as a rising industrial and geopolitical power, was never going to be stymied by the United States, a more careful and nuanced policy could have pursued a modus vivendi, in which the US prevented sensitive technologies that we controlled from being used by China, and demanded more symmetrical behavior with trading partners as a condition of tariff-free access. Instead, Trump imposed and withdrew tariffs willy-nilly.

If a Democratic Administration does take power in 2029, Trump's policies will have left Washington weaker both relative to Beijing and Moscow. His invasion of Venezuela to kidnap President Nicolás Maduro is a virtual invitation for China to take Taiwan and for Russia to take Ukraine. Trump also obliterated what remained of the goodwill built up in the world via agencies of US "soft power" such as USAID.

This is not to say that all was well with the US role in the world before Trump. As hegemonic powers go, the US was relatively benign. But Washington was far more benign in the postwar era. Catastrophic blunders such as the Iraq War made the world a less safe place. A series of US-sponsored coups or attempted coups to protect US corporate interests, in Iran, Chile, Cuba, and Guatemala, mostly backfired. The difference between Trump's military intervention in Venezuela and previous covert operations by the CIA to overthrow several regimes is only that Trump acted openly, flagrantly, and boastfully.

A succession of US administrations poured money into Israel, but allowed Israeli governments to build illegal settlements in the occupied West Bank, and after 2023, to destroy Gaza. Again, Trump was more flagrant in his blank check for Israel. The US also put pressure on the world's nations to subscribe to rules of trade that were tilted to benefit US corporations and banks. If and when a successor government takes office in Washington, the world will be a more dangerous place, and the global rule of law will be that much weaker.

———

I have left the challenge of rebuilding a society of broad economic possibility for last, because it will be the hardest of all. As I wrote in Chapter Two of this book, reflecting on my own early adulthood and the economic experience of my generation, all of the instruments that once made possible an economy of broad prosperity and economic security have been seriously weakened. That package included affordable housing, free public universities, payroll jobs with wages sufficient to support a family, generous pensions, and health coverage increasingly provided either by government or by an employer. A progressive tax system underwrote the public parts of the package without imposing high taxes on working people.

The gradual erosion of this package in favor of a neoliberal system that favored rich people left resentments that culminated in Trump. If a Democratic president and Congress are elected in 2028, but they fail to make palpable progress in restoring an economy of broad possibility, then the cycle of mistrust in liberals and the search for scapegoats will begin all over again.

Even if we can imagine a Democratic President and a Congress with a progressive working majority, the scale of the structural transformation needed to restore anything like the postwar social compact will be massive. Several liberal groups have begun writing versions of a progressive blueprint for 2029, borrowing the Heritage Foundation's Project 2025. While they contain some good ideas, I have not seen one that goes far enough.

Take the case of health care. The problem is not the non-renewal of the Affordable Care Act subsidies, or the withdrawal of aid from rural hospitals, or the assault on Medicaid and the VA, or the degradation of nursing homes. The entire system is unsustainable. It has become a morass of middlemen and entrepreneurs looking for opportunities to profit, while actual caregivers - doctors and nurses - are being squeezed to the point where large numbers are leaving the profession.

Cory Doctorow, a well-informed and witty critic of the predatory business strategies of Google, Amazon, Apple et al, has coined a marvelous term—enshittification. In order to maximize the profits of these platform monopolies, the experience of their customers has become steadily worsened—enshittified. You could say the same of the health care system.

The US spends close to 20 percent of the GDP on health care. Other advanced nations, with vastly less complex and universal healthcare systems, either using nonprofit hospitals and nonprofit insurance systems or fully socialized systems, spend about 13 percent. All have far less waste in the form of private bureaucracies, as well as a far better experience for patients and clinicians alike. The seven percent of GDP saved is about two trillion dollars a year—enough to finance universal health care and a lot more.

Incremental reform won't fix what is broken in the US healthcare system. But a shift to national health insurance would be a massive political lift. Advocates of socialized medicine in the US typically use the term "single payer," meaning that instead of multiple insurance companies and government agencies paying medical and hospital and medical bills, there would be just one payer, perhaps Medicare for All. But even that solves only part of the problem. To impose Medicare for All on top of the existing system of ownership structure of hospitals, medical practices, nursing homes, and middlemen, and the private version of Medicare, mislabeled Medicare Advantage, would leave a wholly dysfunctional system largely intact.

Comprehensive systemic reform would be disruptive—of the private insurance system, the ownership structure and business strategy of hospitals, as well as the current system of employer-provided insurance. There are ways to do some of this piecemeal. We could start by extending Medicare to more age groups, getting rid of Medicare Advantage, and having a five-year transition for all hospitals to become genuine nonprofits.

When I was young, activists for social change read a French theorist named André Gorz. He promoted a strategy of what he termed "non-reformist reform." The idea was that reforms that seemed only modest and incremental, if strategically designed, could become transformative. The Community Reinvestment Act, which I wrote about in Chapter Three, was that sort of reform, in its impact both on banking and on organizing. Transformative incrementalism seems an oxymoron, but it can work.

One of the most illuminating articles I wrote for The Prospect was a profile of the Hotel and Restaurant workers union in New York, one of America's strongest and most creative union locals. The most remarkable thing about the union is its health plan. The union operates four full-service clinics for members and their families and avoids the insurance industry and for-profit medicine entirely. The plan uses salaried doctors. Its costs are about one-third those of New York's other health insurance plans. With some government incentives, this approach could become a model for the entire health system.

Such transformative reforms are far from easy. They will take a large progressive majority and a serious strategic commitment. The combined lobbying power of insurers and organized medicine is immense. It compelled Democratic presidents stretching back from Obama to LBJ to Truman to settle for far less than comprehensive reform.

As I suggested in Chapter Two, the debt-for-diploma system has become unsustainable. It would take on the order of $100 billion a year to restore basically free state universities and community colleges, plus over two trillion to provide serious debt relief. That would leave private colleges and universities as places substantially for children of the rich, with some of the better-endowed ones continuing to provide needs-based financial aid to the poor and the middle class.

Restoring housing opportunity will take lots of public money, both to subsidize the construction of socially owned rental housing and to build new units for home ownership. It will also take judicious use of rent control in areas of the country where scarce supply has given windfall profits to private landlords. While the authors of the "Abundance" doctrine place much of the blame on zoning and other regulations that create obstacles to new construction, even if we could override environmental and other rules to streamline new construction, we'd still need a lot more public investment.

On the employment front, with AI compounding the problem of the scarcity of decent jobs, it will take both stronger wage regulation and the creation of more government-supported jobs that pay decently. While AI is killing some jobs, there is a huge need for jobs in human services. I have written elsewhere that the government could underwrite large numbers of jobs caring for the old, the young, and the sick, all of which would have a salary floor of $35,000 a year and good career ladders. And with private pensions having collapsed, and 401 (k) plans being totally inadequate, we need a second tier of public Social Security to assure decent living standards in old age. Stronger trade unions could help bargain for higher wages and better jobs, and could provide a mobilized constituency of the rest of the progressive program.

All of this needs to be financed by the restoration of a progressive tax system. Given the extreme concentration of wealth and its ostentatious display, that part of the program should be relatively popular politically. Tax reform plus the savings from a shift to socialized health care could produce enough revenue for all of the needs cited here.

And public investment needs to be complemented by public regulation. At the center of an enshittified economy is private equity, an unregulated form of extractive capitalism. Private equity operators borrow money to take over companies, put the debt on the books of the target company, and pay themselves exorbitant fees and dividends. They compensate by selling real estate, laying off workers, raising prices, and cutting wages. Private equity has destroyed many iconic retailers and has moved on to everything from newspapers to veterinarians to nursing homes to trailer parks. Regulation prohibiting debt-financed takeovers and limiting extraction, as proposed by Sen. Elizabeth Warren, could put private equity out of business.

This is not the place for a full-blown policy manifesto. The point is that progressives need to think truly big, as big as the New Deal, or they will fail to restore a decent social compact. And if they fail, we risk getting someone like Trump all over again. The hard part, as always, is the politics. But if Democrats can shake loose the influence of the billionaires that have hobbled their sense of what is politically possible, they can at least think big enough to try. The funny thing about truly progressive policies, like Social Security or Medicare, is that they are hard to enact, but once in place, they are fiercely cherished by citizens.

———

Thus, notes for next time. If we are fortunate and do our jobs during the remainder of Trump's term, there will be a next time.

My own experience suggests a few enduring themes. Good policies require social movements to get them enacted and to keep them honest. I once heard a labor leader, David Rolf of the SEIU in Seattle, say, "Policy is frozen politics." By that, he meant that today's good policies are the fruits of yesterday's struggles. If the politics melt, eventually the policies melt away, too. Struggles are ongoing.

The same is true of public institutions. They need to be defended, vigilantly, by an activated citizenry. One good thing about the struggle against Trump is that it can re-activate citizenship, and defeating Trumpism is only the beginning.

Another core theme that kept recurring during my entire political lifetime: The credibility of Democrats and progressives depends on whether they deliver prosperity, security, and opportunity to ordinary people. Lose that, and the other divisions in a complex society take over. That's why the neoliberal alliance with globalist billionaires was so toxic to Democrats. It will take a long time to win back that trust, but a few bold downpayments would be a start.

And last, let's be hopeful but not wishful. The scale of what needs to be done is massive. That said, I remain an optimist, partly because of the times when I grew up, partly because of my temperament, and partly because of my reading of history.

Taking a long view, I think of the whole American experience:

The stain of slavery, the brilliance of the Constitution, the miracle of Lincoln, the genius of the New Deal, the catastrophe of Vietnam, and, of course, the disgrace of Trump. There were some noble eras, where the rock stayed put for a long while, as well as some shameful ones. This Republic may yet prove resilient enough to survive and surmount Trump. I'd like to be around to see it.

Looking back on my own history, I've had a good life during both hopeful and difficult times for the country. I've built some durable institutions. I've surmounted some personal losses and remained a fundamentally optimistic person. Unlike the experience of one human life, where they don't give you a do-over, I have to believe that the American experiment will endure.

Acknowledgments

This is to thank everyone who has helped me along the way, as well as other friends and colleagues working for a politically possible decent America.

That includes, first, my family: Arthur Kuttner, Polly Kuttner Levy, Adele Kuttner, Eli Levy, Gordon Levy, Ben Levy, Gabriel Kuttner, Jessica Kuttner, Shelly Fitzgerald, Vincent Lorenzo, John Trotter; my grandchildren Owen Stewart, Eli Stewart, Alex Kuttner, James Lorenzo, Amaryah Lorenzo; and especially the two amazing women I've been married to, Sharland Trotter and Joan Fitzgerald.

I thank my teachers, mentors and editors: notably John D. Lewis, George Lanyi, Dick Pollak, Rick Hertzberg, Dorothy Wickenden, Alice Mayhew, Elisabeth Sifton, Drake McFeely, Ash Green, Andrew Miller, Bob Silvers, Emily Greenhouse, Margo Baldwin, Bud Relman, Marcia Angell, William Whitworth, Ernest Painter, Dorothy Connor, Mort Mintz, Bill Greider, Irving Howe, Ross Wetzsteon, Steve Sheppard, Peter Steinfels, Kirk Scharfenberg, Marjorie Pritchard and Renee Loth.

At Pacifica thanks to Larry Josephson, Bill Schechner, Carolyn Goodman, Danice Bordett, Neal Conan, Ed Goodman, Steve

Bookshester, Judy Coburn, Paul Fischer, Margo Adler, among many others.

At the American Prospect: Paul Starr, Bob Reich, Deborah Stone, Mike Stern, David Dayen, Adele Simmons, Harold Meyerson, Mitch Grummon, Jonathan Cohn, Gabrielle Gurley, Jonathan Guyer, Lindsay Owens, Stephen Heintz, Amy Hanauer, Michael Tomasky, Ganesh Sitaraman, Alan Dworsky, Mary Parsons, Bernard Rapoport, Steve Grossman, Shanti Fry, and numerous others.

From Working Papers for a New Society, thanks to editors John Case and Nancy Lyons, and especially to Elinor Langer, whose prescient piece looking back on the Movement in the first 1973 issue was titled "Notes for Next Time."

At Brandeis, thanks to Jack Shonkoff, Lisa Lynch, David Weil, Alexandra Piñeros Shields, Jocie Sobieraj, Mike Doonan, Anita Hill, Mary Brolin, Calla Mattox, and to my students.

At EPI, thanks to Jeff Faux, Larry Mishel, Heidi Shierholz, Thea Lee, Jared Bernstein, Josh Bivens, and the research staff. Other dissenting economists from whom I've learned and who I've counted as friends include Robert Heilbroner, Albert Hirschman, Joe Stiglitz, Bob Pollin, J.K. Galbraith and Jamie Galbraith, Dani Rodrik, John Eatwell, Bennett Harrison, Barry Bluestone, and Simon Johnson.

Ongoing appreciation to a broad circle of friends, colleagues, and co-conspirators: Jim Carroll and Lexa Marshall, Randy Kennedy, Howard Bloch and Ellen Handler Spitz, Connie Bloomfield and Bill McFarlane, Ned Friedman, Kevin Gallagher, Derrick Jackson,

John Shattuck, Ellen Hume, Susan Linn, Chuck Collins, Steve Greenhouse, Todd Gitlin, Ken McLean, Damon Silvers, Elizabeth Warren, Samantha Sanchez and Tim Coulter, Eric and Rae Seitz, David and Sydney Reed, Phil Singerman, Peter Dreier, Jennifer Day and Marc Cendron, Fred DuBow, Peter and Ann Anderson, Deborah Loft, Marc and Barbara Landy, Susan Houseman, Marc Blecher, Norma Percy, Peter Gourevitch, Michael Lipsky, Richard Leone, Richard Valelly, E.J. Dionne, John Judis, Jim Fallows, Larry Aber, Chris Pendry, David Callahan, Buz and Roz Paaswell, Rob Johnson and Alexis McGill Johnson, Anya Schiffrin, Kathy Stone and Matt Drennan, David Howell and Lydia Tugendrajch, Tony Mazzocchi, Les Leopold, Dennis Kelleher, Theda Skocpol, Karen Paget, Tom DeVries, Miles Rapoport, Heather McGhee, Dan Cantor, Maurice Mitchell, Tom Glynn, Tamara Draut, Bob Borosage, Roger Hickey, Kate Milne, Claudia Milne, Sarah Bloom Raskin, Dan McIntosh, Patricia Parsons, Dan Okrent, Becky Okrent, Richard Rothstein and Judi Petersen, Rick McGahey, Teresa Ghilarducci, Derek Shearer, Bharat Ramamurti, Rich Trumka, Doris Kearns Goodwin, Sid Blumenthal, Sam Brown, Ron Grzywinski, Nick Littlefield and Jenny Littlefield, Richard and Robin Parker, Michael Ansara, Bob Ross, Lee Webb, Richard Flacks, Robert Lifton, Heather and Paul Booth, Lori Wallach, Rob Weissman, Ralph Nader, Matt Stoller, Paula Rayman, Richard Herman, Penelope Jencks, Sidney Hurwitz, Jenny Mansbridge, Ed Miller, Teresa Parker, Will Hutton, Pervenche Beres, Poul Nyrup Rasmussen, Peter Coldrick, John Evans, Allan Larsson, Margie Mendell, Peter Kinzler, Ellen Stott, David Feldshuh, Anne and Thea Gelbspan, Carl Salzman, Judy Salzman, Rick and Nonnie Burnes, Rosemary and Lew Lloyd, Ellen Guiney, Suzanne Goldberg, Reuven and Orli Avi-Yonah.

Special thanks to my agent, Felicia Eth, and to Nicco Mele of JP Zenger Books who has invented a new publishing model.

Last and not least, I want to remember dear friends and close associates whom we've lost in just the two years since I began working on this memoir: Sid Wolfe, Ross Gelbspan, Sandy Jencks, Alan Houseman, Nancy Chodorow, Ike Williams, Leslie Epstein, Tim Guiney, Miles and Lise Striar, Stuart Altman.

Index

About the Author

Robert Kuttner is co-founder and co-editor of *The American Prospect*. He holds the Meyer and Ida Kirstein Chair at Brandeis University's Heller School, and is the author of thirteen previous books. He was a co-founder of the Economic Policy Institute and is a former columnist for *BusinessWeek* and the *Boston Globe*.

His other positions have included national staff writer on the *Washington Post*, economics editor of the *New Republic*, and chief investigator of the U.S. Senate Banking Committee. He was educated at Oberlin, the University of California at Berkeley, and the London School of Economics. He holds honorary doctorates from Oberlin and Swarthmore. He lives in Boston.